D0948744

Forgotten Doors

Forgotten Doors

The Other Ports of Entry to the United States

Edited by
M. Mark Stolarik

PHILADELPHIA
The Balch Institute Press
London and Toronto: Associated University Presses

Soc
JV
6450
F67
1988

Associated University Presses
440 Forsgate Drive
Cranbury, NJ 08512

Associated University Presses
25 Sicilian Avenue
London WC1A 2QH, England

Associated University Presses
P.O. Box 488, Port Credit
Mississauga, Ontario
Canada L5G 4M2

The paper used in this publication meets the requirements
of the American National Standard for Permanence of Paper
for Printed Library Materials Z39.48-1984.

Library of Congress Cataloging-in-Publication Data

Forgotten doors.

Includes index.
1. United States—Emigration and immigration
—History—Congresses. 2. Immigrants—United
States—History—Congresses. 3. Ports of
entry—United States—History—Congresses.
I. Stolarik, M. Mark, 1943–   .
JV6450.F67 1988 325.73   87-62319
ISBN 0-944190-00-6 (alk. paper)

PRINTED IN THE UNITED STATES OF AMERICA

Contents

CONTENTS

Illustrations

Preface

The essays that follow were originally presented at a conference entitled "Freedom's Doors: The Other Ports of Entry to the United States" held at the Balch Institute for Ethnic Studies on 13–14 June 1986. The idea for this topic originated with the institute's Academic Advisory Council (Randall M. Miller, chairman). Trustees A. William Hoglund, Edward P. Hutchinson, and Marvin Wachman chaired the sessions of the conference. My colleague James Turk helped with the arrangements.

The conference was part of a larger project that included an exhibit and education programs, all of which were funded by a generous grant from CBS Inc. The institute is very grateful for this enlightened corporate giving and hopes that this book, and the questions it raises about America's past and destiny, will repay, in part, the confidence CBS and other supporters invested in the project.

M. Mark Stolarik

Introduction

M. MARK STOLARIK

In 1986, the United States celebrated the one hundredth anniversary of the Statue of Liberty, and in 1992, it will mark the centennial of Ellis Island. While both these events are noteworthy, they obscure an important part of our history. Millions of Americans are descended from immigrants whose first glimpse of the New World was not the Statue of Liberty, but rather Beacon Hill (Boston), Cape May (Philadelphia), Fort McHenry (Baltimore), Key Biscayne (Miami), the Mississippi Delta (New Orleans), the Golden Gate (San Francisco), and the San Gabriel Mountains (Los Angeles). Furthermore, different kinds of immigrants came to these port cities and gave each a distinctive character, one that would permeate the fabric of these urban areas and make them very different from one another.

Boston, as Lawrence Fuchs reminds us, started out as a quintessential Anglo-American city in the colonial era but lost this characteristic in the nineteenth century. Waves of unskilled immigrants from all over Europe, but particularly Ireland, turned the "Athens of America," into a multicultural metropolis dominated by the Irish. However, as Timothy Meagher adds, relations between the Irish and other ethnic groups, particularly various kinds of Yankees (city versus country and the upper, lower, and middle classes), are not well documented or understood and warrant closer study.

Philadelphia, on the other hand, attracted principally skilled immigrants from northern and western Europe. As Fredric Miller shows in his chapter, the City of Brotherly Love became the workshop of the world by selectively drawing mainly those groups with specific skills needed to staff its many and diverse manufacturing plants. Indeed, as Philip Scranton adds, this labor elite participated in a transatlantic labor market, moving back and forth as economic conditions warranted. Thus, no one group dominated immigration to Philadelphia, leaving the city multiethnic but with a strong British and German element.

Baltimore, as Dean Esslinger observes in his contribution, also attracted immigrants from all over Europe, but the largest number came

11

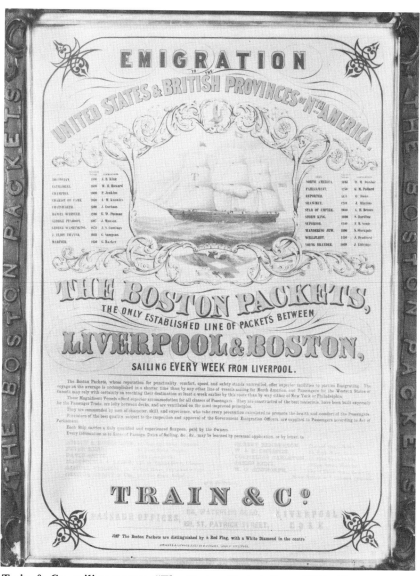

Train & Co. sailing poster, "The Boston Packets," ca. 1850. *(Courtesy of the Bostonian Society Old State House.)*

from Germany. Close ties arose early between merchants in Baltimore and several north German ports—so much so that in the nineteenth century, Baltimore acquired a distinctive German character similar to Cincinnati and Milwaukee. Meanwhile, as Alan Kraut reminds us, other ethnic groups came as well, and relations between these various groups need further study.

Miami, on the other hand, while always multiethnic, has never been dominated by European immigration. Instead, as Raymond Mohl demonstrates in his essay, the Caribbean has traditionally provided the largest number of immigrants (particularly Bahamians, Cubans, and Haitians) to this essentially twentieth-century city. Since Miami has become the gateway to the Caribbean basin in recent years, it differs radically from any other American city. How different, Philip Dolce inquires, still needs to be documented, particularly by comparing the experiences of Caribbean peoples who settled in Miami with those who settled in other, more northern cities.

Radical differences from other American cities also characterize New Orleans, according to Joseph Logsdon and Randall Miller. Having started out as a French, Spanish, and Creole settlement in the eighteenth century, New Orleans, Logsdon points out, began to receive immigrants from all over Europe in the nineteenth and twentieth centuries, making it so unique as to defy easy description. To complicate matters even more, Miller adds, New Orleans was the only Catholic city in the American South, and it drew a disproportionate share of poor immigrants who took advantage of lower fares to this Mississippi destination. Such a combination turned New Orleans into more of a Mediterranean city than any other American metropolis.

San Francisco, by contrast, received most of its European settlers as the result of an overland trek, while its seafaring immigrants were overwhelmingly Asians. The latter, as Charles Wollenberg notes, faced severe discrimination by the Europeans who preceded them and, as a result, the Asians (principally Chinese) formed the largest and most striking ethnic enclave in an otherwise cosmopolitan city. In addition, as Hilary Conroy reminds us, Asians used Honolulu as a vestibule for entering San Francisco after the U.S. Congress banned Chinese immigration in 1882 and Teddy Roosevelt reached the "gentlemen's agreement" with the government of Japan to limit immigration from that country after 1907. Nevertheless, San Francisco remains one of the two most Asian cities in America.

The other Asian city is Los Angeles, which, according to Elliott Barkan, did not really become an important port until air travel after World War II opened her to the Pacific. Largely as a result of the liberalized 1965 immigration act, plus the Vietnam war, large numbers of Asians have entered the United States in the second half of the twentieth century through Los Angeles, and most have also settled there. In addition, hundreds of thousands of Latin Americans (principally Mexicans) have made Los Angeles their chief overland destination (as did European settlers before them). Thus, Los Angeles has become the West Coast's leading port of entry and foremost destination of newcomers in the last two decades. Because several generations of Asians and Latin Americans have settled in Los Angeles in the twentieth century that city, Douglas Massey concludes, will for a long time to come remain fragmented into distinct ethnic enclaves as each generation tries to come to terms with the conflicting goals of assimilation and ethnic persistence.

The contributors to *Forgotten Doors* have introduced us to the one-third of the 50 million immigrants who entered the United States in the last 167 years through Boston, Philadelphia, Baltimore, Miami, New Orleans, San Francisco, and Los Angeles. These seven ports are among America's largest cities, and each has received over a million immigrants since 1820. Moreover, the authors have suggested that, much like their more studied counterparts who came through New York, the new arrivals evinced a startling variety in their reasons for emigrating, responses to the friendly or hostile reception they experienced, and in their impact on the receiving cities. The immigrants' various experiences derived from many factors, including their numbers, ethnic or religious affiliations, and the ethnic makeup of the receiving port. The histories of the forgotten ports of entry are very complex, and this book professes only to outline a story that now demands fuller, deeper, explanation. To do so will not only recover the history of America's forgotten doors of immigrant entry, but allow Americans to discover the variety and complexity of their whole past.

Forgotten Doors

1

Immigration through the Port of Boston

Lawrence H. Fuchs

Boston is self-consciously American as is no other place. Site of the
Boston Massacre (1770) and the Boston Tea Party (1773), Boston was
also the home of the Salutation Tavern, where John Hancock, John
Adams, and other pre-Revolutionary patriots gathered for meetings of
the North End Caucus; and of the Old North Church (1721), where Paul
Revere hung his lanterns before being rowed across the Charles River to
Charlestown to begin his ride to Lexington to warn against the British.

But in the early nineteenth century, the Yankees of Boston's North
End were almost as solidly English in background as its street names—
Hull, Salem, Hanover, Stillman, Endicott, Thatcher, Tileston, and
Sheafe. Sheafe Street alone was home to a half-dozen Protestant clergymen, including Samuel Stillman, Lyman Beecher, Henry Ward
Beecher, Henry Ware, and Dr. Samuel Francis Smith, who in 1832,
wrote "America," or, as it is frequently called, "My Country, 'Tis of
Thee." Leaders of the city were known for their civic consciousness, and
in 1820, British visitor Harriet Martineau said, "I know no large city
where there is so much mutual helpfulness, so little neglect and ignorance of the concerns of other classes."[1] Boston probably had more
newspapers, periodicals, evening schools, libraries, lectures, and con-
certs for its population than any other city in the United States. But it still
had fewer foreigners than most urban areas. For the ordinary emigrant
farmer or artisan, Boston was less attractive than New York, Philadelphia, Baltimore, or even New Orleans, which was a more active port
of immigration than Boston every year from 1828 to 1848, with the
exception of 1844. Farmers could find richer soil much more quickly to
the south or west of other cities, and skilled craftsmen and unskilled
workers were both more likely to locate work within them.

In only three of the twenty years between 1820 and 1840 did Boston
rank as high as third among ports of entry to the United States, and only
once (1822) was it second. The Boston waterfront was the pride of the

Immigrants watching docking in Boston, 1923. *(Courtesy of the Boston Public Library.)*

city, a panorama of masts, spars, and snowy canvas more extensive than that of any other port in the union. Nevertheless, while New York, Philadelphia, and Baltimore depended largely on Boston to import products from far-off countries, they were the principal cities of immigration.

The relatively low incidence of immigration to Boston would have continued had it not been for the terrible Irish potato famine of 1845. Following that tragedy, from 1847 to 1854, no fewer than twenty thousand immigrants arrived in the city annually, and the large majority of them came from Ireland. Because Boston was the terminus for the pioneering steamship service inaugurated by Britain's Cunard Line in 1840 and the rates were subsidized by the British government, even the poor could cross, although it often cost them their last bit of money.

The Irish cottiers and their families who emigrated were among the poorest immigrants ever to come to the United States. The cottier had lived at the mercy of his landowner, who charged high rents, raised them at will, and evicted families without a moment's notice. Disease and infant mortality were high, and when the potato blight came, emigration became not just a choice but a necessity. Having subsisted on potatoes and a little bit of milk, the cottiers and their families could starve, move, or be thrown out. Often, Terrance, Patrick, or Thomas listed under occupation on the ship's manifest the awful word *evicted.*

Sometimes Terrance, Patrick, or Thomas was already dead or had died on shipboard, and large families headed by women made their way to the increasingly congested North End, where the children of poor immigrants—the first of America's street children—were a common sight. Not infrequently, an orphan appears on the manifest, traveling alone or with another family. When they debarked, immigrants sometimes fell prey to dock loafers who plied the port, some of them immigrant ruffians looking for trouble or a way to exploit the ignorance of newcomers.

Barely able to scrape together the $17 to $20 (including provision) for the fare from Liverpool to Boston, increasing numbers came from Cork, Kerry, Galway, Clare, and Donegal in 1850 to 1855—between 21,831 and 27,483 of them annually. Most were too poor to leave Boston and took jobs in the North End, on Beacon Hill, in the South End, or nearby Charlestown, Roxbury, Dorchester, Cambridge, Brookline, or Somerville. Although life was harsh—tuberculosis, alcoholism, and petty crime were common—the status of young women improved from what it had been in Ireland, where they had been wholly dependent on impoverished husbands, fathers, and brothers. In Boston and nearby towns, women could find work as maids or cooks while men settled for less steady employment on the docks or at pick-and-shovel work. Some of the men went as far west as Worcester, where they lived alone in camps and engaged in heavy labor.[2] Ralph Waldo Emerson, writing to Henry David Thoreau about the Irish day laborers in Concord, observed, "Now the humanity of the town suffers with the poor Irish, who receive but sixty or even fifty cents, for working from dark till dark, with a strain and following up that reminds one of negro-driving."[3] Immigrants who went to Waltham, Lowell, Lawrence, Newburyport, and other cities were often recruited for specific mill or construction jobs, a pattern that would continue throughout the nineteenth century. By 1850, two-thirds of the common laborers in Newburyport had been born outside of the United States, nearly all of them in Ireland.[4]

Immigrants from other countries, including Swedes and Germans, came to Boston, too, but the Irish comprised more than three-fourths of the foreign born in the city by 1850 and 25 percent of the population as a whole. The Swedes and Germans tended to move west, so that by midcentury, there were only two thousand Germans and even fewer Scandinavians in the city proper. A scattering of Scots, French, and Italians made up the other minority immigrant populations.

Although Boston, with a population of only 150,000 in 1850, experienced nothing like the economic growth of New York, with its half-million inhabitants in 1850, low wages spurred the growth of the factory system in Boston, particularly in textiles, where intensive cheap labor was vital to success. Manufacturers turned to the Irishmen, who would work for lower wages than even New England farm girls, many of whom would marry and leave their employment anyway. As textile workers, ironworkers, and builders of ships, immigrants worked fifteen hours a day and many times seven days a week, suffering terribly during periods of recession or depression. Not surprisingly, then, most of the immigrants remained crowded in slums that horrified the native-born population.

The Yankees of Boston, who profited from the cheap labor of the Irish, fled the North and South ends in droves. As a result, by 1850, only half of the descendants of the Bostonians of 1820 remained in the city. Violence had broken out as early as the 1830s, and in 1834, in nearby Charlestown, a group of forty or fifty truckmen and some Scotch-Irish brickmakers from New Hampshire burst into a convent school a little before midnight and burned it to the ground. By the 1850s, the American, or Know-Nothing, party gained power in Boston and Massachusetts. Sworn to exclude all immigrants (and Roman Catholics in particular) from places of trust, profit, or honor, the new party carried Massachusetts in 1854, electing the governor, all state officers, the entire state senate, and all but 2 of the 378 members of the state house of representatives.[5] The party tried in vain to convince Congress to restrict immigration, but coincidentally, the number of immigrants coming through Boston began to recede sharply in 1858.

Only in 1865 after the Civil War had ended, did new arrivals to Boston again number more than ten thousand, or nearly one out of every twenty who came to the United States. From that time until 1879, when Boston was clearly established as the second major port of entry to the United States, the annual flow of immigrants fell below ten thousand only twice. From 1870 to 1875, traffic was especially heavy, with Boston receiving about 5 to 8 percent of all immigrants coming to the United States. Far behind New York, whose immigrants usually numbered ten times those of Boston, it easily outdistanced Philadelphia and Baltimore.

The Irish dominated the flow. Economic progress was slow, and Yankee prejudice was still strong, but jobs were much more plentiful than in Ireland. While prejudice limited the mobility of immigrant laborers during this period, as Stephan Thernstrom has shown, there was some movement up the economic ladder despite the barriers ("no Irish need apply").[6] Some companies, such as the Waltham Watch Company, had a decided preference for non-Catholic immigrant labor and imported English, Scandinavian, German, and Swiss workers through the Port of Boston. But the lure of even the most menial jobs and the promise of a better life for their children kept the Irish coming, not just to Boston but through Boston to Waltham, Lowell, Lawrence, Lynn, and smaller cities, such as Newburyport and Chicopee. Although only a small minority of the Irish made their way into nonmanual occupations, the sons of the laborers were much more successful than their fathers in obtaining employment at skilled trades in the 1860s and 1870s, and by 1880, a small group of laboring families had entered the middle class. If data on Newburyport are typical for the Boston metropolitan area, another large body of families now owned property, even though the heads of those households remained in manual occupations. Such information, carried in stories and letters back to the villages of Ireland and other countries in northern Europe, made it clear that opportunities were greater in the New World than in the old.

With the introduction in the 1880s of the type *B* Cunarder ships accommodating fifteen hundred steerage passengers, the Irish emigrant flow to Boston remained high. At the same time, Italians, Greeks, Portuguese, Jews from Poland and Russia, Poles, Armenians, and others came on the ships of other lines, helping to swell the tide. Only three times in the decade did the annual immigration through the port fall below 35,000, and it reached a high in 1882 of 58,186. By 1890, 68 percent of the population of the city was foreign or of foreign parentage, and 45 percent of the male labor force was foreign born.[7]

The flood of immigration diminished sightly in the 1890s, but throughout the decade, more than 200,000 European immigrants arrived at the Port of Boston, the largest contingent of them from Ireland. Some who came through the port went on to other states. For example, of the 17,128 immigrants who arrived in Boston in 1894, 11,748 claimed their destination to be Massachusetts, but 1,011 said they would move to Rhode Island and 832 to Illinois.[8] By the late 1890s, however, Boston was even more a city of immigrants than a port for immigrants. In 1898 and 1899, only 31,498 immigrants came through the port, but nearly 55,000 immigrants from all U.S. ports reported Massachusetts to be their destination. Nevertheless, within ten years, the flow of immigrants through Boston expanded as members of the state's large foreign-born population drew in relatives and friends from abroad. While immigration to the nation as a whole more than doubled between 1899 and 1903, the number of arrivals at the Port of Boston more than tripled, reaching 62,838 in 1903 and highs of 70,164 in 1907 and 69,365 in 1914.[9]

Immigrants landed at the immigration station where they sat on benches and ate and drank refreshments until they were called for inspection. Doctors and immigration officials examined them to make certain they carried no significant diseases nor were otherwise excludable as prostitutes, alien convicts, contract laborers, mentally ill, or likely to become a public charge.

Jewish and Italian neighborhoods grew most quickly. By 1895, there were approximately 7,700 Italians and 6,200 Jews in the North End and 6,300 Jews and 1,100 Italians in the West End. There were also Jews in East Boston, which by 1905 had synagogues, kosher markets and restaurants, dry goods stores, chicken houses, and other Jewish businesses. There, as well as in the North End, the majority of Jewish men were tailors, shopkeepers, peddlers, junk dealers, and industrial workers, a great many of whom eventually saved enough money to move to more desirable neighborhoods in Roxbury, Dorchester, Chelsea, and Revere.

As Jews left the North End, they were replaced mainly by Italians, who first settled on Jeffrey's Point, where there were small gardens and open space, and around Maverick and Cottage streets. But like the Irish before them, many Italian immigrants moved through the Port of Boston to other Massachusetts cities, in this case to Medford, Revere, Arlington, and Waltham, and to Providence, Rhode Island. For the *contadini* (landless peasants) a cash income meant escape from the poverty of Sicily, Calabria, Abruzzi, and Italy's other southern provinces, so these immigrants took what work they could, saved and invested their money, and often returned to Italy for visits or even to stay.

By 1910, the North End was becoming increasingly Italian, but it still had distinctive Irish, Jewish, and Portuguese streets.[11] The West End contained many streets with native-born Americans, including some streets that were predominantly black and others that were almost entirely Irish, Jewish, or Italian. Still others contained British immigrants,

U.S. Immigration Service building, Boston, 1925. *(Courtesy of the Boston Public Library.)*

and at least a half dozen streets were mixed. The South End, which had become increasingly Irish after construction of the new Cathedral of the Holy Cross at the junction of Washington and Union Park streets in 1867, now housed immigrant Jews, Syrians, Greeks, Italians, Chinese, Portuguese, and West Indians as well.[12]

By 1920, Boston was the preferred destination of emigrating Portuguese (mainly from the Azores and Cape Verde Islands) and Finns. The same process of chain migration that had brought over thousands of Irish from Cork and had peopled East Boston's Cottage Street with natives of a few villages in Abruzzi, Italy, was still at work.[13] Portuguese fisherman called their relatives to opportunities in Fall River, New Bedford, Gloucester, and Provincetown; Finns in Fitchburg sent for cousins, aunts, and uncles in the old country. A smattering of Swedes continued to head for Worcester and Waltham, and Lithuanians joined relatives who were working for a rubber company in Hudson. In Boston itself, Chinese merchants and educators, who were not barred by the Chinese Exclusion Law of 1882, and some Chinese laborers who had arrived illegally, had established a small Chinatown in the South Cove.

Reactions varied to the surge of newcomers in the late nineteenth century and into the early twentieth century. Beneficently inclined Bostonians established settlement houses to hasten the Americanization of all major immigrant neighborhoods by offering educational and recreational programs geared especially toward the children. On the other hand, fierce battles took place between Irish and Italians, and Boston blue bloods took the lead in vigorous intellectual and political opposition to immigration, founding the Immigration Restriction League in 1894. For most of the next quarter century, league members advocated a literacy test to keep out the allegedly unassimilable hordes of new immigrants from southern and eastern Europe, even though the distinction between old and new immigrants forced them, as one immigrant historian put it, to accept the Irish as "honorary Anglo-Saxons."[14]

From nearly 70,000 new arrivals in 1914, the port saw only 3,392 immigrants in 1918, compared to nearly 10,000 for San Francisco and almost 30,000 for New York. It was not the literacy test enacted in 1917 but World War I that sharply reduced the immigrant flow. Virtually halted in 1919, immigration picked up again in the 1920s, particularly in 1921 and 1924 just prior to implementation of the restrictionist immigration law of 1924. Ships transporting immigrants were larger now, but except for 1921, the average number of immigrants arriving in Boston in the 1920s was only slightly higher than eleven thousand annually. Due to the Depression, the numbers were reduced even more drastically; in fact, in some years, such as 1933, more foreign nationals left Boston to go home to Italy, Greece, Turkey, and other countries than arrived to take up their lives in the United States. The U.S. Immigration Service building used to process immigrants was no longer needed for its initial purpose. The Depression, World War II, and restrictive immigration laws kept the numbers low before the Hart-Celler Act, passed in 1965 and implemented three years later, plus a series of refugee acts, including the Refugee Act of 1980, resulted in a new influx of immigration through Boston.

Under the 1965 act, quotas and exclusions that for forty some years had skewed the sources of immigration largely to northern and western Europe were abolished, and eventually an equal ceiling of twenty thousand was established for every nation in the world. Under a series of special laws, refugees came to the United States outside of the immigration law until 1980 when the Refugee Act was passed to provide for an orderly, regular annual flow of refugees to the United States, all of whom were permitted to adjust their status to that of immigrant one year after arrival. Although the ethnic makeup of Boston's immigrants has changed radically to include substantial numbers of Asians and Hispanics, the number of new arrivals remains small. Fewer than four thousand arrived through the port of Boston in each of the years 1984 and 1985, dropping Boston from its historic role as second or third largest port of immigration in the United States to fourteenth and sixteenth, respectively, in those years.

Of the 11,584 immigrants admitted in 1982 who chose Massachusetts as a place of residence, more than twice as many came from Mainland China (828) as from the United Kingdom, more than three times as many from Haiti (782) as from Poland, and more than three times as many from India (482) as from Germany. The older countries of immigration—Ireland, Italy, Greece, and the Soviet Union especially—were represented, but the new flows were dominated by people from countries outside of Europe, such as Jamaica (543), Korea (372), Vietnam (352), Iran (212), Colombia (201), Taiwan (192), the Philippines (177), and Guyana (135), many of whom actually had arrived in the United States in Boston or other cities as refugees, tourists, or students and adjusted their status to that of immigrant (resident alien) in Boston.

Sources of immigration are today truly global. The Port of Boston, now its airport instead of its harbor, does not beckon to so many as it did at the turn of the century but to a much greater variety of people, who are drawn to the area's high-tech industries, universities, cultural advantages, hospitals, and school systems. Boston's Vietnamese, Haitian, and Hispanic communities are small and struggling, but their children have performed well in some of the city's most prestigious schools, and an increasing number of these immigrants and refugees are becoming involved in the life of the city. The exclusiveness of Boston—the older, fierce antagonisms between Irish and Yankee, Italian and Irish, Jew and gentile—are largely memories. Individual acts of hostility against Asian and Hispanic newcomers occur, but the full force of the state and the city opposes bigotry, and leading citizens of Boston celebrate the new diversity that stems from the admission of immigrants from over one hundred countries.

Notes

1. Quoted in Oscar Handlin, *Boston's Immigrants: A Study in Acculturation* (Cambridge, Mass., 1941), 23.

2. See Hasia R. Diner, *Erin's Daughters in America: Irish Immigrant Women in the Nineteenth Century* (Baltimore, 1983), 59.

3. Quoted in Stephan Thernstrom, *Poverty and Progress: Social Mobility in the Nineteenth-Century City* (Cambridge, Mass., 1964), 19.

4. Thernstrom, *Poverty and Progress*, 27.

5. For a further discussion of this period, see Lawrence H. Fuchs, *John F. Kennedy and American Catholicism* (New York, 1967).

6. Thernstrom, *Poverty and Progress*, 85.

7. Thernstrom, *The Other Bostonians: Poverty and Progress in the American Metropolis, 1880–1970* (Cambridge, Mass., 1973), 113.

8. *Report of the Superintendent of Immigration, 1894, Table No. 2, Showing the Number of Immigrants Destined to Each State and Territory during the Year Ending June 30, 1894*, 6.

9. Commissioner-General of Immigration, *Report of Nativity and Destination of Alien Steerage Passengers Landing at the Ports of the United States and Canada, Twelve Months Ending June 30, 1898*, 8 and 9; and *Report of Commissioner-General of Immigration, Number of Immigrants Arrived at Ports of the United States and Canada for the Year Ending June 30, 1899, Showing Their Destination by Races*, 20. 21.

10. Diner, *Erin's Daughters*, 37.

11. Robert A. Woods, *Americans in Process* (Boston, 1903), 40, 41.

12. *The South End*, Boston Two Hundred Neighborhood History Series (Boston, 1975), 3.

13. *East Boston*, Boston Two Hundred Neighborhood History Series (Boston, 1976), 7.

14. Maldwyn Allen Jones, *American Immigration* (Chicago, 1960), 259.

"Immigration through the Port of Boston": A Comment

Timothy J. Meagher

Professor Fuchs has provided a comprehensive and emotional depiction of nearly two hundred years of Boston's immigrant and ethnic history. Instead of criticism or praise or simply echoing and lauding his work, then, I have chosen to build on some of the themes of this conference and Professor Fuchs's paper to suggest new areas of exploration and study.

An unstated but certainly an implicit aim of this conference is to compare the immigrant and ethnic histories of freedom's [other] doors with each other and that of their giant sister port, New York. In making that comparison for Boston, I believe we should concentrate on two major points. First, having determined who settled in Boston and for what reasons, we should compare that city's mix of immigrant groups to ethnic populations in other major cities. Second, we should examine in the same comparative way the kind of environment Boston provided for ethnic group development.

"The Massachusetts of the Puritans is as dead as Caesar," thundered James Michael Curley in the early twentieth century, "but there is no need to mourn the fact. Their successors, the Irish, had letters and learning, culture and civilization, when the ancestors of the Puritans were savages running half naked through the forests of Britain. It took the Irish to make Massachusetts a fit place to live in." The bombast, sense of ethnic rivalry, and pretention to historical expertise of Boston's roguish mayor aside, the Honorable James Michael Curley was simply acknowledging an accomplished fact. Massachusetts (or more exactly Boston) had been Yankee; it was now Irish. As Professor Fuchs has noted, the Irish dominated immigration to Boston to a remarkable degree. Indeed, in no other major American city was the proportion of Irish among the foreign born so high. In 1870, for example, nearly two-thirds of Boston's immigrants were Irish. In the same year, the figure for New York was 47 percent and for Philadelphia, 52 percent.[1]

This exceptional Irish preponderance was matched by the equally exceptional virtual absence of Germans in Boston. As Professor Fuchs notes, few Germans came to Boston, and few of those who did come, remained. According to Caroline Golab, that imbalance between large Irish populations and small German ones was characteristic of many eastern cities. Yet in no other major city was the disparity between Irish and Germans so large as it was in Boston. In 1870, for example, Germans accounted for 28 percent of Philadelphia's immigrants and 36 percent of New York's foreign born. In Boston, by contrast, Germans were almost nonexistent, amounting to 3 percent of the immigrant population in 1850 and 6 percent in 1870.[2]

The loneliness of these few isolated Teutons amid a sea of Celts was not the only distinctive or remarkable characteristic of immigration to Boston. The city also attracted a far larger proportion of newcomers from Canada's Maritime Provinces than did any other major American city. In 1890, for example, 24 percent of Boston's immigrants were from Canada's coastal provinces. That same year, the proportion of such immigrants among the foreign born in Baltimore, Philadelphia, and New York barely exceeded 3 percent. In the early twentieth century, there was also a noticeable imbalance between Italian and Polish immigrants in Boston. In 1920, Italians outnumbered Poles in the Hub by nearly seven to one. This discrepancy, however, was not unique to Boston: In New York, the imbalance was even greater and in Philadelphia only slightly less.[3]

It is far easier, of course to point out these differences between Boston's immigrant population and those of other cities than to determine their causes. Logically, there should be some connection between the people who enter a city through its port and the people who settle in its neighborhoods, but such is not always the case. As Professor Fuchs has noted, a number of Swedes arrived in Boston in the 1850s, but few of them settled there. Nearly forty years later, many Russian Jews landing in Boston told customs officials that they were bound for the much larger Jewish settlement in New York. Furthermore, just as those who entered through the port did not always remain there, large numbers also entered America elsewhere and then made their way to Massachusetts. In a number of years in the early twentieth century, the number of immigrants reporting Massachusetts as their destination exceeded the number arriving through the port of Boston by 10,000 or even 20,000 to 25,000 people.[4]

Nevertheless, the relationship between the immigrants entering the port of Boston and the composition of the city's population should not be underestimated. The port's trade connections to foreign cities had a critical impact on the type of immigrants who settled in Boston's neighborhoods. The influx of Canadians from the Maritime Provinces was the clearest example of such an impact. Coastal traffic between Boston and New Brunswick, Nova Scotia, and Prince Edward Island flourished throughout the nineteenth and early twentieth centuries. All during that period, coastal ships carried not merely goods (plaster of paris was an especially important product in the early 1800s) but emigrants eager to find new opportunities in the American city. This immigrant traffic peaked in the last three decades of the nineteenth century when, for example, nearly a third of Prince Edward Island's population fled to the "Boston states."[5]

Canadian coastal traffic was critical not only to the flow of Maritime Canadians to Boston, however, but to the Irish flood to the Hub as well. In the 1820s and 1830s, when Catholic immigration from Ireland had just begun to pick up momentum, the cost of traveling from the United Kingdom to Canada was much lower than the price of shipping out to New York or other ports in the United States. Irishmen who landed in New Brunswick or Nova Scotia could then easily and cheaply make their way to New England. Some walked; others in the 1840s rode the railway. Many, and perhaps most from the 1820s through the 1840s, sailed south on boats engaged in coastal trade with Boston. Marcus Hansen stated flatly that it was the routing of Irish immigrants to Canada and then south by coastal traders that made New England overwhelmingly Irish. Without this Canadian connection, Hansen argued, New England's immigrants would have come through New York and "been more varied as those who advanced from New York into the Middle West."[6]

Hansen's strong assertion has been disputed, but I believe that it is essentially correct. Oscar Handlin puts greater emphasis on the direct connections established between Liverpool and Boston in the 1840s, and those shipping lines did carry the bulk of the famine exiles late in that decade and early in the next one. By that time, however, the Canadian coastal trade had already set a pattern of Irish dominance among Boston and New England's immigrants. Further proof of the importance of the Canadian connection comes from Ruth Ann Harris's statistical analyses of the Missing Friends column in the Boston *Pilot*. Professor Harris had found that of the *Pilot*'s readers placing advertisements in that column in the 1830s and 1840s, the number who had entered North America through Canada was greater than the number who had entered through Boston and New York combined.[7]

German avoidance of Boston, like the Irish attraction to the city, can be explained in a number of ways. Perhaps the Germans detoured around Boston simply because the Irish had settled there so early and in such great numbers. As Caroline Golab has argued, German immigrants might have determined that it was easier to find work in a new, open city than to try to challenge Irish control of Boston's labor market. Handlin suggests that Boston had no opportunities for the Irish or the Germans, but the wealthier Germans could afford to move west to sound economies while the poor Irish could not. Boston's lack of trade connections with German or French cotton ports, such as Le Havre, was also a considerable obstacle to German emigration to Boston. There was, perhaps, not one influence, then, but many that caused the largest group of immigrants to America to bypass one of its most important cities.[8]

So far, I have discussed the composition of Boston's population in terms of nationalities, such as the Irish, Germans, or Italians. Students of Irish or Italian history, however, are well aware of significant economic and even cultural differences among regions in Italy and Ireland. In Ireland, the west, principally the province of Connaught, has been the poorest and most Irish part of Ireland for four hundred years. There, the Gaelic language and traditional folk culture continued among a desperately poor people far longer than in the more prosperous eastern province of Leinster or in much of the southern province of Munster. Italy, like Ireland, was, and still is, divided into two major regions, but in Italy the division has been between a more modern and prosperous North and a traditional but poorer South. To speak of Irish or Italian immigrants in Boston thus may obscure more subtle but nonetheless critically significant patterns of settlement. Indeed, what may have really distinguished Boston from other cities is not the heavy proportion of Irish and Italians, but the number of Irish and Italian immigrants from particular regions or provinces in their homelands.[9]

Determining the regional origins of Irish immigrants to Boston (or to any other city, for that matter) is not easy, and there is so little evidence that it cannot be considered conclusive. The statistics used here are from three sources, all with their own biases: advertisements placed in the Boston *Pilot* in the 1830s and 1840s by readers seeking lost relatives; gravestone inscriptions in the Mt. Auburn Catholic Cemetery from the 1850s, 1860s, and 1870s; and baptismal registers from four Catholic parishes. The parish registers are for St. Peter's, Cambridge, and Immaculate Conception, Newburyport, during the 1870s; and for Mission Church, Mission Hill Roxbury, and Our Lady Help of Christians, Newton, during the 1880s.

Statistics from these sources vary slightly but tend to show the same overall pattern. Irish immigrants from the province of Munster, particularly the counties of Cork and, to a lesser extent, Kerry, made up the largest proportion of the Irish in the Boston area. They constituted 46 percent of the immigrants seeking relatives or friends in the *Pilot* between 1831 and 1850; 53 percent of the men and women interred in Watertown's Mt. Auburn Cemetery in the 1850s, 1860s, and 1870s; and

54 percent of the parents having their children baptized in the four Catholic parishes in the 1870s and 1880s. Nevertheless, the prominence of Munster obscures some important local variations. A number of other sources suggest, for example, that most of the Irish in Boston's North End were from Ulster, largely from the county of Donegal. In addition, Munster's overall hegemony may also mask an important shift in the sources of Irish immigration over time. In the 1880s, for instance, baptismal records from the Roxbury and Newton churches indicate parents born in Connaught far outnumbered even immigrants from Munster.[10]

These numbers are too small and the sources of data too scattered and skewed to support reliable conclusions, but they are nonetheless suggestive. Compared to statistics measuring the flow of emigrants from Ireland's provinces, they suggest that Boston received a disproportionally larger number of immigrants from Munster and, to a lesser extent, Connaught and conversely, a smaller number from Ulster. These discrepancies may, however, be as much the result of biases in the sources as indicators of actual differences between the provincial origins of Boston's Irish and Irish immigrants generally. All of these Boston sources record only Catholics, and because Ulster's emigration was undoubtedly more heavily Protestant, its underrepresentation and the overrepresentation of the other provinces is understandable. In fact, taking note of this correction, the pattern revealed in the Boston figures does not seem peculiar or even distinctive. Instead, it is similar to a count of Irishmen made by a census taker in Milwaukee's Fourth Ward in 1860. Even the possible late nineteenth-century increase in emigration from Connaught revealed in the baptismal records of Roxbury and Newton in the 1880s may simply reflect the general rising rate of emigration from that province in the late nineteenth century.[11]

Defined in the broadest terms, the regional backgrounds of Boston's Italian immigrants likewise appears unremarkable. Working from baptismal registers from the city's two largest Italian parishes, Robert De Marco notes a shift in the sources of Italian immigration to Boston from northern to southern provinces. The first Italians in the city were Genoese, but their little colony was overwhelmed beginning about 1890 by waves of southerners, most of them from Avellino in Campania or from coastal towns in Sicily. Such a shift, of course, was not unique to Italian immigration to Boston, but characterized immigration from Italy to the United States generally.[2]

Examining the provincial or regional origins or Boston's Irish and Italian immigrants seems to shed little light on the process that carried members of these two groups to the Hub. Italian immigration to Boston in broad terms mirrored the general trend of a shift in Italian immigration from northern to southern Italian sources. In more narrowly defined terms, distinguishing not simply between North and South but among provinces or sectors within those two regions, Boston's Italians may have been more distinctive. Neither De Marco nor any other scholar has yet explained why the Avellinese in particular came to Boston. Even here, however, the immigration from a few specific towns in Avellino or Sicily reflects the patterns of long migration chains that scholars have found in Cleveland and other cities. Although it is not clear why Boston's Italians came from Avellino or Sicily, then, the fact that they came from only a limited number of towns in those provinces is typical of Italian migration to America in general.[13]

Similarly, analysis of the county and provincial origins of the Irish appears at first glance to offer few new insights into Boston's exceptionally strong attraction for Irish immigrants. The Irish who came to Boston seem little different from Irish Catholics who went to other cities in America. Yet that conclusion may be more significant than if the backgrounds of Boston Irish had revealed a peculiar or distinctive pattern. The Boston Irish have always occupied a unique place in the history of Irish Americans; they have always seemed the most hapless and hopeless of America's Paddies. Some historians have suggested that they were not simply the poorest but the least talented or adventurous of Boston's immigrants. The richer, brighter, more courageous Celts—so this argument runs—moved west to success, leaving the Hibernian refuse of this Darwinian selection process stranded on the East Coast. If all of this were true, the provincial origins of the Boston Irish might offer a clue. If men and women from Connaught made up the majority or even a plurality of Boston's immigrants, one might conclude that Boston was attracting an exceptional number of immigrants who were from the poorest and most backward of Ireland's provinces. They themselves might not be the least talented of Irish immigrants, but they were likely to be among the poorest and the most poorly prepared to cope with a modern society. Yet Irish immigrants from Connaught made up less than a quarter of Boston's Celts, and the proportions of natives from the four provinces in Boston were very similar to their proportions in Milwaukee, one of the western cities supposedly favored by their "superiors." If the history of the Boston Irish has truly been a tragedy, the fault has not been theirs.[14]

A sense of tragedy has nonetheless seemed to pervade the study not only of Boston's Irish but of all the city's ethnic groups. Handlin set the tone over forty years ago in *Boston's Immigrants*. He seemed to suggest that mass immigration to Boston had been lamentable because the city was not good for immigrants and immigrants were not good for the city. In the 1970s, Stephan Thernstrom appeared to verify the former point with a battery of statistics documenting the economic failures of Boston's Irish and Italians, while the violence of frustrated Irish and Italian Americans during the busing crisis in that same decade seemed to confirm that immigrants and their descendants were still out of place in the Athens of America.[15]

Both Thernstrom's studies and the busing crisis have inspired historians of American ethnicity, especially historians of the American Irish, to reassert a "frontier thesis" of American ethnic history. In simple terms, this thesis suggests that the further west in America a member of an ethnic group went, the greater his or her chances for occupational success, acceptance by nonethnic neighbors, and achievement of self-confidence and self-esteem. Boston, as the easternmost city in the country, symbolized economic failure, rejection, frustration, and despair for eastern ethnic groups, particularly the Irish. Although some historians, as I have noted, toyed with the notion that these Boston failures may have been rooted in the immigrants themselves, the more common explanation has cited the environment of Boston. In sharp contrast to economically dynamic and socially fluid western cities, Boston confronted its newcomers with a well-entrenched, hostile Yankee elite and a sickly economy. Nowhere else in America, it seemed, could immigrants and their children have found a less happy home.[16]

There is something to be said for this interpretation. The rigidity of Boston's social structure has been notorious, and the city's economy was long depressed. Irish immigrants and their children in Boston thus lagged a full generation behind their cousins in San Francisco or even Philadelphia in their efforts to climb their city's occupational ladder. The economic progress of Italian Americans in the Hub also suffered in comparison to achievements of fellow Italians in San Francisco and New York. Frustrations fueled both by this lack of economic success and by vicious battles with the city's Yankee Protestants were also evident. James Michael Curley's rabble-rousing assaults on the Brahmins; Father Coughlin's popularity in the Boston radio market; the vituperative parochialism preached by Father Feeney; the virulent resistance of Irish Charlestown, South Boston, and Italian East Boston to busing; and even recent assaults on Asian immigrants in Dorchester and Revere all seem to reflect the bitterness of defeated people.[17]

If there is much to say for this interpretation, however, there is also much to question as well. Such a perspective, for example, tends to oversimplify and foreshorten Boston's ethnic history, lending it an inevitability that it did not possess. Did the battle against busing begin when the famine Irish crowded into the slums of Fort Hill or when the Avellinese debarked at East Boston a half-century later? Did intervening generations have no influence on their own or their descendants' fate?

Often overlooked in Boston's ethnic history is the thaw in relations between Boston's Irish and Yankees in the 1870s and 1880s. Yankee-Irish political cooperation was the norm, not the exception then. Patrick Collins and John Boyle O'Reilly led a decorous, respectable Irish nationalist movement which won Yankee support in that decade, while the shy Archbishop of Boston, John J. Williams, headed a Catholic Church that was anything but militant. A second problem with depicting Boston's ethnic history as tragedy is that so little is known about the key variable in the Boston environment, the Yankees. Much, of course, has been written about the Brahmins (largely by themselves or their descendants) but far less about the Yankee farm boys and girls who came to Boston to reap the opportunities of city life and became the backbone of the city's native-stock middle class. In particular, it is not clear how the Brahmin elite, this Yankee middle class, and Protestant immigrants from the Maritime Provinces related to each other and how each related to Catholic immigrants.[18]

As important as a reexamination of Boston's history is, it is also helpful to take a second glance at the history of ethnic relations in other cities before reaching conclusions about the Hub's tragic environment. Boston and New England clearly had no monopoly on nativism, which in the 1890s and 1920s actually appeared to be strongest in the Midwest. Nor have Boston's ethnic groups monopolized bitter ethnocentrism. San Francisco has often been depicted as Boston's opposite, an open city of quick mobility, easy social acceptance, and proud pluralism. Yet the Irish in San Francisco were very often as chauvinistic and mean spirited as their Boston cousins, leading the late nineteenth-century racist assault on Chinese and Japanese immigrants. At the turn of the century, the San Francisco Irish boasted a spokesman, Father Peter Christopher Yorke, who was, in the words of his biographer, the prototype of an ethnic militant and as sensitive to ethnic or religious slights as any Boston Irishman. Finally, as Robert Senkiewicz reveals in a study of conflicts over San Francisco's schools in the early twentieth century, as late as 1920, the Irish in the city by the bay seemed no surer of their place and role than did the Irish in Boston or Worcester or any other Massachusetts city.[19]

I do not mean in all this to excuse any of the various people of Boston. I make no apologies for abuse of the city's Irish, Italians, or Poles or for those groups' abuse of others. I believe, however, that the history of immigrants and their descendants in Boston deserves a fresh perspective and new exploration and study. The nature of Boston as immigrant destination needs a finer analysis, perhaps even tracing individuals through the ports of their settlement. Using the research of genealogists may ease the burden of such a painstaking study. Further investigation, especially in the case of the Irish, of where immigrants came from in the old country, what peculiar local conditions drove them to the United States, where they settled, and whom they married once they arrived here is also necessary. The fabled Boston environment, as I have noted, also needs closer scrutiny, particularly the divisions and changes within Yankee society. In terms of the city's ethnic groups, we can no longer accept history that ends with the immigrants and simply projects forward to the present. Each intervening generation and era in Boston's ethnic history demands investigation. Finally, if we are going to compare Boston or other cities with each other, we must know what we think is the norm.

In a play by William Alfred, the main character, Matthew Stanton, describes the embarrassment and discomforts of his journey to the United States. His soliloquy ends as he recalls that "a bitch doctor with his nails too long, dared tell me: 'In America, we bathe!' Matt continues, "I'd have died of shame, had I sailed here to die." Though Matthew Stanton is a tragic figure, his words suggest something of the resilience of immigrant people. They did not sail here to die or be merely passive pawns in a play of forces beyond their control. This was as true of Boston's Irish and Italians as of any other groups in any other city. The hardships these people endured or the frustrations they vented should not let us underestimate them. They deserve neither filiopietism nor patronizing. They deserve only to be depicted truthfully as human beings of courage and cowardice, intelligence and stupidity, compassion and cruelty. They deserve no more, but they deserve no less.

Notes

1. William Shannon, *The American Irish: A Political and Social Portrait* (New York: Collier Books, 1970), 216; U.S. Bureau of Statistics, *Arrivals of Alien Passengers in the United States from 1820 to 1892* (Washington: GPO, 1893), 122–24.

2. Caroline Golab, *Immigrant Destinations* (Philadelphia: Temple University Press, 1977), 168; Bureau of Statistics, *Arrivals of Alien Passengers*, 122–24.

3. Bureau of Statistics, *Arrivals of Alien Passengers*, 122–24; *Fourteenth Census of the United States Taken in the Year 1920*, vol. 1, "Population," part 1, 1007–08.

4. Lists of Alien Passengers Entering the Port of Boston, 1891, reel 114, Boston Public Library, (BPL) Boston, Massachusetts; "Report of the Superintendent of Alien Passengers to the House," *House Documents*, no. 17 (Boston: William White Printers, 1857), 3–4; "Immigration Commission," House Documents no. 67 (Boston: Wright and Potter, 1914), 178–80.

5. Lists of Alien Passengers, 1834, reel 8, BPL: "Report of the Superintendent," *House Documents*, no. 17, 2–3.

6. Kerby Miller, *Emigrants and Exiles: Ireland and the Irish Exodus to North America* (New York: Oxford University Press, 1985), 193–97, 199; Lists of Alien

Passengers, 1834, reel 8, BPL; Marcus Lee Hansen, *The Immigrant in American History* (Cambridge: Harvard University Press, 1940), 159–60.

7. Oscar Handlin, *Boston's Immigrants: A Study in Acculturation* (Boston: Atheneum Press, 1972), 48–49. Fewer than 500 of the readers placing advertisements in the Missing Friends Column entered North America through New York and Boston; fewer than 125 through Boston alone. By contrast, close to six hundred arrived through Canadian ports. The period was 1831 to 1850. Statistics provided by Ruth Ann Harris, Northeastern University.

8. Golab, *Immigrant Destinations*, 24–25; Handlin, *Boston's Immigrants*, 34–38.

9. Miller, *Emigrants and Exiles*, 9–130; Robert De Marco, *Ethnics and Enclaves: Boston's Italian North End*, (Ann Arbor: UMI Research Press, 1981), 1–14.

10.

Pilot		Gravestone Inscriptions	Baptismal
Advertisements		*Mt. Auburn*	*Registers*
Munster	46.1%	53%	54%
Connaught	21.8	8	28
Ulster	14.9	23	9.9
Leinster	17.0	16	7.9
Total (no.)	100%:(713)	(405)	(935)

SOURCES: Statistics from *Pilot* advertisements provided by Ruth Ann Harris, Northeastern University; "Gravestone Inscriptions from Mt. Auburn Catholic Cemetery, Watertown, Mass.," compiled and analyzed by Marie E. Daly; baptismal registers, St. Peter's, West Cambridge, 1872; Immaculate Conception, Newburyport, 1872; Mission Church, Roxbury, 1889; Our Lady Help of Christians, Newton, 1885 to 1886, Archives of the Archdiocese of Boston.

For the North End, see Daly, "Gravestone Inscriptions" and *Golden Jubilee of the Society of Jesus in Boston, Mass. 1847 to 1897, St. Mary's Parish October 3, 4, 5, and 6 1897*. For the rise in emigration from Connaught in the 1880s, note the following breakdown of statistics from the parish baptismal registers:

	St. Peter's, Cambridge and Immaculate Conception, Newburyport (1872)	*Mission, Roxbury and Our Lady Help of Christians, Newton (1889 and 1885–86)*
Munster	67%	30.3
Connaught	16.5	49
Ulster	9.4	10.5
Leinster	6.4	10.2

11. Outflow from Irish Provinces:

	1851–55	*1856–80*	*1881–1910*
Munster	39.6%	33.0%	35.0%
Connaught	13.1	12.6	23.6
Ulster	23.4	13.9	26.6
Leinster	22.9	17.0	14.9

SOURCE: Miller, *Emigrants and Exiles*, 574–75.

Irish in Milwaukee's Fourth Ward:

Munster	41%

Connaught   15
Ulster   11
Leinster   24

SOURCE: Kathleen Neils Conzen, *Immigrant Milwaukee, 1836–1860* (Cambridge: Harvard University Press, 1976), 25–26.

12. De Marco, *Ethnics and Enclaves,* 15–44.
13. Ibid.

14. Handlin, *Boston's Immigrants,* 34–39; David N. Doyle, "The Regional Bibliography of Irish America 1880 to 1930: A Review and Addendum" *Irish Historical Studies* vol. 13, no. 1 (May 1983) pp. 254–55; Lawrence McCaffrey, *The Irish Diaspora* (Bloomington: Indiana University Press, 1976), 77–79; James Walsh, "The Irish in the New America: Way out West," in David N. Doyle and Owen Dudley Edwards, eds., *The American Identity and the Irish Connection* (Westport, Conn.: Greenwood Press, 1976), 165–77; Seamus Breatanac, "Should Irish Eyes Be Smiling?" in James Walsh, *The Irish: America's Political Class* (New York: Arno Press, 1976), 26–29; David N. Doyle, *Irish Americans, Native Rights and National Empires* (New York: Arno Press, 1976), 65–95, 182–200.

15. Handlin, *Boston's Immigrants,* 122–23, 206, 228–29; Stephan Thernstrom, *The Other Bostonians: Poverty and Progress in the American Metropolis, 1880–1970* (Cambridge: Harvard University Press, 1973, 111–75; J. Anthony Lukas, *Common Ground* (New York: Random House, 1985), 139–59; 224–25; 252–76.

16. See especially Doyle, *Native Rights and National Empires* and "Regional Bibliography"; and McCaffrey, *Irish Diaspora.*

17. Stephan Thernstrom, *The Other Bostonians,* 111–75; R. A. Burchell *The Irish in San Francisco* (Berkeley: University of California Press, 1981); Dennis Clark,*The Irish in Philadelphia: Ten Generations of Urban Experience* (Philadelphia: Temple University Press, 1972); Thomas Kessner, *The Golden Door: Italian and Jewish Immigrant Mobility in New York City, 1880 to 1915* (New York: Oxford University Press, 1977); Shannon, *The American Irish;* John F. Stack, Jr., *International Conflict in an American City, 1935–1944* (Westport, Conn.: Greenwood Press, 1979), 50–57; Lukas, *Common Ground, 252–76.*

18. Geoffrey Blodgett, "Yankee Leadership in a Divided City," in Ronald Formisano and Constance Burns, eds., *Boston, 1700–1800: The Evolution of Urban Politics* (Westport, Conn.: Greenwood Press, 1984), 87–110; Donna Merwick, *Boston Priests, 1848–1910* (Cambridge: Harvard University Press, 1973), 69–110; Thomas N. Brown, *Irish American Nationalism: 1870 to 1890* (Philadelphia: Lippincott and Co., 1966).

19. James Walsh, *Ethnic Militancy: An Irish Catholic Prototype* (San Francisco: R and E Research Associates, 1975); Robert Senkiewicz, "American and Catholic: The Premature Synthesis of the San Francisco Irish," in David Alvarez, ed., *An American Church: Essays on the Americanization of the Catholic Church* (Moraga, Calif.: Saint Mary's College, 1979), 141–51.

2

Immigration through the Port of Philadelphia

FREDRIC M. MILLER

Since its founding by William Penn in 1682, Philadelphia has been both an immigrant port and a city of immigrants. In fact, the first major movement of non-British Europeans to an English-speaking colony was the migration to Germantown—now part of Philadelphia—by Dutch and German religious groups beginning in 1683. But that event proved exceptional, for the Germantown settlers not only landed in Philadelphia, but also stayed in the area. Historically, by contrast, most people who arrived in the city soon made their way elsewhere, while most immigrants who settled locally had debarked at another port, usually New York, just ninety miles to the northeast. As a result, ever since the 1820s, the city's immigrant population has been much larger and more diverse than the volume of direct migration would indicate. Philadelphia as an immigrant port of entry has been very different from, and less important than, Philadelphia as an immigrant city.

Nevertheless, the history of Philadelphia as an immigrant port is a rich and complex story of peaks and valleys, false starts, changing economic interests, and perseverance against natural disadvantages. The city is 110 miles from the ocean, up a shallow bay and winding river channel. The Delaware River freezes often, unlike New York's harbor, and the ocean voyage from Europe to Philadelphia is 200 miles longer than the voyage to New York—two serious impediments, especially in the formative years of wooden sailing ships, when the preference for Philadelphia's rival was established. Even so, between 1815 and 1985, more than 1.3 million immigrants entered America through Philadelphia, about a quarter of a million in the period up to 1873, followed by just over a million during the next fifty years. Despite quotas and stricter regulations, yet another hundred thousand immigrants have arrived through Philadelphia since the mid-1920s.[1] From the settlement of Germantown in the seventeenth century to the arrival of Koreans in the 1980s, the city has played a role in every migration to this country.

Accommodations of Emigrant Depot, Philadelphia.

Connected with the Docks and Depot, and under the same roof, are

A Telegraph Office, enabling emigrants to have telegraphic communication with friends and relatives in any part of the United States or Europe.

A United States Letter-Box, for the deposit of letters emigrants may have to send to any part of the United States or Europe.

An Exchange Office, where drafts are cashed and money is exchanged at the most favorable rates.

A Baggage Express Office, for the **cheap** and **speedy transfer** of baggage **to and from** steamer landings, railroad depots, hotels, and private dwellings within the city of Philadelphia and suburbs.

A Ticket Office, at which tickets are issued at very low rates to any part of the United States and Canada, and baggage checked through to destination.

Accommodations of Emigrant Depot, Philadelphia, ca. 1885. American Line broadside. *(Courtesy of the Philadelphia Maritme Museum.)*

Although Philadelphia's role has been continuous, it has also been limited since the 1820s. The city's geographic disadvantages combined with the cautious approach of the city's business community to the risks of both overseas trade and such innovations as steamships to restrict Philadelphia's proportion of immigration. In the three most important periods of immigration through the port—1847 to 1854, 1880 to 1900 and 1910 to 1914—the city's share of the national total reached only 4.4 percent, 5.6 percent, and 4.8 percent respectively. Regardless of very different mixes of immigrants and shipping lines and the fact that each period marked a distinct upswing in local economic activity, the proportion remained remarkably consistent and relatively low. Once the supremacy of New York was firmly established, Philadelphia's subordinate and generally dependent role was also set.

In national terms, Philadelphia certainly had been most important as an immigrant port in the eighteenth century. Beginning about 1717, when the Provincial Assembly ordered ship captains to submit passenger lists to officials, there were true mass migrations of Germans and Ulster's Scotch-Irish directly to Philadelphia, as both groups proved eager to exploit the city's rich farming hinterland. Some thirty-six ships arrived between 1727 and 1733 from Germany alone, and between 1737 and

1754, the average was eleven per year. In 1749, twenty-two ships with seven thousand immigrants from the Rhineland made the seven-week voyage to the city.[2] In all, about seventy thousand Germans landed in the fifty years before the Revolution. Philadelphia also received the largest share of the more than 150,000 Scotch-Irish who migrated to the colonies. In both groups, the majority were so poor that they had come as indentured servants or "redemptioners," who had to work off the borrowed price of their passage.[3] Many were thus forced to stay in the city, helping to make it the largest in the colonies by the time of the Revolution.

Large-scale European immigration to the new United States did not resume until after the end of the Napoleonic Wars in 1815. By then, New York's commercial connections with Europe, its magnificent harbor, and its transportation links with the interior were rapidly making it the nation's largest foreign port while the Philadelphia business community was turning its interest inland. There were still many Philadelphia merchants active in overseas trade, however, and many ships were bringing immigrants to the city. In order to prevent them from also bringing in such contagious diseases as yellow fever, by 1798 a quarantine hospital, or Lazaretto, had been built a few miles below Philadelphia; after 1815, it was busy. Sixty-two ships from Ireland, many carrying immigrants, arrived over the next four years.[4] Between 1820 and 1831, over twenty thousand immigrants came to the city, one-eighth of the national total.[5] Two lines of Philadelphia-owned sailing ships ran regularly to Liverpool, by then the main center for Irish as well as English emigration. Steerage tickets cost between five and seven pounds, at a time when a good British factory wage was one pound per week. Of the two lines, one, belonging to John Welsh, functioned for only a short time. The other, belonging to Thomas Cope, was important and long lasting. Cope, an archetypical conservative Quaker merchant and a descendant of one of Penn's original grantees, began his Liverpool service in 1821, and his ships, the *Tonawanda, Tuscarora,* and *Wyoming* carried thousands to Philadelphia over the next four decades.[6]

Immigration continued steadily in the 1830s and early 1840s, as Cope ships were occasionally joined by other sailings from British and continental ports. Between 1830 and the great famine migration of 1847, about sixty thousand immigrants landed in Philadelphia.[7] But many more people were by this time coming to the city via New York. Philadelphia's share of all immigrant arrivals had fallen to just under 5 percent, where it would stay until the Civil War. One cause of the decline was simply ice in the river for too many months of the year. The city finally bought an ice boat in 1838, but its struggles against five-foot-thick ice ridges were not an ideal inducement to shipping. That same year, moreover, transatlantic steam navigation was proved practicable. Some local businessmen tried to raise funds for a Philadelphia-based line, but in the midst of an economic depression, they failed to find enough investors in the new technology. Thus, the city faced the massive Irish and German migrations of the late 1840s with only its one line of sailing ships to Europe.[8]

However, demand quickly brought forth an increased supply of sailing-ships: Shippers established two new lines from Liverpool, another line plied between Philadelphia and Londonderry, and individual ships arrived from other ports.[9] All told, in the eight years from 1847 through 1854, over 120,000 immigrants arrived in Philadelphia, now just the nation's fourth largest immigrant port. The total for 1853 alone—19,211—exceeded the total for the decade of the 1820s.[10]

The city's first steamship line, officially known as the Liverpool and Philadelphia Steam Ship Company, was owned by the Richardson Brothers, who were Liverpool Quakers. But the real force was their partner, William Inman. In 1850, Inman persuaded the Richardsons to expand their line of sailing packets to buy an advanced new steamship, named the *City of Glasgow*. The ship left Liverpool on 17 December with four hundred passengers and arrived only ten days later in Philadelphia. Within a few years, it had been joined by more "City" ships, named after Manchester, Baltimore, and Philadelphia. A steerage ticket cost eight pounds eight shillings—several months' wages for a laborer—but business was brisk. In 1854, the *City of Manchester* made five trips to Philadelphia, with as many as 532 passengers each time. But that year saw disaster as well: The *City of Glasgow* disappeared in March on its way to Philadelphia with 430 passengers in one of the great sea disasters of the mid-nineteenth century. In September, the *City of Philadelphia* went aground on Cape Race, Newfoundland; passengers were saved, but the ship was lost. The next year, the Richardsons withdrew from the business when Inman violated their Quaker principles by leasing their ships to France for use in the Crimean War. Now on his own and without a Quaker connection, Inman in 1857 dropped service to Philadelphia in favor of New York, and no local entrepreneurs took Inman's place in the steamship business to the city.[11]

Of course, many sailing ships continued to bring immigrants to the wharves lining the Delaware riverfront. Some companies tried to offset the extra travel time by changing fares below those to New York. But the tedious two-week voyage around Cape May and up the river—all the more frustrating because land was continually in sight—continued to limit immigration through Philadelphia.

One company that did operate a profitable, if small, sailing operation was McCorbell & Co. of Londonderry in what is now Northern Ireland.

In July 1851, the emigration officer in Londonderry, Edward Smith, offered a parliamentary inquiry a detailed account of migration to Philadelphia.[12] He noted that most emigrants from Londonderry went to Philadelphia. In the first half of 1851, with the effects of the great famine still evident, thirteen ships had sailed to Philadelphia, compared to four to New York and five to Canada. The year's migration to Philadelphia already totaled approximately 2,500, he explained, and there would probably be seven more voyages to the city before sailings ended in the fall. The emigration officer thought that Londonderry's emigrants were slightly wealthier than the Irish who left from Liverpool, since fares from the latter city were still lower and the range of berths available much greater. Central to the whole link between Londonderry and Philadelphia, Smith explained, was the money for passage remitted by recent arrivals in America. He noted that one firm—probably McCorbell—had received 24,000 pounds from America for tickets in 1850.

The season for emigration from Londonderry to Philadelphia lasted only from April to October, and the trip took a month, according to Smith's testimony. On the McCorbell ships, which accommodated up to four hundred passengers per voyage, a bulkhead divided the one deck into intermediate and steerage classes. Steerage berths were six feet by six feet and held four people each. Although single men and single women were separated, two married couples were sometimes berthed together. On the return trip to Londonderry, Smith concluded, passengers were usually replaced by a cargo of American corn.

The McCorbell line continued to serve Philadelphia until about 1870. As late as 1865, 1,359 immigrants arrived from Londonderry, and one old McCorbell ship, the *Mohongo*, made two voyages with about five hundred passengers on each.[13] But by then, the days of immigration by sail were clearly numbered.

The Cope line from Liverpool was also winding down by that time. Thomas Cope had died in 1854, though Cope company ships remained busy in the 1850s, bringing English and Irish emigrants from Liverpool to Philadelphia. At the same time, continental Europeans coming to Philadelphia numbered only in the hundreds. An official British report of 1855 stated that of 7,206 non-Americans arriving in Philadelphia from all ports, 2,890 were from England and Wales, 3,374 from Ireland, and 425 from Germany.[14] More than three thousand of these passengers had come from Liverpool. On the eve of the Civil War, the Cope line had four ships, each making three voyages and bringing over two thousand each year.[15] The family-owned company never switched to steam. After the Civil War, it was virtually alone in using sail on the North Atlantic immigrant routes, as the grandchildren of Thomas Cope turned from mercantile initiative to philanthropy and culture.[16]

Sporadic voyages were made for the next few years, but even they ended after 1868. The loss of the innovative Inman line to New York and the conservatism of the local Cope enterprise—together with the disruption of the Civil War—had left the country's second largest city virtually bereft of direct passenger and immigrant connections with Europe.

The next five years marked a low point in the history of Philadelphia as an immigrant port. Between 1855 and 1864, more than fifty thousand immigrants had come to the city, about 3 percent of the national total.[17] But from 1865 until the start of new lines in 1873, the total was under ten thousand. By 1872, with over 400,000 people migrating to America, Philadelphia's officially reported share was 154, including 48 Spaniards, 19 Frenchmen, and hardly credible 2 immigrants from Ireland.[18]

The decline of direct immigration stood in marked contrast to Philadelphia's emergence as one of the great immigrant cities of the mid-nineteenth century. What had been a mercantile city of about 30,000 crowded along the Delaware during the Revolutionary War had, by 1850, grown into an industrial metropolis of over 400,000 people. Philadelphia led the nation in many types of modern manufacturing as well as in numerous skilled trades. The urban area stretched all the way to the Schuylkill River on the west and beyond William Penn's old boundaries on the north and south to include the working-class and immigrant neighborhoods of Kensington, Southwark, Moyamensing, and the Northern Liberties. As a result of the immigrant wave of the 1840s, three out of ten Philadelphians in 1850 were foreign born, the highest proportion ever recorded. The Germans and Irish accounted for more than three-quarters of the total, since about twenty thousand of the former and seventy thousand of the latter lived in Philadelphia.[19]

In the absence of significant public transportation, most Philadelphians of all origins and classes lived near their jobs, and immigrants were thus spread around the city far more evenly than later groups would be. There were some ethnic concentrations, though, generally based on job specialization and related income levels. The Irish were initially much poorer than the Germans as a group. In 1850, nearly half of the Irish were engaged in day labor, handloom weaving or carting, with less than a third in skilled trades. Two-thirds of the Germans, by contrast, were employed in skilled trades, such as tailoring, shoemaking, and baking. The Germans settled fairly heavily in the Northern Liberties and other new manufacturing districts to the northeast of the old city. Even so, these areas were neither predominantly German nor home to a large number of the city's German immigrants. The Irish were still more dispersed around Philadelphia. The city's housing and transportation patterns, and their concentration in general construction work, led many of the Irish to live in small houses in alleys or side streets all over Philadelphia, rather than in large ethnic neighborhoods. This pattern was not universal, however, and as early as 1850, Irish concentrations did exist along the southern borders of the city in Southwark, Moyamensing, and Gray's Ferry.[20]

Over the next two decades, Philadelphia's immigrant population continued to grow steadily, but the city's ethnic mix remained stable. By the mid-1870s, Philadelphia had grown by 350,000 people and was home to about three-quarters of a million residents. It remained the second largest city in the United States. Its economy was firmly based on dozens of major enterprises in the textile, metal products, machine goods, printing, and chemical industries. Over a quarter of the population was foreign born, with a hundred thousand Irish and fifty thousand Germans accounting for more than five-sixths of all the city's immigrants, while almost all other immigrants were from England and Scotland. In 1858, horsecar lines had begun running on iron rails, and soon after, the Civil War developers had started building large tracts of uniform row houses in north and south Philadelphia, especially east of Broad Street, and across the Schuylkill in west Philadelphia.[21] Farther to the northwest, Germantown became a middle-class commuter suburb.

In the 1870s, as at midcentury, Germans and British immigrants were much more common in the skilled trades than were the Irish. While more of the Irish now had good factory jobs, many remained in building and unskilled labor.[22] The difference in Philadelphia was partly the continuation of differences in Europe. Most Irish immigrants had come from rural areas rather than industrial cities, though there was a steady influx of skilled English factory workers. In 1855, 3,508 immigrants, predominantly Irish, who had arrived in Philadelphia directly from Europe reported their occupations to American authorities. The largest group, numbering 1,459, were laborers, while there were also 686 female domestic servants, 359 farmers, 643 mechanics, mostly from England, 171 miners, and 37 mariners.[23] Twenty years later, similar backgrounds still defined some ten thousand immigrants who landed in Philadelphia: Laborers numbered 1,650, and there were 895 farmers and 851 domestics. But the list of other occupations illustrates the wide range of skilled people drawn from the British Isles to Philadelphia in the 1870s. It included 13 confectioners, 109 shoemakers, 52 musicians, 170 carpenters, 20 cooks, 67 blacksmiths, and even 9 clergymen.[45]

Unable to afford the horsecar fare or the new houses, most laborers and industrial workers remained tied to the neighborhoods in which they worked, while more affluent Philadelphians of all ethnic groups were moving out of the old parts of the city to the northwest and west. German-born Philadelphians now lived all over the city, although the concentration of the German population in the Northern Liberties and Kensington had not only persisted but expanded into other parts of north and northeast Philadelphia. The Kensington mill district also had a significant population of British immigrants. At the same time, a large community of Irish skilled workers and middle-class families had developed west of Broad Street on both sides of South Street, but that was by no means a predominantly Irish area. Likewise, there was no Irish ghetto—or German ghetto—in the later sense of the term. Like the Germans and the British, the Irish lived all over the city. Some Irish businessmen and professionals moved to the suburbs, while others lived downtown in the traditional style of wealthy Philadelphians.[25]

The glaring contrast in the early 1870s between Philadelphia's immigrant-based expansion and its moribund immigrant port did not last long. Two modern steamship companies were established locally in 1873. Their operations ushered in a fifty-year period of active immigration through Philadelphia, during which just over a million immigrants arrived in the city. By the early 1880s, Philadelphia had reclaimed its place as the fourth largest immigrant port of entry in the country.

The more important of the two companies was the American Line, which dominated the city's immigrant traffic until World War I. It was founded by the locally dominant Pennsylvania Railroad, whose owners saw a need for a direct freight and passenger link with Europe, bypassing New York. The line soon opened the city's first immigrant station at a railroad-owned pier at the foot of Washington Avenue in south Philadelphia. Launched the previous August at Philadelphia's Cramp's Shipyard, in May 1873 the *Ohio* began the line's regular service to Liverpool, via Queenstown in the south of Ireland. Three other modern iron steamers—the *Pennsylvania, Indiana,* and *Illinois*—soon joined the fleet, each carrying up to four hundred passengers. The line also leased up to half a dozen other ships in the 1880s, so that it could offer three sailings per week to Liverpool. By 1882, when the American Line carried 17,342 passengers to Philadelphia, it was the most important and technologically advanced American-owned steamship company.[26]

Although the American line began servicing New York in the 1890s, it never abandoned Philadelphia, because of the Pennsylvania Railroad connection. New ships with such local names as the *Kensington, Southwark, Haverford,* and *Merion* were added to the Philadelphia run around the turn of the century. By then, the American Line's prosperity was firmly based on new waves of immigrants coming from eastern and southern Europe to America via Britain. After World War I, the American line briefly resumed its immigrant service from Liverpool but leased it in 1921 to the British White Star Line, which only maintained it for another three years.[27] Throughout the period from 1880 to 1910,

Washington Avenue Immigration Station, Philadelphia, 1913. *(Courtesy of Philadelphia City Archives.)*

however, the American Line accounted for the bulk of roughly twenty thousand immigrants per year arriving annually in Philadelphia.[28]

The American Line's major local competitor was the Red Star Line, which connected Philadelphia with the Continent directly through Antwerp, Belgium, traditionally a major center for German and northern European migration. Red Star's service began in 1873, also with strong backing from the Pennsylvania Railroad, and it was maintained with several ships on a regular basis until World War I. While the traffic was never extensive, there was enough business to justify purchasing two new ships specifically for the Philadelphia line in 1906 and 1907.[29]

The success of the Red Star and American Lines encouraged other larger companies to extend service to the city. As early as 1884, the Allan Line began service from Glasgow. In 1898, the largest German company—the Hamburg-American Line—started a run between Hamburg and Philadelphia that drew directly on the great Jewish and Polish migrations from Russia and Austria-Hungary. Previously, few German passenger or immigrant ships had come directly to Philadelphia, but by the eve of World War I, four Hamburg-American ships were sailing regularly to Philadelphia with a stop in Boston.[30] They had been joined by ships of the Holland-America, Italia, and North German Lloyd lines by then, but only the American Line offered weekly sailings.[31]

After nearly fifty thousand immigrants arrived at the port in both 1911 and 1912, immigration through Philadelphia peaked at over sixty thousand in 1913. Between 1910 and 1914, about a quarter of a million immigrants arrived in Philadelphia, nearly 5 percent of the national total. Philadelphia had become the third most important immigrant port in the country at the very height of immigration from southern and eastern Europe.[32]

The First World War put an abrupt end to this growth. By 1923, only the old *Haverford,* now leased by Britain's White Star Line, carried large numbers of immigrants.[33] Restrictive immigration quotas enacted the next year ended even that activity, reducing the booming immigration of only ten years earlier to nothing more than a memory.

Fifty years of large-scale immigration had naturally had a profound effect on the city's immigration facilities. In the nineteenth century, Pennsylvania required almost all ships from Europe and the South coming to Philadelphia between the spring and the fall to stop first for a health inspection at the Lazaretto in Essington, eight miles down river from the city. There, passengers from vessels carrying people with infectious diseases could be isolated for up to several months. The Lazaretto hospital could accommodate five hundred passengers, while the steam disinfecting plant heated their clothing and baggage to 220 degrees.[34] Nevertheless, in 1884 the federal government established a National Quarantine Station of its own at the mouth of Delaware Bay near Lewes, Delaware, to check ships coming from ports with reported infections. Nine years later, in the midst of a cholera scare, the government set up another national station—mainly for disinfecting—at Reedy Island, some forty-five miles below Philadelphia. Duplicate inspections by state and federal authorities continued to annoy passengers until 1913, when inspections were centralized at a new state facility at Marcus Hook, twenty miles from the Philadelphia docks.[35] Finally, in 1919, the state ended its inspection service. In any case, Philadelphia had been more than adequately protected against disease and, after 1866, experienced no epidemics of the cholera prevalent in many European ports.[36]

Very few people, however, were kept out by either health precautions or federal laws from 1872 on barring paupers and criminals. By various means—not all of them strictly legal—immigrants passed inspection. From 1901 to 1902, for example, of 17,175 arrivals in Philadelphia, though many were detained for questioning or investigation, only 107 were debarred from entering the country—twenty-six for diseases, eighty as paupers, and one as a convict.[37] For the latter two groups and other illegal aliens, the city maintained a detention center at Second and Christian streets.[38]

Almost all immigrants made their first contact with America at the piers and immigrant stations. And according to all accounts, for most who came through Philadelphia, it was their only contact with the city, since they were quickly taken elsewhere by relatives or employers. But between the 1870s and the early 1920s, the Delaware River waterfront was a bustling place, especially around the Washington Avenue wharves where the American and Red Star lines docked. This was an area of warehouses, factories, sugar refineries, freight depots, and grain elevators, all connected to the vast rail yards of the Pennsylvania Railroad. The railroad owned the wharves and effectively controlled the immigrant traffic. In the 1870s, it had constructed a two-story facility for receiving immigrants. Having already had their medical examinations downriver, at Washington Avenue passengers proceeded through customs inspections and then went downstairs to a ticket office and reception area, from which they could board trains and leave the city.[39]

As immigration increased, it outgrew the capacity of the Washington Avenue building. In 1896, the railroad spent $10,000 to expand that capacity from three hundred to fifteen hundred people and modernize the whole facility, equipping it with electric lights and steam heating. Passengers now disembarked directly in the building's second story for medical examinations and questioning. The first floor had a ticket office, money exchange, women's dressing room, waiting room, and travel information bureau. As up to eight inspectors greeted each ship, it was estimated that three hundred English speaking or one hundred fifty non-English speaking passengers could be processed each hour.

The station naturally became one of the most colorful places in Philadelphia. For example, one part of the examination room was called the altar because under some conditions single women were prevented from landing, so that many hurried unions were celebrated on the spot. Outside, there was usually a crowd of entrepreneurs eager to charge newcomers exorbitant rates for a variety of needed and unneeded services.[40]

Just before World War I, the surging immigrant traffic spread to other Philadelphia piers. By 1912, the Red Star Line had a pier on Reed Street in south Philadelphia, the North German Lloyd landed north of Washington Avenue at Fitzwater Street, and the Allan Line docked north of the downtown at Callowhill Street. In addition. a municipal immigrant station, on a 571-foot-long pier at Vine Street, served the Italian ships. The station had no regular staff, however, and as at the other piers, federal inspectors were sent from Washington Avenue whenever a ship arrived.[41]

Just as work at Vine Street was starting in 1909, Philadelphia's immigration facilities became embroiled in a three-year-long regional controversy. In an attempt to divert some immigrant traffic away from New York's Ellis Island, Congress funded the construction of new immigrant stations around the country. But the $250,000 it appropriated for Philadelphia was not enough to purchase a riverfront site within city limits. A political boss from Gloucester City, New Jersey, named William Thompson, sold his own five-acre estate to the government some two years later, but World War I interrupted construction. The one building finished before the war was used as a detention center and immigration service offices. Meanwhile, since the Washington Avenue station was torn down in 1915, inspections now took place on the ships after they had docked. With immigration reduced after the war, work at Gloucester City was not resumed, and the Delaware Valley never had its anticipated equivalent of Ellis Island.[42]

Although the immigrant quotas of the early twenties which killed that project had brought a sudden end to the era of direct immigration to Philadelphia that had begun with the American and Red Star lines in 1873, in those five decades Philadelphia had again been transformed by immigration. At first, Great Britain, Ireland, and Germany continued as sources of immigrants to Philadelphia. In 1881, nearly 15,000 of the city's total of 21,712 new arrivals were from those countries, while another 5,000 were Scandinavian.[43] The 1880 census had revealed that more than 90 percent of the city's two hundred thousand foreign-born residents were from Germany or the British Isles, half of them from Ireland alone.

But a massive change began in the eighties. In 1882, the American Line's *Illinois* brought to Philadelphia 360 Russian Jews fleeing po-groms.[44] Ten years later, the number of Russian Jews arriving directly in the city exceeded three thousand, almost equaling the Irish immigration. When the Red Star Line's *Nederland* inaugurated the new Washington Avenue station in 1896, its 568 passengers from Antwerp were mainly Hungarians, Poles, Russians, and Germans.[45] The bulk of the more than four hundred thousand immigrants who arrived in Philadelphia between 1890 and 1910 were from central and eastern Europe, and they had come to the city after making their way to such ports as Hamburg, Antwerp, and Liverpool. The start of regular service from Italy in 1908 led to a rapid increase in direct Italian immigration. By 1914, most of Philadelphia's 68,837 foreign passengers were from Russia (29,000), Italy (19,000), and the Austro-Hungarian Empire (13,000). Only five thousand were from Great Britain and Ireland.

Most immigrants who settled in the city still came via New York rather than directly to Philadelphia, but their backgrounds had changed as had those of the direct immigrants. As late as 1900, Germans, Irish, and British still made up over two-thirds of Philadelphia's foreign born, though nearly thirty thousand Russian Jews and twenty thousand Italians already lived in the city. Only twenty years later, Italians nearly equaled the Irish at about sixty thousand each, while Russian Jews numbered almost one hundred thousand. There were now more Philadelphians who had been born in Poland (31,112) than in England (30,886), and Germans numbered less than forty thousand.[46] After the final burst of immigration in the early 1920s, immigrants and children of immigrants accounted for nearly a million Philadelphians—half the city's total population—including about 200,000 Italians and an equal number of eastern European Jews.

Industrial expansion and an abundance of cheap and available housing had fueled the growth of this "workshop of the world." At the turn of the century, Philadelphia led the nation in such diverse industries as the production of locomotives, streetcars, saws, rugs, hosiery, hats, leather goods, and cigars. It was second in sugar and petroleum refining and the production of drugs and chemicals. Because most of the city's industries relied on skilled and semiskilled workers rather than on massive concentrations of unskilled laborers, Philadelphia attracted fewer Slavic immigrants than such cities as Pittsburgh, Detroit, and Chicago.

Philadelphia's relatively skilled workers were fairly well paid, so they could afford to buy many of the several hundred thousand row houses built between 1880 and 1920. In the 1890s, the electrification of the horsecar trolley lines greatly extended practical commuting distance and rowhouse development rapidly spread until it filled the areas between the city's industrial belts, which extended for miles along rivers and rail lines. By the twenties, nearly half of all Philadelphians owned their own residences, and the city's population density was remarkably low.[47]

A complex mixture of ethnic relationships, customs, occupational specializations, and neighborhood settlements now characterized immigrant Philadelphia. In the early twentieth century, Irish and Germans remained fairly evenly distributed around the city, with few of them in recognizable ethnic enclaves. Both groups were now comparatively prosperous, mostly employed in skilled industrial or white-collar occupations. Along with those of British background, they tended to predominate in the commuter developments being constructed along the new trolley and subway lines extending through west Philadelphia and such parts of northern Philadelphia as Olney, Oak Lane, and Logan. For these groups, ethnic, religious, cultural, social, and political ties remained important, but these were far from dominant in their lives.

The situation of the new immigrant groups was very different. In the first decades of this century, Italians, Poles, and Jews were much more concentrated in traditional ethnic neighborhoods and streets. Comprising a large portion of the city's laborers, unskilled workers, and small merchants, they still generally had to live close to their jobs. Both Jews and Italians initially crowded into the old streets and alleys not far from the Delaware. But by 1930, the two groups had diverged. the Italians,

now well established in the garment, construction, and waterfront industries enlarged their settlement in south Philadelphia further to the south
and west. In contrast, Jews had moved to several different parts of north
and west Philadelphia, leaving only modest communities in the old
neighborhoods they had shared with the Italians. Poles, a much smaller
group, followed yet another pattern, settling near their jobs in outlying
industrial areas, such as Manayunk, Nicetown, and Bridesburg; like the
Italians', their settlements were long lasting. In addition, the new immigrant groups preserved their unity through family ties, fraternal groups,
and religious congregations, so that by the 1920s, Philadelphia had as
rich and complex an ethnic life as any city in the country.[48]

Philadelphia, however, was no longer a significant immigrant port of
entry. The effect of quotas limiting immigration from southern and
eastern Europe was to kill an already ailing immigrant business. The
9,555 immigrants of 1924 were followed by just 731 in 1925, and the
total did not exceed a thousand for nearly twenty years. By 1929, more
aliens were being deported through the Gloucester City detention center, classified as criminals or mental defectives, than were being admitted
through the port.[49] Total immigration to Philadelphia for the forty-five
years from 1925 to 1970 was only thirty thousand. Philadelphia's decline
was much steeper than the national decrease in immigration. Although
the city had received 5 percent of all immigrants from the 1870s to
World War I, in the postwar years it received less than 1 percent.[50]

Unlike any previous trough, this decline has never been reversed.
Instead, hundreds of thousands of blacks migrated from the American
South to Philadelphia over the next half-century, filling many of the
roles once occupied by earlier European immigrants. Yet Philadelphia
has continued to receive some members of each major foreign influx,
including up to sixteen thousand Displaced Persons from eastern Europe after World War II and much smaller numbers of Hungarians from
1956 to 1957, Cubans in the early sixties, Soviet Jews in the early
seventies, and Indochinese refugees after 1975.[51] There was also a small
continuing stream of immigrants in the 1950s and 1960s from Germany,
Ireland, Italy, and Britain. After the reform of the immigration laws in
the late 1960s, they were joined by Greeks, Filipinos, and Koreans. By
then, the international airport had become the center for immigration to
Philadelphia. The overall total of direct immigrants remained low, however, numbering about thirty-five thousand for the entire decade of the
seventies, despite liberalized legislation and special refugee provisions.[52]

Today, the contrast between the immigrant port and the immigrant
city still characterizes Philadelphia. For instance, there were 127,000
foreign-born Philadelphians in 1970, but many more people were being
naturalized in the city than actually arrived through the airport. By
1980, when the largest single group naturalized were Koreans,[53] the

census showed that the city contained over twenty thousand people of Asian ancestry and over two thousand Cubans. Visible Irish, Italian, Jewish, and Polish neighborhoods, such as Gray's Ferry, south Philadelphia, Oxford Circle, and Bridesburg remained. And there were far newer communities of Koreans, Vietnamese, and Greeks in such areas as Olney, Logan, and west Philadelphia, which had housed earlier waves of immigrants.

Although ships no longer bring immigrants to the banks of the Delaware, the legacy of the immigrant port is very much alive. Philadelphia remains a city of ethnic traditions and associations. The Irish, Jews, Italians, and Poles whose ancestors crowded onto ships of the Cope, Inman, McCorbell, American, and Red Star lines, or who came to the city after landing in New York, still form the largest and most visible groups among the city's white population. As an immigrant port, Philadelphia played a subordinate, though not unimportant, role in the massive immigration from Europe to the United States. But the immigrants who settled in Philadelphia created what continues to be not only one of the nation's largest cities, but also one of its most diverse.

Table 1
Immigration to Philadelphia, 1820–1930[a]

Years	Arrivals in Philadelphia	Annual Average	National Immigration (in 000s)	Philadelphia % of National Immigration
1820–31	24,231	2,019	200.4	12.1
1832–46	58,297	4,164	1,227.5	4.7
1847–54	124,583	15,572	2,817.3	4.4
1855–66[b]	54,600	4,550	2,199.0	2.4
1867–73	7,093	1,013	2,380.6	0.3
1874–79	42,310	7,051	1,168.7	3.6
1880–89	276,229	27,623	4,910.2	5.6
1890–99	208,234	20,823	3,694.2	5.6
1900–1909	204,265	20,426	8,202.4	2.8
1910–14	248,223	49,644	5,174.7	4.8
1915–24	55,977	5,598	3,947.1	1.4
1925–30	2,447	408	1,762.4	0.1

[a]See note 1 in text.
[b]This is an estimate. See note 17 in text.

Notes

1. See Table 1. Immigration statistics are unfortunately inconsistent. In general, local figures from 1820 to 1867 indicate alien passengers arrived; from

1868 to 1905, they include all new arrivals; and after 1906, they include all immigrant and nonimmigrant aliens. However, the vast majority of all these groups in Philadelphia were, in fact, immigrants. Sources include William J. Bromwell, *History of Immigration to the United States* (New York, 1856); United States Department of the Treasury, *Foreign Commerce and Navigation of the United States*, (1868–92); *Annual Report of the Commissioner General of Immigration* (1892–1940); and *Annual Report* or *Statistical Yearbook of the Immigration and Naturalization Service* (1941–   ). National totals can be found in Bureau of the Census, *Historical Statistics of the United States from Colonial Times to 1970* (Washington, 1976): 105–6.

2. Russell Weigley, ed., *Philadelphia: A 300–Year History* (New York, 1982): 37, 61, 74–75; Gary Nash, *The Urban Crucible* (Cambridge, Mass., 1986): 66, 67–68.

3. R. C. Simmons, *The American Colonies: From Settlement to Independence* (New York, 1976): 182–84.

4. Dennis Clark, "The Irish in Philadelphia, 1840–1870" (Ph.D diss., Temple University, 1969), 29.

5. Bromwell, *History of Immigration*, 21–65.

6. J. Thomas Scharf and Thompson Westcott, *History of Philadelphia* (Philadelphia, 1884), 2216. Great Britain, Parliamentary Papers, 1826, IV, *Report from the Select Committee on Emigration* 297.

7. Bromwell, *History of Immigration*, 65–129.

8. Weigley, 272.

9. Weigley, 323.

10. Bromwell, *History of Immigration*, 161.

11. N. R. P. Bonsor, *The North Atlantic Seaway* (New York, 1975), 218–22; Terry Coleman, *Going to America* (New York, 1972), 236–37, 240–41.

12. Parliamentary Papers, 1851, XIX, *Report from the Select Committee on the Passengers' Act*, 618–42.

13. Parliamentary Papers, 1866, XVII, *General Report of the Emigration Commissioners*, 107.

14. Parliamentary Papers, 1857, Session 2, XXVIII, *Commercial Reports, Pennsylvania*, 267.

15. See the appendices to the annual General Report of the Colonial Land and Emigration Commissioners in the Parliamentary Papers. The reports list every passenger ship, and the number of passengers, from Liverpool and Londonderry to Philadelphia for the years 1854 to 1866.

16. Scharf and Westcott, *History of Philadelphia*, 2216; Henry Simpson, *The Lives of Eminent Philadelphians* (Philadelphia, 1859), 248–56.

17. The local figures for the years 1856 through 1866 are estimates to fill the gap between Bromwell's book and the start of government reporting. They are based on the known figures of emigration from Liverpool and Londonderry, which were about half the Philadelphia total in 1855, and the known total immigration to the United States, of which Philadelphia contributed about 3.5 percent in 1854 and about 1 percent in 1867.

18. *Foreign Commerce and Navigation of the United States*, 1873, 65.

19. Alan N. Burstein, "Residential Distribution and the Mobility of Irish and German Immigrants in Philadelphia, 1850–1880" (Ph.D diss., Univ. of Pennsylvania, 1975), 77.

20. Ibid., 130–40.

21. Theodore Hershberg, ed., *Philadelphia: Work, Space, Family, and Group Experience in the Nineteenth Century* (New York, 1981), 135–37, 165–66.

22. Ibid., 106–13.

23. Parliamentary Papers, 1857, Session 2, XXVIII, 257–58.

24. *Foreign Commerce*, 1876, 81.

25. Hershberg, *Philadelphia*, 188–99.

26. Bonsor, *North Atlantic Seaway*, 920–21; Scharf and Westcott, *History of Philadelphia*, 2170; *British Parliamentary Papers Relating to Emigration*, vol. 26 (Shannon: Irish University Press, 1971), 74.

27. Bonsor, *North Atlantic Seaway*, 927, 931.

28. *Annual Report of the Commissioner General of Immigration*, 1880–1910.

29. Bonsor, *North Atlantic Seaway*, 829–41.

30. Ibid., 293–94, 366.

31. Ibid., 533, 1270, 1383–84; *Second Annual Message of Rudolph Blankenburg, Mayor of the City of Philadelphia*, Philadelphia, 1912: v 2, 483–485 (Report of the Department of Wharves, Docks, and Ferries).

32. *Annual Report of the Commissioner General of Immigration*, 1910–14.

33. Bonsor, *North Atlantic Seaway*, 945.

34. Edward Morman, "Guarding against Alien Impurities: The Philadelphia Lazaretto, 1854–1893," *Pennsylvania Magazine of History and Biography* 108 (April 1984): 132; *Handbook of the Lower Delaware* (Philadelphia: Maritime Exchange, 1895), 18–19.

35. *Handbook*, 23–34; Frank Taylor and Wilfrid Schoff, *The Port and City of Philadelphia* (Philadelphia, 1912), 37–38.

36. Morman, "Guarding against Alien Impurities," 135–36.

37. *Annual Report of the Commissioner General of Immigration*, 1902, 9.

38. *The Port of Philadelphia; Its History, Advantages and Facilities* (Philadelphia: Department of Wharves, Docks, and Ferries, 1926), 37–45.

39. Minutes of the Board of Public Charities, 23 October 1882, Philadelphia City Archives (copy in Balch Institute).

40. Immigration file, Philadelphia *Bulletin* clipping collection, Temple University Library.

41. *The Port of Philadelphia: Its Facilities and Advantages* (Harrisburg, 1914), 49–51; *Annual Report of the Mayor of Philadelphia* 1911, Department of Wharves, Docks, and Ferries: 450.

42. See the file of documents on the Gloucester City immigrant station at the Balch Institute, including memoirs and correspondence copied from the National Archives.

43. *Foreign Commerce and Navigation*, 701ff.

44. Maxwell Whiteman, "The Eastern European Jew Comes to Philadelphia," unpublished paper from Conference on the History of the Peoples of Philadelphia, 1971, 10.

45. 1896 clipping in *Bulletin* clipping file on "Immigration," Philadelphia *Bulletin* collection, Temple University Library.

46. For ethnic change in Philadelphia, see appendix A in Caroline Golab, *Immigrant Destinations* (Philadelphia, 1977), 168

47. See Fredric Miller, Morris Vogel, and Allen Davis, *Still Philadelphia: A Photographic History, 1890–1940* (Philadelphia, 1983), 3–7, 31–33.

48. In addition to Golab and Miller et al., see Stephanie Greenberg, "Industrialization in Philadelphia: The Relation between Industrial Location and Residential Patterns, 1880–1930," (Ph.D. diss., Temple University, 1977).

49. *Annual Report of the Commissioner General of Immigration*, 1925–26, 1930; Philadelphia *Bulletin*, 8 April 1919.

50. *Annual Reports* of the Commissioner General of Immigration to 1940 and

the Immigration and Naturalization Service since 1941.

51. Nationalities Service Center Collection, Temple University Urban Archives, box 21.

52. *Annual Report* and *Statistical Yearbooks of the Immigration and Naturalization Service,* 1970–80.

53. *Statistical Yearbook of the Immigration and Naturalization Service,* 1981, 75–81.

"Immigration through the Port of Philadelphia": A Comment

PHILIP SCRANTON

As often as not in discussions of immigration and particularly in treatments of immigrant cities, historians who focus with such clarity and subtlety on aspects of the immigrant experience seem to have only the most passing acquaintance with the economic context within which that experience takes shape. A week or so ago, Fredric Miller sent me a letter that supplemented his written presentation. It was a fairly direct request to develop what he termed a macroexplanation for the consistency of Philadelphia's share of the immigrant flow in three very different eras. As that is the sort of challenge an economic historian can hardly resist, I will try to offer a sense of how I would address this issue, reflecting on some of the ways in which it might be useful for all of us to place patterns of the numbers in a broader context.

Two points raised in the letter are emphasized in the paper at hand. First, in three periods of Philadelphia's history—roughly the 1830s to 1850s, later from the 1880s to about 1900, and in the last years before World War I—the city consistently received 4–6 percent of the total U.S. immigrant influx, a proportion amounting to two hundred to two hundred fifty thousand people per decade toward the end of the prewar years. These were much large percentages of the national figures than in other eras, a variation that needs explanation. Second, after the decay of the Cope family's transatlantic line, Philadelphia merchants and traders failed to create other parallel and competitive shipping companies that would have solicited direct immigrant arrivals here. Consequently, not until the Pennsylvania Railroad took action in the 1870s was the absence of a locally sponsored line remedied. Why did local capital miss out on this opportunity and concede the focus as an immigrant destination to New York?

On the first matter, I would suggest we look closely at the dates when Philadelphia's share of the immigrant traffic became most prominent. In the overall pattern, these are periods when the city's economic, indeed

industrial, base was expanding most rapidly. The initial industrial concentrations in Philadelphia were taking shape in the period from the
1830s to the mid-1850s, with the remarkable elaboration, on one hand,
of handcraft production and, on the other, of steam-powered operations
in manufacturing sectors. Of course, the late fifties proved to be a period
of sharp economic crisis in Philadelphia followed almost immediately by
the dislocations of the first years of the Civil War, not the best time for
immigrants to arrive there. The war and Philadelphia's reputation as a
center of Southern sympathizing may have had something to do with the
decline as well. In the latter 1870s, which were highlighted by the
Centennial Exposition, however, Philadelphia's economy moved forward again.[1] After 1880, the city gained its reputation as a massive
workshop; the numbers of industrial workers increased from perhaps
140,000 to nearly a quarter-million after the turn of the century.[2] Again,
in the final period before World I, there were major surges in the
regional industrial economy, the expansion of Midvale Steel, and substantial business at the navy yard, the arsenals, Cramp's shipyards, and so
on. In addition, the construction of public works, a trade in which Italian
immigrants were much engaged, flourished, giving us the Benjamin
Franklin Parkway, as one example. Third, what some would call the
second industrial revolution arrived here as electrical plants, scientific
instrument firms, and chemical works (for example, Rohm and Haas)
rooted themselves in area neighborhoods. These large-scale plants were
in a position to demand the labor of sizable numbers of both skilled and
unskilled immigrants, perhaps providing a link to the third period of
heavier arrivals.[3]

These are very rough ways of linking numbers and the structure of
the regional economy, but it is worth exploring what kind of industrial
base Philadelphia possessed in this period in order to frame some
thoughts that historians of ethnicity and immigration might wish to
pursue. Philadelphia's manufacturing system was a veritable wonder,
producing an extravagant variety of high-quality products from pianos
to carpets and books to battleships. Virtually every nineteenth-century
skilled trade was practiced here; virtually every twentieth-century skilled
trade found a place as well. Skill was the critical element. Local firms
turned out batch lots of precisely specified goods for highly differentiated markets. That is to say, Philadelphia's manufacturing was dramatically different from Pittsburgh's, with its tonnage steel mills, or of New
England's, with its bulk-staple textile cities, such as Lowell, Lawrence,
and Fall River.[4]

The operation of an economy relying on batch production necessitates
hiring people who have far more skill than is needed for industrial
processes based on machine tending, heavy-duty common labor, and the

like. Because outputs are constantly changing, batch production requires workers who are schooled in the factory, either through apprenticeship or by classic informal learning that transmits know-how across generational and ethnic boundaries. Philadelphia relied so heavily on its workers' capacity to handle complexity and solve new problems that it became known as the paradise of the skilled workman in the late nineteenth century. Thus, it might be interesting for someone to examine passenger registers for the port of Philadelphia in these decades, and given that they list occupations, to develop a sense of the fit between the arrivals' talents and the job structure of the city. One might then readily compare the Philadelphia data with patterns of occupation among immigrants landing in Boston or Baltimore for a sense of whether close-at-hand labor opportunities are related to distinctive immigrant flows. One might also see how representative are the stories that immigrants landing in Philadelphia quickly boarded trains to the West. It would be relatively simple to compare some of the passenger lists for the 1880s with occupational data from the Philadelphia Social History Project or with data samples derived from city directories.

In this regard, I was encouraged to find in Timothy J. Meagher's response to the paper on Boston attention to districts within the countries of origin instead of general references to undifferentiated Irish, Germans, or Poles. In Temple University's Urban Archives, interviews from the 1930s indicate that many of the Poles who worked in Philadelphia's textile mills were not from peasant backgrounds but instead came from the area surrounding Lodz, the center of cotton textile manufacturing.[5] Similarly, in my own research on Paterson, New Jersey, I discovered from secondary sources and newspaper accounts that its Italian population was quite distinct from Italian communities in New York and Philadelphia, being heavily drawn from northern districts where textile trades and indeed silk manufacture were both prominent and during the later nineteenth century, in crisis.[6] Therefore, it would be well worth exploring the hint that the region of origin and its occupational and industrial structure are linked with final destination, particularly for industrial workers. This line of inquiry would suggest that the economic dimension of immigration can be seen in a more particularized way, that specific opportunities and specific places were part of the mechanism of chain migration. It is important to appreciate that people go to new places not just to flee trouble, but to seek gain in a very concrete fashion by using their skills.

Although immigrants coming into the United States in the early nineteenth century may have been a very talented and relatively prosperous group, I would suggest that, no matter how many peasants arrived in later decades, there was a similarly able component among the subsequent immigration as well, skilled individuals who by one means or another arrived in Philadelphia or Worcester, Brooklyn, and a variety of east coast cities where the skilled crafts were a solid part of the economic base. Immigrants did not automatically take the Pennsylvania Railroad or the New York Central to Cleveland or Chicago. On the contrary, I suspect that the Midwest and its opportunities were attractive to those immigrants who could not readily enter the skilled-labor economies of eastern industrial cities. Thus, a perception of regional differences in labor market structure within the U.S. manufacturing belt may be important in understanding the geography of settlement.

The second important issue is why Philadelphia merchants, the old financial and importing elite of Digby Baltzell's classic study, failed in the 1840s to build a steamship line from this city to Britain or the Continent. An immediate answer is that they built the Pennsylvania Railroad instead. Mercantile capitalists are risk takers, but they also wish to minimize the hazards they face. In the environment of the 1840s in Pennsylvania, both the railroad business and speculation in coal lands in northeastern Pennsylvania held acceptable risk levels and promised return relatively higher than did venturing into transatlantic steam transport. If one looks at *Philadelphia Gentlemen*, the lure of these opportunities is evident in Baltzell's cross-generational table of family interests. Indeed, the Copes were much involved in creating the "Pennsy," as were their elite colleagues of the period.[7] The success of these activities, including development of the Reading line as a coal delivery system, is one reason why houses on the Main Line are not built out of cardboard. Later, after the Civil War, these same elite capitalists found that their business acumen would be well rewarded in insurance, banking, urban real estate development, and in creating the street railway system that immigrants rode daily to work. Economic alertness is not a regionally specific phenomenon, but the set of differentiated opportunities for economic activity is regionally distinct.

In addition to exploring these two questions, I would like to address briefly two other concerns of my own. First, we need to broaden our thinking in order to consider Philadelphia not only as a port of entry but as a port of exit and reentry, as well. It is well known that many Italians and Poles in their later years returned to their lands of origin, but still too little appreciated is the routine transatlantic crossing by workers responding to changes in the labor market. In the late nineteenth and early twentieth centuries, it was not at all unusual for workers in Philadelphia and other major east coast cities to return to the old country, not to buy land and retire, but to find jobs, sometimes even better jobs. Two brief examples illustrate the point.

In 1903, a general strike in Philadelphia lasted five-and-a-half months, and within two weeks of the strike's beginning, trade newspapers in the textile industry announced that freighters and passenger ships leaving Philadelphia were crammed with workers going to Britain, where they could work or visit kin during what promised to be a long and bitter battle here.[8] Passage was cheap and the pace of work in Britain less enervating than in the United States. One could stay abroad for six months or a year and still return with good prospects for employment, for there were some eight hundred textile mills in Philadelphia then and two hundred more in the adjacent counties of Pennsylvania. Two years later, the English industrial economy was improving while the American one was flattening out after a period of expansion. At that time, the editor of Boston's the *American Wool and Cotton Reporter* wrote of a difficult strike in Fall River,

> as if this were not unfortunate enough, the new factor has appeared in the movement . . . back to the old country. The fact is the textile industry in England was never in better condition than at present. . . . thus probably it is explained that on one recent steamer bound for England, there were a thousand, mostly textile help, from many of the different American centers.[9]

Although it was not well recognized until after World War II, a trans-oceanic labor market already existed at the turn of the century, but Americans, with a sense of their own magnetism dominant, have often failed to realize that that market operated in both directions. It was entirely plausible for immigrants, especially single men, to look elsewhere, for the Statue of Liberty alone did not guarantee steady work.

Finally, entry is dramatic: Transatlantic passages, steerage stories, the many experiences people relate provide touchstones we cannot ignore. Moreover, in the last academic generation, say, since the late 1960s, there has been an explosion of powerful and evocative studies of ethnic community life, its structures, values, and institutions. Yet between the two, there remains a hole, representing how one goes from *A* to *B*. How does the amorphous mass of humanity landing on the docks translate into the dynamic, integrated, or, at times, fractious ethnic communities spread across a nation and the deserved object of so much admiration and study? It seems to me that it would help to know something about the structure and process of dispersion from the ports of entry in order to link the ships to the savings banks and political clubs. There may well be research tools to be developed here, but a marvelous example of how one writer has appreciated the problem lies in the book *La Merica* by Michael LaSorte, recently published by Temple University Press.[10] Using diaries and autobiographical accounts, LaSorte imaginatively reconstructs the tracks followed by Italian immigrants in order to find where those bonds of association and caring could be articulated. LaSorte is conscious of this missing middle term, and if his accounts are at all representative, it is plain that far more American immigrants than we have imagined were still in motion long after the assembly rooms in the dockside processing centers had emptied. Until we have a firmer grasp of processes that followed passage through the golden doors, we will not be fully in touch with the dynamics of immigrant settlement, economic change, and community building.

Notes

1. Russell Weigley, ed., *Philadelphia: A 300-Year History* (New York: W. W. Norton and Co., 1982).

2. The figure for 1905 was 228,809, with an additional 22,839 white-collar workers in Philadelphia manufacturing establishments. See Department of Commerce and Labor, Bureau of the Census, *Bulletin 60: Census of Manufactures: 1905, Pennsylvania* (Washington, D.C.: General Printing Office, 1906), 2.

3. Philip Scranton and Walter Licht, *Work Sights: Industrial Philadelphia, 1890–1950* (Philadelphia: Temple University Press, 1986).

4. Ibid.

5. W.P.A. Project Files (Palmer surveys), Urban Archives, Paley Library, Temple University.

6. See Philip Scranton, ed., *Silk City: Studies on the Paterson Silk Industry, 1860–1940* (Newark: New Jersey Historical Society, 1985).

7. E. Digby Baltzell, *Philadelphia Gentlemen: The Making of a National Upper Class* (New York: Free Press, 1958), 71–77, 92.

8. *Philadelphia Public Ledger*, 9, 22 June 1903.

9. *American Wool and Cotton Reporter*, 6 July 1905, 752.

10. Michael LaSorte, *La Merica: Images of Italian Greenhorn Experience* (Philadelphia: Temple University Press, 1985).

3

Immigration through the Port of Baltimore

DEAN R. ESSLINGER

Baltimore's image in the twentieth century, before its recent renaissance, was that of a working man's city made up of dozens of closely knit neighborhoods. It was a place to pass through on the way to or from Washington, having neither the political importance of the nation's capital nor the financial nor historic importance of New York or Philadelphia. Yet for those who chose to stop, Baltimore revealed itself as a city of pleasant living, a city of comfortable red brick row houses set on rolling hills around a busy harbor. This contrast between image and reality, between the traveler's impressions and the resident's loyalty, is indicative of Baltimore's past as well as its present. In particular, this contrast reflects Baltimore's past as an immigrant port of entry where many passed through but some stayed. Why nearly two million immigrants chose to enter the United States through the port of Baltimore is the subject of this essay.

Immigrants who came to Baltimore immediately after the American Revolution and before the War of 1812 were much like their predecessors of the colonial period, English or Irish men and women who arrived by ship or Germans who drifted southward from Pennsylvania. Although Baltimore had profited from the Revolution by becoming a supply center for the Continental Army and from the War of 1812 by serving as the home base for a third of the nation's privateers, its real expansion as an immigrant port of entry came in the more peaceful years after 1820. By this third decade of the nineteenth century, the city's business leaders had begun to see their city as competing with New York and Philadelphia for western trade. When, on their initiative, the Cumberland Road was completed in 1818 linking the Chesapeake Bay to the Ohio River at Wheeling, Baltimore's role as a port of entry was immediately enhanced. As Englishman James Flint wrote at the time:

> The completion of the new road will make Baltimore the most popular landing place for Europeans who would settle in Western America.

61

Immigrants disembarking at Locust Point, Baltimore, ca. 1904. *(Courtesy of the Peale Museum, Baltimore.)*

At present the carriage of goods from Baltimore to Wheeling is cheaper than from Philadelphia to Pittsburgh. It is evident that the new route is already the shortest and cheapest.[1]

After 1820, there was a noticeable increase in the number of European immigrants who turned to Baltimore as a gateway to the American West. From only a few hundred immigrants per year, the total of newcomers climbed to nearly two thousand by the end of the decade. In 1828, Baltimore further improved its position by establishing the nation's first commercial steam railroad. Worried that Baltimore would be surpassed by Georgetown to the south, which was the terminus of the new Chesapeake and Ohio Canal, or overwhelmed by Philadelphia to the north, the city's business leaders organized the Baltimore and Ohio Railroad. And Baltimore continued to expand its transportation network in the next two decades by funding other canal and railroad projects northward along the Susquehanna River and east toward Delaware Bay.

This early focus on improving transportation provides the best clue as to why immigrants chose Baltimore: Its location as the westernmost seaport along the East Coast combined with adequate highway, canal, and rail connections to give the city the basis for attracting both trade and immigrants. But it would be misleading to suggest that immigrants chose Baltimore as a port of entry only because of its closer proximity to the farmlands and cities of the West or because of its transportation facilities. In fact, the rail link to the Ohio River at Wheeling was not completed until 1853, after Philadelphia had built its own railroad to Pittsburgh, and for years, the jobs that the construction of railroads and canals created were just as important in attracting immigrants to Baltimore. Thousands of young German, Irish, and English men chose Baltimore because the prospects of employment in the region were good for those who had few skills and little capital. Others may have discovered the advantages of the Baltimore job market purely by accident rather than by choice. Ludwig Strassfort, a young German immigrant in the 1840s, complained of the cheats and swindlers who took the newcomer's money and left him in debt:

> So, he says, "abandoned by everyone, there is nothing left to be done but to seek work on the canal or the railroad, where are to be found a goodly mixture of every class. Those who in Germany mayhaps have been lawyers, preachers, merchants, craftsmen and farmers, vie with each other in pushing a wheelbarrow."[2]

Additional workers were needed to build the city itself. Baltimore was clearly a boom town in the first half of the nineteenth century as its population soared from 13,503 in 1790 to 212,418 by 1860.[3] In the early 1830s, Hezekiah Niles commented frequently on the shortage of housing in Baltimore and on the need for more workers.[4] No doubt many immigrants whose original intentions had been to move west to take up land or employment in the interior found that jobs were available in Baltimore and moved no further. They were a welcome addition to the city's work force not only in the construction trades but in opening shops as merchants, booksellers and bookbinders, saddlers, bakers, locksmiths, and shoemakers. For example, Engelhard Yeiser, a German architect, built the canal to straighten out the Jones Falls, a stream that passes through the center of the city and was the source of power for the budding textile industry.[5]

Although both the state of Maryland and private companies advertised the amount of land and the number of jobs available and Baltimore's transportation advantages were well known, it is possible to overemphasize the degree to which immigrants made a conscious or well-planned decision about where they would land in America. Certainly, those newcomers who were following friends and relatives to the United States profited from their predecessors' experiences that were described in letters to the homeland. But it is just as likely that as many or more immigrants were brought to Baltimore by trade patterns between the city and northern Europe.

In the 1820s, a new generation of businessmen was aggressively expanding Baltimore's manufacturing and commercial base. Robert and Alexander McKim, for example, took advantage of new technology and their connections abroad to develop the Baltimore Steamworks factory into the largest cotton textile factory in the city. The older Union Manufacturing Company, Washington Cotton Manufacturing Company, and the Powhattan Cotton Mills also expanded and added to the exports Baltimore had to offer.

By 1830, Baltimore had firm trade links with Liverpool and Bremen, both major ports for emigrants leaving northern Europe. Many immigrants no doubt ended up in Baltimore simply by chance as a result of the shipping patterns that existed. Just as Maryland tobacco, which was finding a growing market in northern Europe after 1812, and Baltimore's cotton goods formed a strong basis for overseas trade, the same combination of local manufacturing and regional agriculture was the driving force behind Baltimore's urban growth in the first half of the nineteenth century. And when tobacco and textile ships returned from Europe, they brought with them a cargo of new immigrants to people the burgeoning city.

There is no question that Baltimore eagerly sought to increase its contacts and trade with Europe. Like the colonial merchants before them, Baltimore's business leaders of the nineteenth century were well connected by family and ethnic ties to their counterparts across the Atlantic. In fact, those who were immigrants themselves sometimes gained an advantage in business by maintaining their relationships with friends and family in the mother country. Alex Brown, for instance, was an Irish immigrant who found success in dominating Baltimore's Irish linen trade, but his wealth and power increased even more when he shifted his attention to investments in foreign bills of exchange.[6] In time, Alex Brown and Sons would become one of the most prominent names in the city's financial circle. Another successful immigrant was Albert Schumacher, son of a Bremen city counselor. He came to Baltimore in 1826, on the advice of a friend who had done well there. Going to work for his friend C. A. Heinecke, Schumacher became a traveling agent who made contacts throughout the world and later took over the business. He eventually became a consul general for Bremen and Hamburg and served on the boards of the Baltimore and Ohio Railroad, the Baltimore Chamber of Commerce, and several local banks. He was socially active as the president of the German Society and was prominent in the Germania Club and other ethnic organizations.[7] Indeed, it was Schumacher who later was instrumental in creating a link between German steamship lines and the Baltimore and Ohio Railroad.

Although Brown's and Schumacher's success were exceptional, of course, their examples suggest yet another reason why immigrants came to Baltimore: It was a city where immigrants eventually found a degree of mutual support and protection. Unemployment, overcrowded housing, and even violent opposition were sometimes part of the newcomers' lot in attempting to adjust to American society, but they also found help in Baltimore. This was especially true for the four largest groups who arrived before the Civil War: the English, French, Irish, and Germans.

Because the majority of Baltimore's residents were either English born or descended from English ancestors, immigrants of that nationality tended to be quickly absorbed into the social and economic structures of the city.[8] Rather than forming separate organizations, English newcomers joined the native-born majority in the local political parties and social organizations. Even so, there was a constant complaint in the press about the influx of English paupers who arrived regularly at the docks. The trustees of the city almshouse in 1832 tried to persuade the government to put a limit on the number of indigent English who seemed to be "dumped" on Baltimore.[9] The prejudice, however, was directed more toward those who were likely to become a burden on the community than against the English generally.

The French, whose largest migration came before 1830, were welcomed in Baltimore; often, they were refugees from political or religious disorder. In 1792, for example,the first members of the Sulpician Order arrived after having been expelled from France and invited to stay by Baltimore's new bishop, John Carroll. Then, on 9 July of the following year, when fifty-three vessels carrying a thousand and five hundred black refugees from the revolution in Santo Domingo sailed into the harbor, local residents took them into their homes and raised $12,000 to take care of them. Although many of these French refugees were only temporary inhabitants of the city, they had a noticeable impact. Businesses began advertising in French, and Baltimore society became more conscious of "gentlemanly" behavior.[10]

The French influence was only temporary, however, and did little to attract new immigrants to Baltimore. Far more important were the Irish and Germans who became the predominant groups after 1830. Twenty-five percent of the city's population of 212,418 was foreign born by the time of the Civil War, including 15,536 Irish and 32,613 Germans but not counting their thousands of native-born descendants.[11] In both cases, as the numbers grew, immigrant communities made a strong effort to welcome new arrivals and help them adjust.

The Irish were the first to organize, forming the Ancient Order of Hibernians in Baltimore in 1803 for the purpose of providing aid to new immigrants. Dr. John Campbell White, the first president of the society, joined several prominent businessmen of diverse ethnic backgrounds, such as John McKim, Robert Oliver, William Patterson, John Pendleton Kennedy, and J. H. B. Latrobe, in providing relief to the poor.[12] In 1817, they tried to assist Irish immigrants by petitioning Congress to set aside land for them, and in 1824, John Oliver gave $20,000 to the Hibernian society for the establishment of a school for the Irish poor.[13]

But not everyone in the Baltimore community regarded the growing number of Irish immigrants as a blessing. Rapid population growth brought crowding, epidemics, and sometimes violence. In the 1830s, when most of the numerous inmates of the almshouse were Irish, the city imposed a head tax of $1.50 on immigrants and allotted the funds to the almshouse, the Hibernian, and German societies. Dysentery, cholera, and respiratory diseases struck hard in immigrant neighborhoods, and in the 1830s, Baltimore's reputation as mobtown stemmed in part from violence between Irish immigrants and native-born workers.

Nevertheless, the Irish established a foothold in the city, and occasionally their contributions were recognized. Matthew Arnold remarked in 1826 that the "Irish labourers are found uncommonly handy and active, and for years have done a large portion of the work on canals and turnpikes."[14] Baltimore's Hibernian society acted as an employment agency and by the 1850s, was helping about twenty-five immigrants per month to find jobs on the railroad.[15] The Irish also prospered as storekeepers, clerks, craftsmen, and tavern owners and were important in the city's politics.[16] After having been clustered together in the old eighth and tenth wards and around St. Patrick's and St. John's churches in the antebellum period, after the Civil War, the Irish spread north into the suburbs, where they worked in the cotton mills, foundries, and machine shops of Woodbury and the rock quarries of Cockeysville.[17]

Even greater in number and thus more influential than the Irish were the Germans. Many had come to Baltimore before the American Revolution, moving down the Susquehanna Valley from central Pennsylvania or coming directly from Europe by sailing ship. George Rapp and a few of his early followers passed through the port of Baltimore in 1804, and his later disciples duplicated his route on their way to his nineteenth-century utopian community.[18] The significant increase in German immigration, however, came after the War of 1812 and especially after 1830.

The German society of Maryland, first organized in 1783 to help new arrivals, was incorporated and made more effective in 1817, in response to the sometimes brutal treatment of German redemptioners or indentured servants.[19] On 7 February 1817, the *Baltimore American* ran a story that shocked the German-American community into action:

> A ship with upward of 300 German men, women and children has arrived off Annapolis where she is detained by ice. These people have been fifteen weeks on board and are short of provision. Upon making the Capes, their bedding having become filthy, was thrown overboard. They are now actually perishing from the cold and want of provision.[20]

Several prominent leaders, including General John Striker, commander of the Maryland Militia during the Revolution, called for a meeting at Kaminsky's tavern. Revived and incorporated as a result of that outrage, the German society became one of the most effective organizations in the city. Principally, it furnished either legal protection or financial aid to the poorest immigrants from Germany and within a year had persuaded the Maryland legislature to regulate labor contracts of the redemptioners and provide for the education of those under twenty-one. Under the new laws, no immigrant was to be kept on board a ship for more than thirty days after arrival; the sick were to be placed ashore immediately, and family members could not be held liable for passage money of their kin. The society was quick to bring to trial any ship captain who violated the protective laws.[21]

With equal vigor, the German society raised funds to help newcomers. Between 1817 and 1888, it spent $253,190.67 hiring physicians, paying for medicine, and distributing wood, coal, and clothes to thousands of Germans. But equally important was its role as an employment agency that placed immigrants in jobs in other states as well as in Maryland and Baltimore. The society's Intelligence Bureau was formed in 1845 and by 1846, had found jobs for 3,500 immigrants. Such effort and success could only have bolstered Baltimore's reputation as a favorable port of entry when immigrants wrote home to their friends and relatives.[22]

From about 1840 until late in the nineteenth century, Germans continued to build a strong community that attracted more immigrants each year. By the time of the Civil War, probably one-quarter of Baltimore's population was of German ancestry, and more immigrants were coming each year. The community, which was based on a combination of German churches, schools, social organizations, and political groups, made Baltimore an attractive alternative to the more popular port of New York.

As in most immigrant communities, the church played a major role, but for Baltimore's German Catholics, there was an especially strong link with Europe. In 1840, Baltimore became the home of the Congregation of the Holy Redeemer (or Redemptorists). Headquartered at St. James Church, this missionary order stayed in close touch with its members in Germany and Belgium while founding new churches, schools, orphanages, and perhaps even the first savings and loan institution in Baltimore and the surrounding region.[23] Both money and ideas flowed along the network that connected Baltimore's German Catholics with their coreligionists in Europe.

Other religious groups likewise developed strong centers from which they cared for local residents and assisted newcomers from abroad. For the Lutherans, Zion Church became a focal point for social and cultural activities, but there was an abundance of other Protestant congregations, including those of the Evangelical and Reformed denomination.[24]

Intolerance in Europe, especially in Bavaria, combined with the Baltimore-Bremen tobacco connection to bring most of Baltimore's early Jews to the city.[25] Those who fled discrimination probably gave less thought than others to the relative merits of the city of debarkation, but as the number of German Jews grew to at least seven thousand by the time of the Civil War, Baltimore developed characteristics and attractions that would have appealed to Jewish newcomers.[26] The Lloyd Street Synagogue, the oldest in Maryland, was only the first of many that served the needs of Orthodox, Reform, and Conservative Jews. Soon there were so many schools, charitable societies, literary clubs, and other organizations that when large numbers of Russian Jews began to arrive in the late nineteenth century, they found a sizable Jewish community already flourishing in east Baltimore.

In addition to religious congregations, schools were a key element in the prosperous German community of the nineteenth century. Whatever their religion, Baltimore's Germans were enthusiastic supporters of education, whether for the purposes of preserving the German language and culture or helping their children compete more successfully in American society. At their peak in the second half of the nineteenth century, the schools of the Redemptorists and the Sisters of Notre Dame had three thousand students, Pastor Scheib's Lutheran school had eight hundred, and Friedrich Knapp's secular one, seven hundred. By 1872, the German influence was strong enough so that the public school system established a number of tax-supported German-English schools in which all subjects were taught in both languages.[27]

After the churches and schools came the German community's social organizations. The Baltimore Liederkranz, founded in 1836, was the second German singing society in the United States.[28] The Germania Club, a social organization made up mostly of merchants, appeared by 1848, and the Concordia Club for German music and theater provided outstanding entertainment.[29] The Grand National Sängerbund assembled in Baltimore in 1854 and 1859 and filled the city with music.[30] The various Schützen organizations, or shooting clubs, sponsored tournaments and picnics with brass bands, athletic contests, and plenty of food and drink. As no holiday or special occasion went by without German songs, parades, music, and speeches, by the 1870s, Baltimore was a city with a distinct German flavor.

Political clubs and associations were also an important part of the complex network that gave strength to the German community in Baltimore and tied it to nationalist movements in Europe. Refugees from the rebellion in 1848 passed through Baltimore, and many of them stayed to add their liberal viewpoints to the political scene. Carl Heinrich Schnauffer, for example, in 1851 established a German-language newspaper, *Die Wecker*, which spoke out boldly against slavery.[31] In 1849, the Turnverein of Baltimore was founded and began to attract to its membership a number of the new immigrants who were politically active in liberal causes. This increased activity was not without its hazards. On several occasions in the 1850s, German newspaper offices and German workers were attacked by southern sympathizers who resented the Germans' foreign birth and antislavery views. At the height of Know-Nothing strength in the 1850s, the Germans were sometimes attacked as they paraded on festival days or celebrated in their parks on the outskirts of the city, and they found that their shooting clubs and rifle companies became effective escorts for German families at the end of a Sunday outing.[32] But perhaps nativist opposition to the German community might have been even greater if the German speeches and editorials had been in English.

Just how influential Baltimore's reputation was in drawing Germans and others is, of course, difficult to assess accurately. It can be assumed, however, that frequent contacts of businesses, churches, and ethnic organizations with their counterparts in Europe as well as advertisements by the state government and private companies, newspaper articles, and letters from friends and relatives must have played an important role in each immigrant's decision to emigrate and the selection of a route to follow.

The choice of Baltimore as a port of entry was made easier after the Civil War when the city improved its transportation connection with the Baltic ports of northern Germany. On 21 January 1867, the Baltimore and Ohio Railroad signed an agreement with the North German Lloyd Steamship Line allowing immigrants to buy a single ticket that would carry them across the Atlantic by ship and then west by train. On 24 March 1868, the first steamer, the *Baltimore*, arrived with its cargo of immigrants and German manufactured goods.[33] On its return voyage, the ship carried Maryland tobacco and lumber. This convenient transportation arrangement was a direct result of close links between German businessmen in Baltimore and their non-German associates, in particular, between Albert Schumacher, the consul for Bremen, Hamburg, and Luebeck, and his Baltimore friend, John W. Garrett, president of the Baltimore and Ohio Railroad.[34] Soon, other steamship concerns, such as the Hamburg-American Line and the Baltimore Mail Line, followed a similar route.

This improvement in regular transportation coincided with a rise in the number of immigrant passengers arriving at the port of Baltimore. Over ten thousand travelers came through the port in 1867 compared to fewer than four thousand the year before. The number peaked at nearly 18,000 in 1873, then rapidly dropped, probably as a result of the economic depression in the United States, before increasing again to a new high of 41,739 in 1882.[35]

With the improvement of its transportation facilities and this increase in passengers in the late 1860s, Baltimore entered what might be called its modern period as an immigrant port. If ever Baltimore as a port of entry resembled a smaller version of New York, complete with its own Castle Garden, it was in the years between 1868 and 1914. Unlike New York, however, Baltimore depended on privately run facilities to care for the new arrivals.

In 1869, several of the steamship companies signed a contract with a Mrs. Koether to run a large boarding house at Pier 9 on Locust Point, where immigrants debarked from ships and boarded trains going west. And on 23 March, she served her first meal to 350 newly arrived steerage passengers. For each immigrant she fed and housed, she received $.75 a day. Over the next half-century, Mrs. Koether, described as a small German woman with blond hair and blue eyes, received as many as forty thousand per year at her boarding house.[36]

For those who were traveling west to the farmlands and cities of the interior, the stop at Mrs. Koether's was only for a meal or a brief rest. The boarding house was hardly an inspection center in the same way that Castle Garden and Ellis Island were. Rather, because of Baltimore's unique location near the northern end of the Chesapeake Bay, doctors and immigration officials boarded the ships as they slowly made their way up the bay and examined passengers on deck, often completing the entire inspection process before ships docked at Pier 9. Only steerage passengers were required to pass through the examination procedures, and even they were looked at only casually. One employee of the German steamship lines, later an immigrant himself, described the experience:

The quarantine men boarded the boat on its way up the bay. Every immigrant went through a quick medical examination. Checking of

Locust Point Immigration Station, Baltimore, ca. 1916. *(Courtesy of the Maryland Historical Society.)*

the luggage by Customs was a quick and cursory affair. From that point, most of the immigrants who landed in Baltimore stepped aboard B. & O. trains and traveled on to Chicago, St. Louis or Cincinnati.[37]

Baltimore was probably fortunate because the majority of its immigrants came from northern German ports where inspection for disease was rigid and facilities for caring for outbound passengers were as good as any in Europe.[38]

Those immigrants who were not processed by immigration and health officials on board the ships would have faced the inspection as soon as they landed at piers 8 or 9 at Locust Point on the south side of Baltimore's Inner Harbor. The Baltimore and Ohio Railroad had constructed two large buildings that served as a terminal for both the steamship lines and the railroad. Some immigrants therefore could move directly from the ships to the trains that would carry them west. By 1873, in fact, the Baltimore and Ohio had built special cars to carry large numbers of immigrants headed for the Midwest.[39] Others might have to wait for hours or even a day or two before completing immigration procedures and boarding the train for their particular destination. If that was the case, Mrs. Koether's nearby boarding house was a welcome establishment. Those who were detained there for several days for health reasons or because they were suspected of violating immigration restrictions were given adequate food and had the use of a large yard for fresh air and exercise. Many apparently spent their hours in detention enjoying the fishing off the pier.[40]

By 1913, when the number of immigrants arriving in Baltimore was averaging about forty thousand per year, the federal government built three large buildings at Locust Point to take over the functions of Mrs. Koether's boarding house and the Baltimore and Ohio terminal. But just as the buildings were completed, World War I closed off the flow of immigrants. During the war, these structures were converted for use as a military hospital, and at the end of the war, there were not enough new immigrants arriving to justify opening them as a reception center.

The reasons immigrants chose Baltimore as their port of entry during the period between the Civil War and World War I remained much the same regardless of where they came from in Europe. After 1877, the number of Polish immigrants increased as did the number of Czechs, Russian Jews, Ukrainians, Greeks, and Italians. Like the Germans before them, they came to Baltimore because of existing trade routes that tied northern German ports to the Chesapeake and because of regular passenger service offered by steamship and railroad companies. Many immigrants especially Poles, were looking for land to farm and passed through Baltimore to the Midwest. But those who lacked the capital or the desire to move on stayed to build the strong ethnic communities that by the beginning of the twentieth century characterized the city. As Baltimore shifted its economic base from commerce to a greater dependence on industrialization, newcomers found jobs in the textile mills, clothing factories, canning plants, and steel mills. Each group developed distinct neighborhoods centered around religious institutions and close to the places of work. For example, the Poles were clustered around St. Stanislaus, Holy Rosary, and St. Casimir Catholic churches in East Baltimore, and while the German Jews moved northwest toward Eutaw Place and beyond, the newer Russian Jews crowded around the sweatshops and synagogues in Old Town east of the Jones Falls. As each ethnic community grew, it developed newspapers, schools, social clubs, beneficial societies, and other self-help organizations that made it attractive to newcomers. In time, then, each community itself became something of a magnet drawing new arrivals and encouraging them to choose Baltimore as their home.

In sum, before 1920, Baltimore's foreign business connections combined with good transportation facilities and an attractive local environment to draw immigrants through its port of entry. The majority of the newcomers passed through the city on their way somewhere else, but those who stayed made Baltimore a city of ethnic neighborhoods and strong community life.

Notes

1. Ruben Gold Thwaites, ed., *Early Western Travels, 1748–1846* (Cleveland: Arthur Clark, 1904), XIX, 105.

2. *Society for the History of Germans in Maryland*, 16th annual report, 1907, 20.

3. Waring, George E., Jr., *Report on the Social Statistics of Cities*, part II (Washington: Government Printing Office, 1887), 3.

4. *Niles' Register*, (Baltimore) 23 January 1830, 23 April, 30 July, and 20 August 1831.

5. J. Thomas Scharf, *History of Baltimore City and County* (Philadelphia: Louis H. Everts, 1881), 82; Dieter Cunz, *The Maryland Germans: A History* (Princeton: Princeton University Press, 1948), 161; and James V. Crotty, "Baltimore Immigration, 1790–1830, with Special Reference to Its German, Irish, and French Phases" (M.A. thesis, Catholic University, 1951), 42.

6. Gary L. Browne, *Baltimore and the Nation, 1789–1861* (Chapel Hill: University of North Carolina Press, 1980), 173–75.

7. Cunz, *Maryland Germans*, 241.

8. The English were the most numerous immigrants in 1820 and 1830, but they were surpassed thereafter by Irish and the Germans in the antebellum period. Crotty, "Baltimore Immigration," xxxvi.

9. *Niles' Register*, 15 September 1832.

10. Crotty, "Baltimore Immigration," 22–24.

11. U.S. Census Bureau, *Population of the United States, 1860*, xxxi.

12. Christine M. Arnold, "Baltimore's Invisible Irish: Patterns of Assimilation and Mobility, 1850–1929" unpublished paper, 15.

13. Crotty, "Baltimore Immigration," 53–55.

14. Matthew Arnold, *Reflections on the Subject of Emigration from Europe*, (Philadelphia: Carey and Lea, 1826), 22.

15. Suzanne Ellery Greene, *Baltimore: An Illustrated History* (Woodland Hills, Calif.: Windsor Publications, 1980), 92; and Sherry H. Olson, *Baltimore: The Building of an American City* (Baltimore: Johns Hopkins University Press, 1980), 118.

16. Arnold, "Baltimore's Invisible Irish," 32.

17. Ibid, 20.

18. Crotty, "Baltimore Immigration," 35.

19. Morgan Pritchett and Raymond M. Frampton, *A Compendium of German-American Organizations in the Baltimore Area* (Baltimore: Historical Records Committee of Deutsch-Amerikanischer Biergerverein von Maryland, 1960), 31.

20. Louis P. Hennighausen, "The Redemptioners and the German Society of Maryland, an Historical Sketch," *Society for the History of Germans in Maryland*, 2d annual report, 1877–88, 40–41.

21. Hennighausen, "Redemptioners," 42–48.

22. Cunz, *Maryland Germans*, 203.

23. Scharf, *History of Baltimore*, 541; and Olson, *Baltimore*, 124–25.

24. Scharf, *History of Baltimore*, 568–73.

25. Moses Aberbach, "The Early German Jews of Baltimore," *Society for the History of Germans in Maryland*, 35th annual report, 197, 27–29.

26. Isaac Fein, *The Making of an American Jewish Community* (Philadelphia: Jewish Publishing Society of America, 1971), 41–42, 77, and 93; and Aberbach, "Early German Jews," 30.

27. Ernest J. Becker, "History of English-German Schools in Baltimore,"

Society for the History of Germans in Maryland, 25th annual report, 1942, 13–17; and Olson, *Baltimore,* 182.

28. Cunz, *Maryland Germans,* 30.

29. Ibid., 323. See also Cunz, *A History of the Germania Club* (Baltimore: Society of the History of Germans in Maryland, 1940).

30. Scharf, *History of Baltimore,* 673.

31. Dieter Cunz, "The Baltimore Germans and the Year 1848," *American-German Review* (October 1943): 33; and Scharf, *History of Baltimore,* 630.

32. Louis P. Hennighaussen, "Reminiscences of the Political Life of the German-Americans in Baltimore during 1850–1860," *Society for the History of Germans in Maryland,* 11th and 12th annual reports, 1897–1898, 3–14; and Augustus J. Prahl, "History of the German Gymnastic Movement of Baltimore," *Society for the History of Germans in Maryland,* 26th annual report, 1945, 16–17.

33. Edward Hungerford, *The Story of the Baltimore and Ohio Railroad, 1827–1927,* 2 vols. (New York: G. P. Putnam's Sons, 1928), vol. 1, 79; Scharf, *History of Baltimore,* 306.

34. "Laurels and Bays to the Living," *Society for the History of the Germans in Maryland,* 24th annual report, 1939, 32.

35. Enoch Pratt Free Library, vertical file, "Emigration and Immigration."

36. Henry C. Raynor, "Immigrant Tide Here Is Slowly Rising Again," Baltimore *Sun,* 8 March 1925.

37. Anton Hagel, "When Immigrants Poured into Baltimore," Baltimore *Sun,* 19 August 1973.

38. Alan M. Kraut, *The Huddled Masses: The Immigrant in American Society, 1880–1921* (Arlington Heights, Ill.: Harlan Davidson, Inc., 1982), 48.

39. Baltimore *Sun,* 19 August 1973.

40. Raynor, "Immigration Tide," Baltimore *Sun,* 8 March 1925. Stephen Basarab et al., *The Ukrainians of Maryland,* (Baltimore: Ukrainian Education Association of Maryland, Inc., 1977), 138–40; describes the dilemma of 102 Austrians who were detained under the belief that they had been recruited to work as strikebreakers in the steel industry in 1901. They had arrived from Bremen on the North German Lloyd steamer *Hannover.*

"Immigration through the Port of Baltimore": A Comment

Alan M. Kraut

I second Professor Esslinger's objection to those who mistakenly characterize Baltimore as "a place to pass through on the way to or from Washington." As any Washington baseball fan can tell you, Baltimore is an oasis in that vast major league desert that extends from the green diamonds of New York and Philadelphia southward to Atlanta. Indeed, it was on my very first pilgrimage to see the Orioles play in 1975 that I became aware that H. L. Mencken's beloved city was a place deserving my attention as an immigration historian as well as a baseball fan.

The sign on the Baltimore-Washington Parkway welcomed me to a working American city. I was intrigued, especially when I learned that the door prize at Memorial Stadium was a Black and Decker drill, but being an immigration historian rather than a labor historian, I awaited further evidence that it was worth turning a professional eye on the city.

That evidence came inside the ball park. There, a beer vendor accosted me with "Hey Bud, want a Bo?" He was referring to National Bohemian Beer, which I later discovered was the house brew at Memorial Stadium and tasted especially good with the kosher hot dogs sold in the park. Baltimore once had many breweries, a fellow fan volunteered, and many of the beers reflected the national identities of those who brewed and drank them. The same fan scoffed at my hot dog and suggested that I would have done better to have stopped for a sandwich at Jack's, located on Corned Beef Row on Lombard Street, one of the few such places left in the old Jewish quarter. At the very least, I should eat dinner in Little Italy before returning to Washington. No question, there had been immigrants in Baltimore. The only event that left me somewhat puzzled occurred during the seventh-inning stretch when local fans—these descendants of Germans, Bohemians, Irish, Italians, and East European Jews—rose to their feet, clutching their cups of National Bohemian Beer and bellowed a chorus of "Thank God I'm a Country Boy" to the accompaniment of the stadium organ.

Baltimore's ethnic flavor comes from having been both a major entry point for new arrivals, especially in the nineteenth and early twentieth centuries, and an industrial magnet for low-cost immigrant labor. In his essay, Dean Esslinger offers an overview of this important port and the immigrants who arrived there. With broad brush strokes, he sketches the history of Baltimore and its role as gateway to the American West for new arrivals. Esslinger describes how "thousands of young German, Irish, and English" workers chose Baltimore as a destination in the midnineteenth century because of jobs in this growing city and its ideal transportation links to points inland. Though he admittedly has little evidence, he further speculates that the existing trade pattern alone between Maryland merchants and their counterparts in Europe brought ships filled with immigrant labor as well as other commodities to harbor in Baltimore. Esslinger offers such immigrants as Irishman Alex Brown, who dominated the linen trade, and German entrepreneur Albert Schumacher as examples of the opportunity for upward socioeconomic mobility that Baltimore provided immigrants who remained in the city.

By 1860, a quarter of Baltimore's population was foreign born, mostly Irish and German, a pattern not dissimilar from that in New York, Boston, and Philadelphia. As in other cities, newcomers formed communities and organized to battle the sickness, poverty, and nativism that were obstacles to all newcomers in all ports. As in other cities, too, the Irish were laborers in foundries and mills and early entered the city's politics. The German community, larger, wealthier, and older than the Irish community, was even more effective than the Irish in sponsoring voluntary self-help organizations and such cultural clubs as the Liederkranz, the Germania Club, and the many Schützen organizations.

The cohesiveness of the German community in Baltimore attracted other Germans. By the Civil War, over 25 percent of all Baltimoreans were either German immigrants or of German ancestry. And as among the Irish, religious institutions, especially the Roman Catholic church, were the nexus of community. According to Esslinger, there is even a claim that the German Catholic congregation of the Holy Redeemer started Baltimore's first savings and loan institution. The German immigrants also included Jews. Although not so large as the communities in New York or Philadelphia, the German Jewish community in Baltimore built synagogues, such as the Lloyd Street Synagogue, Maryland's oldest Jewish house of worship. The first great wave of immigration had left its mark on Baltimore. It was a major mid-Atlantic coast immigration port and a city flavored with the cultures of northern and western Europe.

The second great wave of immigration, which Esslinger dates as early as 1868, made even more dramatic changes in the port. Esslinger suggests that the state of Maryland played less of a role in protecting the immigrant from society and vice versa than did the state of New York, but he really does not compare the two. He cites the private contracts that some shipping lines signed with private concessionaires in Baltimore to house and feed immigrants passing through on their way west. New York State did not house and feed immigrants either, although state officials eventually did contract with and license privately owned board-inghouses to shelter immigrants after arrival. As for the inspection process, Esslinger says that it was usually carried out by Maryland of-ficials on board ship or at piers 8 and 9 at Locust Point. As in other ports, there were delays, and some new arrivals waited as long as several days before resuming their journey.

When the federal government assumed responsibility for the immi-gration process in 1890, inspection was regularized and new facilities were required. With Baltimore averaging about 40,000 arrivals per year by the second decade of the twentieth century, as compared to Ellis Island's 600,000, there was no need for a massive facility. The federal government built three buildings at Locust Point, but they were not even completed until the eve of World War I, when immigration was dis-rupted by the conflict in Europe. After the war, the structures were never put into service.

Esslinger only briefly summarizes the impact on Baltimore of the southern and eastern European immigrations of the late nineteenth and early twentieth centuries. He mentions, but does not develop, a portrait of an industrializing city that could offer jobs in factories and mills to new arrivals. Likewise, he locates, but does not describe at length, the Polish and east European Jewish neighborhoods that displaced German enclaves of an earlier generation.

The essay concludes with the provocative notion that Baltimore, a port of choice for millions of immigrants prior to 1920, was perhaps more popular because of other possible destinations from the port than be-cause of the city's desirability as a first residence after migration. Unfor-tunately, the paths away from Baltimore, important as they may be to the port's significance for immigration historians, are roads not taken by the author in his study.

I am quite intrigued by Professor Esslinger's paper. It is a serviceable introduction to a city that deserves much more scholarly attention than it has received as an immigrant port or a first place of settlement. Just as importantly, the essay raises questions that will be part of the agenda for those studying this mid-Atlantic port in the future. High on that list of topics should be the individual immigrant who disembarked in Bal-timore. Where did members of different groups live? What businesses and industries offered employment opportunities? What public and private agencies offered help? Also, there is as yet no published book

that gives the newcomer's perspective on Baltimore as a chosen destination, a port of entry, and a first residence after arrival. Those who comb
the letters and diaries of new arrivals or conduct interviews and oral
histories among surviving immigrant residents of Baltimore's distinctive
row houses will enrich our historical understanding of Baltimore with
the immigrant's view.

And what of the native born who watched the character of the city
change as two great waves of immigrants redefined the Baltimorean?
Was there a nativist backlash in Baltimore? How did the long Roman
Catholic presence in Maryland affect reactions to Irish and German
Catholic immigrants and later Italian and Polish Catholics? In her book
Ambivalent Americans, the Know-Nothing Party in Maryland, historian Jean
Baker offers an in-depth analysis of how the passage of immigrants
through Baltimore's port shaped the politics of the entire state in the
1850s.[1] And what of the later period? How active was the Immigration
Restriction League in Baltimore?

Especially useful would be a comparative perspective on Baltimore as
a port. Ellis Island was called the Isle of Tears by some new arrivals, did
the immigration depot in Baltimore have a similar reputation? What
problems did it share with much larger and busier ports, such as the port
of New York? Both were east coast ports drawing immigration from the
same countries. Prior to 1890, what were the similarities and differences
in how the states of New York and Maryland treated immigration? After
1890, how were newcomers treated in each depot? Did an immigrant
with trachoma or an unsavory past have a better or worse chance of
entering America at Baltimore than at Ellis Island? Were support services the same? Were the Hebrew Immigrant Aid Society and other such
groups as active in Baltimore as New York? Was their corruption at the
Baltimore depot in the early twentieth century as there was in New York?
How was it handled? What changes occurred in procedure as the immigration depot became busier? Information on different ports can be
found in papers of the Immigration and Naturalization Service and
those of the Public Health Service in the National Archives.

Also, we need to know more about how Baltimore coped with influxes
of immigrants from different corners of the world? How did newcomers
from different immigrant groups find jobs, lodging, and education in
Baltimore? According to historian Isaac Fein, who chronicled the history
of Baltimore's Jewish community, on landing, immigrants were met by
agents of large factories, known as inside shops, and proprietors of small
establishments, the outside shops. Clothing manufacture had become
the city's leading industry, and green hands were hired on the spot to
help meet the great demand for ready-made clothes[2] Baltimore, in Fein's
description, thus provides quite a contrast to such a city as New York,

where the crush of competition for jobs often caused new arrivals to pound the pavement for days before finding work.

Esslinger says little about the impact of immigrants on the port city's politics. In his autobiography, however, H. L. Mencken describes how in the 1880s, Mayor Ferdinand C. Latrobe extended himself to the newcomers:

> I heard him [Latrobe] claim not only Irish, Scotch, Welsh, Dutch, and other relatively plausible bloods, but also Polish, Bohemian, Italian, Lithuanian, Swedish, Danish, Greek, Spanish, and even Jewish. Once I heard him hint that he was remotely Armenian. . . . The best he could do for the Chinese, who were then very few in Baltimore, was to quote some passages from the Analects of Confucius, which he had studied though the medium of a secretary.[3]

Whatever his native-born constituents might think, Mayor Latrobe sought a close relationship with the newcomers, especially as elections neared.

Professor Esslinger tells us that many immigrants chose Baltimore because of its convenient transportation links to the West and, he might have added, to the South. Nevertheless, we need to know more about the permanent networks that developed between immigrants who remained in Baltimore and those who undertook a secondary migration immediately or years after arrival. During the mid-1970s, I was doing research on the Jewish community in rural North Carolina. Again and again, older residents described to me how second-generation Jewish women of marriageable age were sent to live with relatives in Baltimore in the hope that the young ladies would find Jewish husbands. There were always stories of kosher meat sent by a Baltimore butcher or of Passover delicacies ordered from Baltimore. We need to know more about how Baltimore became a hub for those smaller enclaves of immigrants who ventured into rural America.

Thus far, there have been few articles or monographs published on the ethnic communities of Baltimore. Fein's history of Baltimore Jewry and Dieter Cunz's book on Maryland's Germans are two of the few.[4] There is a master's thesis by Kathleen Neils Conzen on the mid-nineteenth-century immigrant experience in Baltimore and one on Baltimore's Italian immigrant community in the late nineteenth and early twentieth centuries by Diane Carrick that are suggestive.[5] Undoubtedly, fresh ground will be broken as scholars mine the rich vein of primary sources available for the study of immigration ports in federal records at the National Archives and articles in English and foreign-language newspapers that chronicled the arrival of the "huddled masses" at the port of Baltimore.

As for me, I am most interested in knowing more about those ethnic breweries and kosher hot dogs. Every spring, I feel the need to study ethnicity in Baltimore close up.

Notes

1. Jean H. Baker, *Ambivalent Americans: The Know-Nothing Party in Maryland* (Baltimore, 1977), passim.

2. Isaac M. Fein, *The Making of An American Jewish Community: The History of Baltimore Jewry from 1773 to 1920* (Philadelphia, 1971), 165.

3. H. L. Mencken, *Happy Days* (New York, 1940), 47.

4. Fein, *The Making of an American Jewish Community*, passim. Dieter Cunz, *The Maryland Germans: A History* (Princeton, 1948).

5. Kathleen Neils Conzen, "Trade Relations between Bremen and Baltimore, 1828–1840: Immigrants and Tobacco" (M.A. thesis, University of Delaware, 1966). Diane Carrick, "Residential Persistence of Baltimore's Italians, 1880–1920" (M. A. thesis, University of Maryland, 1977).

4

Immigration through the Port of Miami

Raymond A. Mohl

Since the Cuban Revolution of 1959 Miami has emerged as one of the most distinctive of the nation's new immigrant cities. Over a twenty-five year period, more than 800,000 Cubans left their homeland for the United States; virtually all of them were processed by U.S. immigration authorities in Miami, and a large portion of them settled there permanently. As the Cubans gradually changed Miami into a bilingual city, tens of thousands of legal and illegal immigrants from other Latin American and Caribbean nations were attracted to the south Florida metropolis. Impoverished Haitian boat people, exiles from revolution in Nicaragua, farm workers from Mexico, working-class people from Colombia, professionals from Jamaica, wealthy businessmen from Venezuela—these and many others have found a haven in Miami.

The new immigration of the past twenty-five years has brought a veritable demographic revolution to the Miami metropolitan area. In 1980, according to the U.S. census, the foreign born made up about 54 percent of the population of the city of Miami and almost 36 percent of the population of the entire metropolitan area. No other major American city even came close to Miami's foreign-born proportion. By comparison, the 1980 census revealed that the population of Los Angeles was 27 percent foreign born, while that of New York City was about 24 percent. As these statistics suggest, Miami now commands attention as an important immigration center and a vital gateway for the millions from Latin America and the Caribbean who equate the United States with the land of opportunity.

Bahamian Immigration

The magnitude and diversity of current immigration to Miami tends to mask the fact that Miami has always had a substantial foreign-born

Cuban refugees arriving in Miami, 1979. *(Courtesy of the Historical Association of Southern Florida.)*

ingredient. The city had only a few hundred people when it was incorporated in 1896, but by 1900, the population had increased to 1,681, including a sizable number of black immigrants from the Bahamas. Over the next twenty years, the Bahamian influx helped to swell the local population. By 1920, the foreign born made up one-quarter of the Miami population; more than 65 percent of the immigrants were blacks from the West Indies. In that census year, 4,815 black islanders, almost all from the Bahamas, comprised 52 percent of all Miami's blacks and 16.3 percent of the city's entire population of 29,571. By 1920, Miami had a larger population of black immigrants than any other city in the United States except New York.[1]

Bahamian blacks had been coming to Florida's lower east coast long before the building of Miami. In the early nineteenth century, when Florida was isolated and undeveloped, the area was frequented by Bahamian fishermen, wreckers, and seamen. According to one Bahamian writer, these early visitors regarded Florida "much as another island of the Bahamas." By the late nineteenth century, Bahamian blacks were migrating to Key West, where they worked in fishing, turtling, and sponging. They also began coming to Florida's lower east coast to work in the region's important agricultural sector. The distance from the islands was short, and the cost of the journey relatively cheap. As a result, after about 1870, these newcomers from the Bahamas served as an early migrant labor force in Florida agriculture. Until about 1900, one chronicler of early south Florida has noted, "All of our heavy laborers were Bahamian negroes." The scrubby pine and coral rock topography of south Flordia was similar to that of the islands. Bahamians "knew how to plant" on this land, and they brought in "their own commonly used trees, vegetables, and fruits." Thus, they demonstrated to native American planters the rich agricultural potential of what seemed at first a desolate and forbidding land.[2]

The building of Miami created new opportunities for Bahamian immigrants. Indeed, black Bahamian immigrants were attracted to Miami for the same reasons that European immigrants poured into the industrial cities of the Northeast and Midwest during the same decades at the turn of the century. The new and rapidly growing resort center provided opportunities for better jobs and higher wages than they had known at home. As one writer put it, "Wonderful things were going on in Miami, and there was a great demand for labour there. . . A remarkable building boom was on, and any Bahamian who wanted a job could find it." One Bahamian immigrant who arrived in Miami in 1911 noted that agriculture was depressed and job prospects discouraging in the Bahamas, but "Miami was a young Magic City where money could be 'shaken from trees.' Home-returning pilgrims told exaggerated tales of their fame and fortune in the 'promised land' "—a familiar tale in immigrant literature. Between 1910 and 1920, the total population of the Bahamas declined more than 5 percent, and many islands lost 10 percent or more of their inhabitants as a result of emigration to Florida.[3]

Bahamians were noted for their masonry skills; in particular, they were adept at building with the coral rock and oolitic limestone common to the Bahamas and south Florida. Thus, Bahamian blacks came to Miami after its founding in 1896 to work in the burgeoning construction industry. They also worked on the railroads, the docks, in lumber yards and gravel pits, and as day laborers. The emergence of Miami as a tourist resort provided still further opportunities for Bahamians, especially as maids, cooks, and service workers in the city's new hotels and restaurants, or as domestic servants for wealthy whites with permanent or winter residences in Miami.[4]

The area's agriculture continued to prosper as well. Bahamians worked in the local citrus industry, particularly in Coconut Grove, a community near Miami where Bahamians had been living since the 1880s. Their presence in Coconut Grove, one recent study has noted, gave the area's black community "a distinctively island character that is still evident." They also labored in the expanding vegetable farms on

Miami's agricultural fringe. Many Bahamians came as migrant laborers during harvest season, returning to the islands each summer. This pattern was especially evident during the years of World War I, when the federal government sought to boost Florida's agricultural production. In the years before effective federal regulation of immigration, Bahamian blacks moved easily and at will between south Florida and the islands.[5]

Manuscript census schedules give a more detailed picture of black Bahamian immigrants in Miami. In 1900, the McCloud family typified the early Bahamian presence in south Florida. Hiram McCloud, a forty-eight year-old Bahamian, had come to the United States in 1878. The census described him as a common laborer. He was a naturalized U.S. citizen. He rented his house in Coconut Grove; he could read but not write, and he had been unemployed for two months during the year. His thirty-nine-year-old wife, Clotilda, also came to the United States in 1878, but she had not yet become a citizen. A washerwoman who worked continuously throughout the year, Clotilda could read and write. During twenty years of marriage, she had given birth to eight children, but only five were still living in 1900. The oldest child, Curtis McCloud, had been born in Florida in 1881 and was also working as a laborer. Four other children, ranging in age from five to fifteen, had all been born in Florida; two were attending school.[6]

The McClouds came to Florida before the establishment of Miami in 1896. Many other Bahamians arrived during the 1890s, typically single males who worked as farm laborers or fruit pickers. Few were naturalized American citizens. They lived together in groups of four and five in rented premises or lodged with Bahamian families. Other occupations listed by census enumerators for Bahamians included carpenter, fisherman, boatman, blacksmith's helper, deck hand, seamstress, dressmaker, cook, chambermaid, house servant, and odd jobs.[7]

By 1910, the Bahamian community in Miami had increased substantially to well over fifteen hundred. A veritable wave of new Bahamians had arrived in 1908 and 1909, an early boatlift from the islands that captured the attention of the city's leading newspaper, the *Miami Metropolis*. According to the paper, more than fourteen hundred Bahamians arrived in Miami during the single year after July 1908, many of them temporary farm workers. They came fifty or sixty at a time on small schooners, often "so crowded with people that there was barely standing room on their decks." Apparently, these new arrivals were processed by immigration authorities, for the *Metropolis* noted that about 10 percent of the Bahamians were sent back to the islands after "failing to meet the requirements of the immigration laws."[8]

The new wave of Bahamians worked extensively in citrus groves and vegetable fields. As census schedules suggest, these immigrant farm workers tended to be young, single men living in boarding houses; most of them had been in Miami less than a decade, and a large proportion had applied for citizenship, perhaps in order to obtain or retain an agricultural laboring job. Another large segment of the Miami Bahamian community worked in the resort town's service economy as maids and porters in hotels, cooks and waiters in restaurants, servants and housekeepers in private homes, and the like.

In the census of 1910 a typical Bahamian household was that of Albert A. Taylor, a thrity-eight-year-old car cleaner in a local railroad shop. Taylor had entered the United States in 1898 and at the time of the census was renting a house at 721 Third Street in what was known as Miami's Negro section. Taylor lived with his Bahamian-born wife, two American-born children, a sister (a cook for a white family), a brother (an odd-job laborer), and two cousins (both laborers). Completing this extended Bahamian household were three boarders, two young men who worked as laborers, and a twenty-one-year-old girl who worked as a maid for a white family.[9]

The boom years of the 1920s brought tremendous population growth and urban development to south Florida; Miami more than tripled its population to over 110,000. Bahamians continued to flow into Florida, too, although at a slower pace. Officially, about 1,800 new black immigrants arrived in Miami in the 1920s, giving the city some 5,512 foreign-born blacks in 1930. The islanders, according to census reports, comprised about 22 percent of Miami's black population. Some evidence, however, suggests that additional large numbers of Bahamian farm workers had been brought into the area illegally. Newspaper reports in August 1921, for instance, revealed that "the smuggling of negroes from the Bahama Islands has attracted the attention of the immigration department in the past few weeks."[10] Bahamian immigration tapered off in the 1930s, but Miami still had 4,063 foreign-born blacks in 1940.[11]

The Bahamian presence made Miami's black population distinctively different from that in most southern cities. Bahamians had an impact on food ways, cultural patterns, work habits, educational aspirations, musical and artistic activities, and other social characteristics. Unaccustomed to racial prejudice and segregation in the islands, Miami's Bahamians resented the color barrier they found in the United States. Independent and footloose, Miami historian Paul S. George has written, "These British subjects were less obsequious toward whites than native blacks." As a result, many Bahamians not only preached but sought to practice racial equality in Miami long before the walls of segregation crumbled in the 1950s.[12] A definable Bahamian presence continues in Miami to this day, testimony to the powerful surge of immigration from the islands in the early years of the twentieth century. Coconut Grove, in particular, retains the "indelible imprint" of the Bahamas. As one writer put it recently in the *Nassau Tribune*, the Grove still has "an atmosphere more akin to a Bahamas settlement than an American neighborhood." An annual Bahamian Goombay Festival in Coconut Grove reflects local enthusiasm for the celebration of black ethnicity in modern Miami.[13]

Cuban Immigration

The Cuban Revolution in 1959 ended the long regime of Fulgencio Batista and brought Fidel Castro to power. Most Cubans at first welcomed the new revolutionary government, but the implementation of socialist policies soon turned the Cuban elites, professionals, and the urban middle class against the new regime. A great exodus began, one that transplanted hundreds of thousands of discontented Cubans to Miami in the space of a few short years.

Actually, Florida had been providing a place of refuge for Cubans since the nineteenth century. In 1868, at the beginning of Cuba's Ten Years' War, Cuban political exiles began immigrating in large numbers to Key West; by 1870, some two thousand Cubans had settled in Florida's southernmost city. By the late 1880s, about ten thousand Cubans lived in Key West and Tampa, where they were employed mostly in the burgeoning tobacco industry.[14]

Few Cubans came to Miami in these early years. The 1910 census reported only three Cuban-born immigrants in the Miami area. A Cuban community began to emerge in Miami in the early 1930s, however, as exiles from the Cuban Revolution of 1933 arrived in the city. By January 1934, a Miami newspaper could refer to the city's hundreds of Cuban exiles. According to the 1940 census, as many as eleven hundred Cuban-born immigrants made Miami home.[15]

Miami's Hispanic community continued to grow throughout the 1940s, reaching about twenty thousand by 1950. Most of the Hispanics were Puerto Ricans, but a colony of several thousand Cubans was well established by the time the anti-Castro exodus began in 1959. There is even some evidence to suggest that a concentrated area of Cuban settlement had begun to take shape just to the southwest of Miami's central business district and native Miamians were already calling the area Little Havana. Thus, the exiles who flowed from Cuba in such astonishing numbers during the 1960s and 1970s were only the latest in a long line of Cubans who sought refuge in Florida.[16]

Cuban immigration to the United States since 1959 has stemmed from the revolutionary upheaval in Castro's Cuba. As one study put it, "A massive restructuring of the social and political order . . . was under way, and millions of lives were being transformed or at least profoundly affected by government action." The business and propertied classes were the first to leave, along with the professional and managerial elites, white-collar workers, and the urban middle class. A study of early Cuban émigrés noted that "the great preponderance of the refugees are drawn from the wealthier, the better educated, the more urban, and the higher occupational sectors." Later refugees tended to be more similar demographically to the Cuban population as a whole.[17]

The exiles came to the United States in several waves over two decades, an erratic immigration dictated by the state of United States-Cuban relations at any particular time. This relationship has also determined the form of the movement, since at various times, Cubans have arrived in Florida by boatlift, airlift, or traveled through a third country.

The first great wave of Cuban refugees came to the United States between January 1959 and October 1962. Some 215,000 Cubans arrived in the United States during this period, most coming by commercial aircraft to Miami. Because they wre fleeing a communist country, they were admitted to the United States outside the regular immigration quota and granted a special parolee status. The Cuban Missile Crisis in October 1962 ended direct flights between Cuba and the United States and brought the first Cuban exodus to a close. As one writer put it, "Cuba was shut tight, and no one could get in or out."[18]

Ultimately, however, about thirty thousand Cubans did leave over the next few years, either clandestinely or by traveling to third countries, such as Spain or Mexico. During 1965, for example, the U.S. Immigration and Naturalization Service (INS) reported that some eleven hundred Cubans escaped from the island in small boats during the year. Most were picked up at sea by the U.S. Coast Guard and granted asylum in the United States.[19]

Not until December 1965 did the two governments reach an agreement ending the hiatus in Cuban emigration to the United States. During the next eight years, a second wave of over 340,000 Cubans arrived in Miami by way of an airlift—two daily freedom flights from the Cuban town of Varadero that brought in three to four thousand people each month. A priority was placed on family reunification in issuing exit visas from Cuba, so most of these new exiles had relatives already in the United States.

Early in 1973, Castro abruptly ended the airlift, and Cuban emigration declined drastically. By the end of the 1970s, only a few thousand Cubans were arriving in the United States each year, mostly in small boats or by way of third countries. But in 1980, when most thought the migration of Cubans to the United States was over for good, Castro opened the gates once again. The Mariel boatlift of May to September

1980 brought 125,000 new Cuban exiles to Miami. This massive third wave of Cuban newcomers, moreover, created controversy and anger because Castro had filled the freedom flotilla with thousands of criminals and other undesirables. About half of the new arrivals, those with family and relatives here, were quickly absorbed by Miami's Cuban community. Federal officials dispersed the rest to camps as far away as Wisconsin, Arkansas, and Pennsylvania, but once released, most of them drifted back to Miami.[20]

The great exodus of Cubans to Miami reflected growing disenchantment with the outcome of the Cuban Revolution. Revolutionary goals led to the expropriation of property and the redistribution of wealth. The rural poor and the urban working classes benefited from the new social policy, but established elites felt betrayed. As one study put it, "The radicalization and eventual communization of the Cuban government alienated large sectors of the population." Optimistic expectations for the revolution were shattered, leaving many disillusioned and disaffected. Cubans who did not fall in line with the revolution were harassed, threatened, persecuted, and imprisoned. The earliest exiles were ideological opponents of Castro's revolution; later exiles were more likely to have been initial supporters whose revolutionary zeal had been eroded by pragmatic experience in the new Cuba. More recent immigrants may have been pulled more by economic opportunity in the United States than pushed by political or social conditions in Cuba. Whatever the reasons for departure, becoming an exile usually involved a wrenching personal or family decision.[21]

Virtually all of the Cuban émigrés entered the United States through Miami. Cubans had already established a small community in the city; the climate was agreeable, and it was only a few hundred miles from home. Miami seemed a logical place to "wait out" the Cuban revolution or to organize to overthrow Castro and eventually return to the island. Federal policy opened the gates to Cuban exiles, who entered the United States without immigration quotas or restrictions. In the era of the Cold War, Americans at first welcomed the anticommunist Cubans with open arms.

As a result of this unprecedented migration of exiles, Miami emerged after 1959 as one of the chief immigration ports in the nation. Annual reports of the INS confirm Miami's prominence as a port of entry; from 1960 through 1969, only New York City surpassed Miami as an immigrant port. From 1970 to 1976, reflecting the surging migration of Vietnamese, Chinese, and other Asians into the United States, Honolulu replaced Miami as the second busiest immigration port. In 1977, however, the INS once again reported Miami to be in second place. The INS records for this period also demonstrate that substantial numbers of the newcomers entering through Miami remained in the south Florida region and particularly in Miami itself.[22]

Beginning in 1960, the federal government's Cuban Refugee Program (CRP) handled the actual processing and resettlement of Cubans in Miami. After initial security screening of exiles by the INS, the CRP's Cuban Refugee Emergency Center provided them with a variety of social services, educational programs, medical assistance, job training and placement, and the like. By 1973, more than $1 billion had been spent by the federal government to assist Cuban resettlement in the United States. The center also coordinated private aid from numerous religious and voluntary agencies, such as the Catholic Diocese of Miami, which played an especially important part in Cuban refugee settlement.[23]

By 1962, the Cuban refugee center was located in the former Miami News building, a distinctive downtown skyscraper modeled after a fifteenth-century tower in Seville, Spain, and completed in 1925. Soon renamed the freedom tower, the historic building where most of the newcomers were processed became an important symbol of the migration of Cuban exiles. As former Miami Mayor Maurice Ferre said recently of the freedom tower, "For Miami's Cubans, it is our Ellis Island, our Statue of Liberty."[24]

One important goal of the CRP was to resettle the Cubans throughout the United States. It was believed that such a dispersal would not only relieve the economic and social burden on Miami but also speed the assimilation of Cubans. Within two days of their arrival in Miami, tens of thousands of Cubans "were on their way to somewhere else," one journalist wrote in 1966. But Miami had a magnetic pull for Cuban exiles, and a large portion of those resettled elsewhere eventually returned to their original port of entry. By the 1980s, more than 60 percent of all the Cubans in the United States resided in the Miami metropolitan area.[25]

Given the professional and business backgrounds of the early exiles, the dimensions of resettlement assistance, and their concentration in a single city, it is not really surprising that Cubans have adjusted well and prospered in their new home. They have built a thriving ethnic community in Miami's Little Havana, in Hialeah, and other sections of the metropolitan area. After a period of initial adjustment, Cubans have been successful economically, creating an enclave economy that maintains the Spanish language and provides jobs for Cuban newcomers. Cubans, then, have been instrumental in turning an aging and declining tourist town into an exciting, vibrant, and bilingual city. Their presence has been partly responsible for the recent emergence of Miami as an important center of international banking, trade, finance, and tourism. As Cubans gradually accepted the permanence of their stay in the

"Freedom Tower" Cuban Refugee Center, Miami, 1985. *(Courtesy of Balch Museum Collection; photo by Elliott Barkan.)*

United States, a large number of the community became naturalized citizens, and now Cubans are a powerful force in the volatile urban politics of the Miami metropolitan area. Despite the leveling tendency of Cuban emigration over time, Cubans are markedly different from other Hispanics in the United States: Statistical evidence suggests that they have more education, better jobs, higher incomes, and lower fertility rates than the Hispanic population generally.[26]

The migration of Cuban exiles to the United States is surely one of the unique chapters in the history of American immigration. And by most measures, it would seem the Cuban story has been a huge success, clearly demonstrating how newcomers seize opportunity in America. The Mariel boatlift in 1980, with its attendant problems, represented a temporary setback, but it seems likely that most of the newest Cuban refugees will ultimately share the positive experiences of those who came in the earlier waves of Cuban immigration to Miami.

Haitian Immigration

A third group of island immigrants—Haitians—has added to the diversity of the recent Caribbean influx into the south Florida area. As noted earlier, Miami's black population has always had a substantial foreign-born element—first Bahamians, more recently Jamaicans, and black Cubans. Thus according to the 1980 census, over 22 percent of Miami's blacks were foreign born. The arrival of about 25,000 Haitians in 1980 alone has pushed that figure substantially higher now, and as a result of this immigration over many years, the black population of the Miami area is much more ethnically diverse than that in most metropolitan areas.[27]

The rise of François "Papa Doc" Duvalier to power in Haiti in 1957 stimulated the first sizable Haitian migration. Early exiles sought to escape the brutality of the Duvalier dictatorship, with its "peculiar combination of terror, repression, anomie, and exploitation." Haitian political exiles, along with urban professional and business elites, settled primarily in New York City in the 1960s, and by the early 1980s, about 450,000 Haitians and Haitian Americans resided there. Smaller Haitian communities sprouted in Montreal, Boston, Philadelphia, and Washington. Miami's Haitian community initially was quite small; the 1960 census reported only 239 Haitians in the entire Miami metropolitan area.[28]

The Haitian exodus continued throughout the 1960s. By mid-decade, some 80 percent of the country's engineers, lawyers, physicians, teachers, and other professionals had been driven out of Haiti by Papa Doc's ruthless dictatorship. The business and professional elites who came in the early wave of Haitian immigrants generally entered the United States legally, or at least with legal-looking papers, and they came by air. By the mid-1960s, people of more modest means were joining the wealthy and the well educated in the flight from poverty and repression, although generally they were forced to leave in clandestine fashion by small boat to the Bahamas or south Florida. As early as 1965, according to the INS, Haitians were being smuggled into Florida by boat from the Bahamas.[29]

Intensified political repression and economic deprivation from the early 1970s until the overthrow of the Duvalier family's regime in 1986 prompted a further exodus from Haiti of the urban lower classes and the rural poor. Most of these Haitians arrived by small boat, either directly to south Florida or by way of the Bahamas, where tens of thousands of Haitians searching for a better life have settled temporarily. In their desperation, Haitian refugees have been willing to risk all in a dangerous, eight hundred-mile journey to South Florida. Since 1975, at least forty thousand black boat people, probably many more, have completed this perilous trip in tiny, overcrowded, and barely seaworthy sailboats. Some immigration experts report that at least an equal number have died at sea, and many have drowned within sight of their goal when high seas caused their boats to founder on Florida beaches.[30]

Miami has become a symbol of hope and the good life for the poor and depressed masses of Haiti. Journalist Kristine Rosenthal captured the allure of Miami for Haitians in a recent article:

> The image of Miami rises like a specter over all of Haitian consciousness. Whatever one can accomplish, obtain, or develop is dwarfed and made insignificant by the possibilities of Miami. Miami is the place where you can make a month's wages in a day or a year's wages in a week. . . . So if you are ambitious and willing to take a risk, you can better your life by getting to Miami.

For Haitians, over the past decade or so, going to the United States has meant going to Miami. By the mid-1980s, at least sixty thousand Haitian refugees had settled in Miami's Little Haiti, while another thirty thousand resided just to the north in Florida's Broward County (Fort Lauderdale, Hollywood, and Pompano Beach).[31]

Haitian newcomers have received a less than enthusiastic welcome in the United States. Even objective observers detect a double standard in American immigration policy—one that welcomes mostly white refugees from Cuban communism, for instance, but rejects black immigrants from Haiti who also claim to be political exiles from a totalitarian government. The INS has refused to accept Haitian appeals for political asylum because Haitians, the INS has argued, are seeking economic opportunity in America and not fleeing political persecution. Thus, the thousands of Haitians who arrived in 1980 were officially detained—imprisoned, really—by the INS in the Krome Refugee Camp west of Miami or, for a while, at another camp in Puerto Rico. By contrast, the Cuban *marielitos* without criminal records went free immediately. As one writer said in 1979, these political refugees were "from the wrong place." He might have added that they were also the wrong color.[32]

Because the Haitian boat people were considered illegal immigrants by the INS, it became official policy to deport them as soon as possible. Beginning in the 1970s, many Haitians were pressured or coerced into accepting immediate voluntary return to Haiti. For those who claimed political asylum, however, immigration law gave them the right to demand a deportation hearing. By the end of the 1981, almost forty thousand Haitian refugees were awaiting exclusion or deportation proceedings.[33]

Several thousand Haitian detainees ended up in the squalid and depressing Krome camp, some for as long as eighteen months. If the freedom tower served as a symbol of hope for Cuban exiles, Krome camp became a symbol of hopelessness and despair for thousands of Haitians. Demonstrations by Haitian supporters focused public attention on the Krome situation, and legal action by the Haitian Refugee Center, a private Miami advocacy organization, forced the issue into federal courts. In 1982, a federal judge ruled against the INS detention policy and released all Haitian detainees pending individual deportation hearings. Congressional immigration reform would have normalized the immigration status of most Haitians, but the legislation failed in 1984.[34]

Meanwhile, as a further deterrent to Haitian immigration to the United States, the Reagan administration in 1981 implemented an interdiction policy to halt the flow of boat people on the high seas. The policy involved sending coast guard ships to the Windward Passage near Haiti, seizing the boat people at sea, holding INS hearings on ship, and returning the voyagers to Haiti immediately. The interdiction policy remains in effect, and it has probably caused a reduction in the number of Haitian boat people arriving in south Florida. During the last four months of 1984, for instance, more than two thousand Haitians were picked up by the coast guard and returned to Haiti. Occasionally, the interdiction policy has had disastrous results, as in June 1984, when a Haitian boat stopped by the coast guard overturned and a dozen or more of its passengers drowned. As the interdiction policy suggests, the United States "is no longer so anxious to welcome the tired, the wretched and the poor of other nations." Nevertheless, Haitians continue to drift up to Florida beaches in rickety, leaking boats in their search for a better life.[35]

Despite their problems with the INS, Haitians have begun to build a new ethnic community in Miami. The new Haitian immigrants have settled heavily in the Edison-Little River section of Miami, one of the city's oldest neighborhoods, where cheap and run-down housing, white flight, and nearby job opportunities in the garment industry, warehousing, and light industry have attracted newcomers. Prior to the Haitians' arrival, the area was described as "a blighted tri-ethnic community [characterized by] high rates of housing turnover and residential instability." Now known as Little Haiti, the community is over 40 percent Haitian.[36]

Researchers are just beginning to sketch out the full dimensions of Haitian community life in Miami. Miami Haitians are relatively young, in their prime working years, and at least one generation removed from rural peasantry. One study revealed a group of immigrants who were mostly semiskilled rather than unskilled workers in Haiti and who had achieved a substantial level of education (7.6 years of schooling) in a country where 80 percent of the people receive no formal schooling whatsoever. The Haitian boat people, it has been argued, are "positively selected"—that is, they are risk takers, ambitious and willing to take chances and work hard in a struggle to get ahead.[37]

The Miami Haitians have demonstrated not only a powerful work ethic but a strong commitment to education as well. One study reported that 55 percent of all Miami Haitians had enrolled in some sort of school or educational program since their arrival in the United States. As a group, they have picked up English, and Spanish, too, remarkably well. They have a growing entrepreneurial sector in Little Haiti, although it tends to consist almost entirely of small retail and service businesses or other kinds of informal enterprises, all generally marginally profitable. Because Haitians lack the sort of self-sufficient enclave economy the Cubans have created in Miami's Little Havana, they have experienced severe unemployment problems as a result. Under the circumstances, however, Haitians have adjusted remarkably rapidly. Moreover, Haitian culture remains strong in Miami, and the community is constantly being replenished by new arrivals from Haiti. The anti-Duvalier politics that marked the Haitian community in Miami have now died down, but many observers believe that these newcomers will become new players in the old game of ethnic politics in Miami, a development that is certain to sustain the powerful sense of ethnic identity among the Haitian people.[38]

The odyssey of the Haitian boat people has not finished. Even after the overthrow of the repressive regime, black boat people have continued to make the difficult journey to south Florida. In the near future, at least, Miami will retain its allure for poverty-sticken Haitians.

Few American immigration ports have matched Miami's ethnic diversity in the post–World War II era. Black Bahamian immigration gave Miami its special character early in the twentieth century. By the 1930s and 1940s, Miami and Miami Beach had also attracted foreign-born retirees, especially European Jews, who had immigrated earlier to New York and other northern cities, but Miami's role as an immigrant port did not emerge again until the Cuban Revolution in 1959. The massive migration of Cuban exiles and Haitian refugees over the past twenty-five years has created a demographic revolution in the Miami metropolitan area. Miami has been unalterably changed and reshaped in the process. Newcomers from all over the Caribbean, Central America, and South America are adding to the ethnic diversity of the area. The census of 1980 reported about 174,000 non-Cuban Hispanics in the Miami metropolitan area. Immigration officials admit to tens of thousands of illegal and uncounted aliens as well. Every Latin American revolution or coup d'état produces a new exile community in Miami. The Sandinista revolution in Nicaragua, for example, has resulted in a new community of some seventy to eighty thousand Nicaraguan exiles since 1979, most settling in a section west of Miami now called Little Managua.[39]

Diversity marks the Miami area, but the city is also unique in the ways that Cubans, Haitians, and others have arrived. The Cuban airlift between 1965 and 1973, the astounding Mariel boatlift, the dramatic arrival of the Haitian boat people—these events have shaped American images about Miami as an immigration port. Miami business leaders long have boasted of their city as the gateway to Latin America. It is perhaps even more apparent now that Miami has been the gateway to the United States for hundreds of thousands of upwardly striving people from the Caribbean and Latin America, and there is little to suggest that this immigration pattern will change in the near future.

Notes

1. U.S. Bureau of the Census, *Thirteenth Census of the United States Taken in the Year 1910*, vol. II, *Population 1910* (Washington,D.C.: U.S. Government Printing Office, 1913), 332; U.S. Bureau of the Census, *Fourteenth Census of the United States Taken in the Year 1920*, vol. II, *Population 1920* (Washington, D.C.: U.S. Government Printing Office, 1922), 760, 795.

2. Larry Smith, "Coconut Grove: Bahamian Roots in Florida," *Nassau Tribune,* 12 October 1977, clipping file, Miami-Dade Public Library; Sharon Wells, *Forgotten Legacy: Blacks in Nineteenth-Century Key West* (Key West: Historic Key West Preservation Board, 1982), 7–13; George E. Merrick, "Pre-Flagler Influences on the Lower Florida East Coast," *Tequesta: Journal of the Historical Association of Southern Florida* 1 (1941): 5; Thelma Peters, *Biscayne Country, 1870–1926* (Miami: Banyan Books, Inc., 1981), 229, 239; Charles Garofalo, "Black-White Occupa-

tional Distribution in Miami during World War I," *Prologue: Journal of the National Archives* 5 (1973): 98–99.

3. Paul Albury, *The Story of the Bahamas* (London: Macmillan, 1975), 168–69; Ira De A. Reid, *The Negro Immigrant: His Background, Characteristics, and Social Adjustment, 1899–1937* (New York: Columbia University Press, 1939), 184–85; Michael Craton, *A History of the Bahamas* (3d ed.; Waterloo, Ont.: San Salvador Press, 1986), 241; Government of the Bahamas, *Demographic Aspects of the Bahamas Population, 1901–1974* (Census Monograph no. 2; Nassau, Bahamas: Department of Statistics, 1976), 5.

4. Thelma Peters, *Lemon City: Pioneering on Biscayne Bay, 1850–1925* (Miami: Banyan Books, Inc., 1976), 230.

5. Arva Moore Parks, "The History of Coconut Grove, Florida, 1821–1925" (M.A. thesis, University of Miami, 1971), 38–41; Bruce Porter and Marvin Dunn, *The Miami Riot of 1980: Crossing the Bounds* (Lexington, Mass.: Lexington Books, 1984), 2; Paul S. George, "Criminal Justice in Miami, 1896–1930" (Ph.D. diss. Florida State University, 1975), 185; Peters, *Biscayne Country*, 264; Helen Muir, *Miami, U.S.A.* (Coconut Grove, Fla.: Hurricane House Publishers, Inc., 1963), 11.

6. Manuscript census schedules, Dade County, 1900, microfilm ed., roll 167, National Archives.

7. Ibid.

8. *Miami Metropolis*, 12 June 1909; Albury, *Story of the Bahamas*, 168–69.

9. Manuscript census schedules, Dade County, 1910, microfilm ed., roll 158, National Archives.

10. U.S. Bureau of the Census, *Fifteenth Census of the United States: 1930. Population*, vol. II (Washington, D.C.: U.S. Government Printing Office, 1933), 562; *Palm Beach Post*, 29 July 1921; Chas. S. Thompson, "The Growth of Colored Miami," *Crisis* 49 (1942): 83.

11. U.S. Bureau of the Census, *Sixteenth Census of the United States: 1940. Population*, vol. II, *Characteristics of the Population* (Washington, D.C.: U.S. Government Printing Office, 1943), 142.

12. "Folklore," typescript, c. 1936, in "The Florida Negro" file, collections of the Florida Historical Society, University of South Florida Library, Tampa, Florida; Reid, *The Negro Immigrant*, 189; *Nassau Tribune*, 10 November 1913; James A. Bryce to Edward Grey, 13 April 1911, Colonial Office Records, microfilm ed., CO 23/268, Bahamas Public Records Office, Nassau, Bahamas; George, "Criminal Justice in Miami," 185–86.

13. *Nassau Tribune*, 12 October 1977. For a more detailed treatment of Bahamians in Miami, see Raymond A. Mohl, "Black Immigrants: Bahamians in Early Twentieth-Century Miami," *Florida Historical Quarterly* 65 (1987): 271–97.

14. Michael J. McNally, *Catholicism in South Florida, 1868–1968* (Gainesville: University Presses of Florida, 1984), 15, 21; Gerald E. Poyo, "Cuban Communities in the United States: Toward an Overview of the Nineteenth-Century Experience," in Miren Uriarte-Gastón and Jorge Cañas Martínez, eds., *Cubans in the United States* (Boston: Seminar on Cuban-American Studies, Boston University, 1984); Louis A. Pérez, "Cubans in Tampa: From Exiles to Immigrants, 1892–1901," *Florida Historical Quarterly* 57 (1978): 129–41.

15. U.S. Bureau of the Census, *Thirteenth Census, 1910*, 332; *Friday Night* (Miami), 12 January 1934; U.S. Bureau of the Census, *Sixteenth Census, 1940*, 144.

16. Thomas D. Boswell and James R. Curtis, *The Cuban-American Experience: Culture, Images, and Perspectives;* (Totowa, N.J.: Rowman & Allanheld, 1983), 72–74; Morton D. Winsberg, "Housing Segregation of a Predominantly Middle-

Class Population: Residential Patterns Developed by the Cuban Immigration into Miami, 1950–74," *American Journal of Economics and Sociology* 38 (1979): 408–10.

17. Richard R. Fagen et al., *Cubans in Exile: Disaffection and the Revolution* (Stanford: Stanford University Press, 1968), 4, 23; Silvia Pedraza-Bailey, *Political and Economic Migrants in America: Cubans and Mexicans* (Austin: University of Texas Press, 1985), 18–52; Alejandro Portes and Robert L. Bach, *Latin Journey: Cuban and Mexican Immigrants in the United States* (Berkeley: University of California Press, 1985), 84; Boswell and Curtis, *The Cuban-American Experience*, 49, 51.

18. José Llanes, *Cuban Americans: Masters of Survival* (Cambridge, Mass.: Abt Books, 1982), 8; Portes and Bach, *Latin Journey*, 85–86.

19. U.S. Immigration and Naturalization Service, *Annual Report of the Immigration and Naturalization Service, 1965* (Washington, D.C.: U.S. Government Printing Office, 1965), 4.

20. Portes and Bach, *Latin Journey*, 86–88; Llanes, *Cuban Americans*, 98–101, 141–42; Roberto E. Hernandez, "The Origins of the Mariel Boatlift," in José Szapocznik et al., *Coping with Adolescent Refugees: The Mariel Boatlift* (New York: Praeger, 1985), 3–21.

21. Fagen et al., *Cubans in Exile*, 34. See also Lorrin Philipson and Rafael Llerena, *Freedom Flights: Cuban Refugees Talk about Life under Castro and How They Fled His Regime* (New York: Random House, 1980).

22. U.S. Immigration and Naturalization Service, *Annual Reports, 1960–1977* (Washington, D.C.: U.S. Government Printing Office, 1960–77); Unpublished tables for immigration to Florida, INS computer tapes, 1972–77.

23. John Thomas, "Cuban Refugee Program," *Welfare in Review* 1 (1963): 1–20; John Thomas, "Cuban Refugees in the United States," *International Migration Review* 1 (1967): 46–57; David R. Colburn and George E. Pozzetta, eds., *America and the New Ethnicity* (Port Washington, N.Y.: Kennikat Press, 1979), 108; McNally, *Catholicism in South Florida*, 127–66.

24. Milton Bracker, "Cuba's Refugees Live in Hope—and Despair," *New York Times Magazine*, 30 September 1962, 84; Howard Kleinberg, *Miami: The Way We Were* (Miami: Miami Daily News, Inc., 1985), 110–ll; *Miami News*, 26 December 1983; *Miami Herald*, 30 July 1985.

25. Tom Alexander, "Those Amazing Cuban Emigres," *Fortune* 74 (1966): 148; Portes and Bach, *Latin Journey*, 88–89.

26. Raymond A. Mohl, "Miami: The Ethnic Cauldron," in Richard M. Bernard and Bradley R. Rice, eds., *Sunbelt Cities: Politics and Growth since World War II* (Austin: University of Texas Press, 1983), 58–99; Raymond A. Mohl, "An Ethnic 'Boiling Pot': Cubans and Haitians in Miami," *Journal of Ethnic Studies* 13 (1985): 55–63; Kenneth L. Wilson and W. Allen Martin, "Ethnic Enclaves: A Comparison of the Cuban and Black Economies in Miami," *American Journal of Sociology* 88 (1982): 135–60; Raymond A. Mohl, "The Politics of Ethnicity in Contemporary Miami," *Migration World* 14, (1986): 7–11; Portes and Bach, *Latin Journey*, 200–239; A. J. Jaffe et al., *The Changing Demography of Spanish Americans* (New York: Academic Press, 1980), 245–78.

27. U.S. Bureau of the Census, *1980 Census of Population*, vol. I, *Characteristics of the Population*, PC80-1-C11, *Florida* (Washington, D.C.: U.S. Government Printing Office, 1981), 11–278, -281; Thomas D. Boswell, "The New Haitian Diaspora: Florida's Most Recent Residents," *Caribbean Review* 11 (1982): 18–21; Mohl, "An Ethnic 'Boiling Pot,'" 63–67.

28. Robert I. Rotberg, *Haiti: The Politics of Squalor* (Boston: Houghton Mifflin Company, 1971), 243; Michel S. Laguerre, *American Odyssey: Haitians in New York*

City (Ithaca, N.Y.: Cornell University Press, 1984); Alex Stepick, *Haitian Refugees in the U.S.* (London: Minority Rights Group, report no. 52, 1982); U.S. Bureau of the Census, *U.S. Census of Population: 1960. Detailed Characteristics. Florida.* Final report PC(1)-11D (Washington, D.C.: U.S. Government Printing Office, 1962), 11–306.

29. Rotberg, *Haiti*, 243; INS, *Annual Report, 1965*, 8.

30. Alex Stepick, "The New Haitian Exodus: The Flight from Terror and Poverty," *Caribbean Review* 11 (1982): 14–17, 55–57; *USA Today*, 6 February 1985; *Miami Herald*, 27 October 1981; *Miami News*, 31 March 1982.

31. Kristine Rosenthal, "In the Shadow of Miami: Haitian Sojourn," *Working Papers Magazine* 9 (1982): 25; *Miami Herald*, 24 February 1985; *Miami Review*, 28 February 1985.

32. Patrick Lacefield, "These Political Refugees Are from the Wrong Place," *In These Times*, 7 November 1979, 11, 13; INS, *Annual Report, 1980*, 9; Virginia R. Dominguez, *From Neighbor to Stranger: The Dilemma of Caribbean Peoples in the United States* (New Haven: Antilles Research Program, Yale University, 1975), 16–18; Jake C. Miller, *The Plight of Haitian Refugees* (New York: Praeger, 1984), 79–101; Bryan O. Walsh, "The Boat People of South Florida," *America* 142 (17 May 1980): 420–21.

33. Alex Stepick, "Haitian Boat People: A Study in the Conflicting Forces Shaping U.S. Immigration Policy," *Law and Contemporary Problems* 45 (1982): 163–96; Thomas Brom, "Haitians Jam the Gears at INS," *In These Times*, 7 April 1982, 7; Miller, *Plight of Haitian Refugees*, 103–22.

34. *Miami Herald*, 1 November, 28 December 1981; Larry Mahoney, "Inside Krome," *Miami Herald, Tropic Magazine*, 10 January 1982, 7–15; Miller, *Plight of Haitian Refugees*, 127–30; *Miami News*, 18 June 1982.

35. *Miami Herald*, 1 October 1981, 7 June 1984; *USA Today*, 6 February 1985; Miller, *Plight of Haitian Refugees*, 72–75; Jacob Wortham, "The Black Boat People," *Black Enterprise* 10 (1980): 32.

36. Mohl, "An Ethnic 'Boiling Pot,'" 63–67; Yetta Deckelbaum, "Little Haiti: The Evolution of a Community" (M.A. thesis, Florida Atlantic University, 1983).

37. Alex Stepick, "Haitians in Miami: An Assessment of Their Background and Potential," *Occasional Paper Series*, dialogue no. 12 (Miami: Latin American and Caribbean Center, Florida International University, December 1982); Robert A. Ladner et al., *Demography, Social Status, Housing, and Social Needs of the Haitian Population of Edison-Little River* (Miami: Behavioral Science Research Institute, 1983); Thomas D. Boswell, "In the Eye of the Storm: The Context of Haitian Migration to Miami, Florida," *Southeastern Geographer* 23 (1983): 67.

38. Alex Stepick and Alejandro Portes, "Flight into Despair: A Profile of Recent Haitian Refugees in South Florida," *International Migration Review* 20 (1986): 329–50; Alex Stepick, *The Business Community of Little Haiti* (Miami: Haitian Task Force, 1984); Ellen Hampton, "Little Haiti: The City Within," *Miami Herald, Tropic Magazine*, 3 July 1983, 7–26.

39. *Miami Herald*, 23 December 1985; *Miami News*, 21 June 1986; Marshall Ingwerson, "Miami a Rebel Base Again," *Christian Science Monitor*, 30 May 1986, 3; "Behind the Hibiscus and the Potted Palms," *Economist*, 19 July 1986, 22; Tom Morganthau et al., "Miami: America's Casablanca," *Newsweek*, 25 January 1988, 24, 28.

"Immigration through the Port of Miami": A Comment

Philip C. Dolce

Although Raymond Mohl's essay "Immigration through the Port of Miami" presents a good overview of this important topic, it leaves the reader with a number of questions about the key themes of location, people, and policy that are critical to any study of immigration.

Miami as an American immigration center is intriguing because it seems vitally different from most urban locations traditionally associated with this type of research. Unlike New York, Boston, Baltimore, or San Francisco, Miami is truly a twentieth-century city, with a fairly unique economic base. As Professor Mohl points out, Miami was established very late in the nineteenth century, and by 1900, its population totaled fewer than 2,000 people. This was a time period when many industrial urban areas had well-established populations that included large immigrant groups. Moreover, Miami's economy has always rested on its reputation as a resort community. Thus, it would be important to know more about the impact of the city's unusual time scenario and economic base on its immigrant population. For instance, whom (if anyone) did various immigrant groups displace in Miami's neighborhoods and work places, and how did immigrants interact in the politics of the city? Likewise, we need much more information about both the importance of location and the degree of opportunity offered by the city.

Miami is really a center of immigration for three major Caribbean cultural groups. These groups are latino (mainly Cubans), French Creole (Haitians), and Afro-English (Bahamians). The latino cultural impact on Miami is predominant, but scholars need more information about the cultural impact of the other groups on the city. Comparative data from other cities that have experienced similar types of immigration would be helpful in such research. For instance, because the largest immigration to New York City in the last twenty years has been from the Caribbean and composed of the same three cultural groups, it would be interesting to compare how newer cultural patterns are changing these two cities.[1]

99

Each group's contribution to Miami seems to be different; for instance, as Professor Mohl points out, "The Bahamian presence made Miami's black population distinctively different from that in most southern cities." Such statements, however, deserve further elaboration because of the significance they bear not only for immigration history but also for Afro-American history. During the period when Bahamians were settling in Miami, most black immigrants to the United States also came from the West Indies, so comparisons with other centers of West Indian settlement would make Miami's situation much more understandable.[2]

Miami's appeal as a settlement area and the degree of opportunity found there seem to vary for the three major immigrant groups. The city's allure to Cuban immigrants is well known and extensively documented. Interestingly, by contrast, Miami seems to have less appeal for Haitians than does New York City. Over three-quarters of all Haitians reside in New York City, and apparently a large number of Haitians entered the United States through Miami and then settled in New York. It is important, therefore, to determine what kinds of opportunities were available to each group in Miami and how immigrants responded to them.[3]

One way of testing the importance of location is to compare the same immigrant group in different American cities. For instance, a comparison of the Cuban population in Miami with that in Hudson County New Jersey, might prove fruitful, for both arrived at the same time and had a similar class background. While Miami has the largest Cuban population in the United States, the second largest Cuban community is located in Hudson County, New Jersey. Both physically and historically, these communities are very different from one another. The Cuban settlement in New Jersey centers around two towns, West New York and Union City, and three adjacent communities. West New York is less than one square mile wide and the most crowded town in the most crowded county (Hudson) in the most crowded state in the union. The second most crowded municipality is Union City, which borders West New York and is only seven blocks wide and forty-nine blocks long.[4]

These densely populated urban areas were well-established industrial cities at the turn of the century and populated chiefly by successive waves of German, Irish, and Italian immigrants. In 1960, census data revealed that more than half of West New York's population was still made up of foreign stock, although Cubans were too few to be listed as a separate group. By 1970, however, approximately one-third of West New York's population was Cuban. Eight years later, two-thirds of West New York's population was Hispanic, and Cubans comprised the vast majority of that group.[5]

Cubans established a strong economic, cultural, and later political base in the West New York-Union City area largely as a result of government assistance, the disproportionate number of upper- and middle-class refugees in their midst, and fortunate timing. The first waves of Cuban refugees arrived during the "crisis of American cities," when older ethnic groups were fleeing West New York and Union City. The Cubans, often credited with redeveloping the economic structures of these cities, revived some of the economic functions that had traditionally supported residents of these locations, such as small shops along the main thoroughfare (Bergenline Avenue), light manufacturing, and the garment industry. The garment industry in particular provided jobs for Cuban women, who earn one-third of the family income in West New York and have one of the highest rates of participation for women in the American labor force. Not surprisingly, then, 73 percent of all Hispanic businesses in Hudson County are owned by Cubans, and most of them are located in Union City and West New York.[6]

Cubans may not only have revived the economic base of the area, but also helped transform its political orientation. Traditionally, Hudson County was overwhelmingly Democratic, but in 1984, President Reagan carried eleven of Hudson County's twelve municipalities with all communities with a significant Cuban population voting Republican. Indeed, 85 percent of the adult Cubans who are citizens are registered to vote, and 70 percent of these registrants regularly do vote. Cuban influence in the social and religious life of these communities has also been noted. Therefore, a comparison of Cubans in West New York and Miami might reveal important information about the impact of location on immigrants in the United States. It might also demonstrate that the position immigrants find themselves in within the community relative to other groups helps determine which of their prior resources can be used and what new ones must be acquired.[7]

The third issue I would raise concerns immigration policy. Professor Mohl's essay properly points out the double standard of federal immigration policy that gives little or no assistance to refugees from friendly nations, such as Haiti, in contrast to the extensive aid given to refugees leaving communist nations, such as Cuba. Nevertheless, this fact should be placed in a more detailed context. The anticommunist bias in the U.S. immigration policy, which dates back to the Displaced Persons Act and continues to this very day, has enjoyed substantial popular support for most of a forty-year period. One has only to recall that in 1956, the Hungarian freedom fighter was *Time* magazine's "man of the year" in order to understand that continuity. Thus, the friendly reception and high degree of government aid given to Cuban refugees were really an expansion of U.S. immigration policy that later extended to Vietnamese and Soviet refugees. In fact, the liberalization of immigration policy has always proceeded much more rapidly within an anticommunist context.[8]

Although in 1980, the U.S. refugee law changed to include people from any communist or noncommunist country who had a well-founded fear of persecution, the liberalization of the law did not change government policy. It was this contradiction between law and government policy that created the Krome refugee camp outside Miami and other camps that held detained Haitians. No doubt, the Refugee Act of 1980 was a partial cause of massive boatlifts from Haiti because the new law gave Haitians hope that the United States would accept them. Prior to liberalization of the refugee law, there would have been no such hope and no detention camps. Instead, Haitians would have been placed on the next available plane back to Haiti because they could not have been classified as refugees.[9]

The harsh tactics used by the federal government to stem the tide of Haitian immigration must not only be condemned but also explained. The reason the Reagan Administration ordered Haitians to be interdicted at sea rather than questioned on landing in Florida was another result of this conflict between law and government policy. During the 1960s, a series of landmark Supreme Court cases vastly expanded procedural rights that applied to all people, not just U.S. citizens. As a result, potential refugees, including Haitians, gained legal rights under both the Fifth and Fourteenth amendments on landing on Florida's beaches. The federal government had to contend with these procedural rights, and the result was long periods of detention in the Krome refugee camp while claims of refugee status were evaluated. Clearly, the Reagan Administration was looking for a way of turning back Haitian refugees while avoiding legal problems. Interdicting Haitian ships at sea achieved that goal.[10]

While the Immigration Reform Act of 1986 has resolved many issues, it has not solved all refugee problems. The conflict between law and government policy concerning refugees continues, as a recent study by the General Accounting Office (GAO) has shown. The study demonstrates that Central Americans are more likely to be refused asylum than immigrants from other regions even when their claims are similar. According to the GAO study, 82 percent of requests for asylum processed by the INS came from El Salvador, Nicaragua, Iran, and Poland. The approval rates for Poland (49 percent) and Iran (66 percent) were much higher than those for El Salvador (2 percent) and Nicaragua (7 percent), and the discrepancy by country did not change even when applicants cited torture and imprisonment to support their claims for asylum.[11]

Despite all of its glaring inadequacies, however, U.S. refugee policy has admitted over 1.5 million people to the United States in the last twenty-five years. Recently, Japanese Prime Minister Nakasone commented that the high level of educational achievement in Japan was due to the nation's monoracial society. While the outcry over these racial remarks centered on genetics and education, Nakasone's remarks are an accurate reflection of Japan's immigration policy. For years, Japan has fulfilled its refugee obligations "by check" and been completely unwilling to accept foreign settlers. In a nation where 98 percent of the population is native born, it is impossible to conceive of the diversity found in Miami or West New York. It also reminds us that harmony between law, government policy, and public attitudes does not always achieve a positive result.[12]

Miami's immigrant communities are intimately affected by current events. Over the last thirty years, many Haitians fled the tyranny of the Duvalier dictatorship. Yet even though that dictatorship has ended, Haiti is still in economic and political turmoil with unforeseeable consequences for immigration trends.[13]

Relations between Havana and Washington, which can never be predicted with great accuracy, are crucial to the resumption of fullscale immigration from Cuba. Because Cubans from the Mariel boatlift were permitted to apply for permanent residency under the 1966 Cuban Adjustment Act, they will eventually attain citizenship and the ability to bring relatives from Cuba to the United States. Approximately 300,000 Cubans could enter the country as a result, and most of them would probably settle in either Miami or the West New York area. The controversy over Radio Marti, however, has interrupted the immigration program. In fact, an international twist affects virtually every aspect of Cuban life in America, especially in politics. Recently, for example, the last two prisoners of the Bay of Pigs invasion were released from Cuban jails, one settled in Miami and the other in Union City, New Jersey.[14] Although this gesture could signal the end of an era for Cuban Americans, it also serves as a reminder of the importance of international relations to these immigrant communities. Likewise, the Sandinista Revolution in Nicaragua has not only resulted in the establishment of a new exile community but may also have reinforced the anticommunist attitude of Cuban Americans.[15] At the center of these developments, Miami offers a unique opportunity for the study of immigration that increases our desire to know more about the city and it immigrant population. Professor Mohl's essay is a good starting point for subsequent research.

Notes

1. David M. Reimers, "Recent Third-World Immigration to New York City, 1945–1988: An Overview," paper presented at the New York Historical Society (May 1986), 11.

2. Lawrence D. Hogan, "Afro-American History as Immigration History: The Anguillians of Perth Amboy," paper presented at the Immigration Studies Curriculum Conference (Jersey City State College, June 1986), 81–83; Gilbert Osofsky, *Harlem: The Making of a Ghetto* (New York: Harper and Row, 1979), 131–35.

3. Thomas D. Boswell and James R. Curtis, *The Cuban-American Experience: Culture, Images, and Perspectives* (Totowa, N.J.: Rowman and Allanheld, 1983), 71–96; Elliott Robert Barkan, "Portal of Portals: Speaking of the United States as Though It Were New York—and Vice Versa," paper presented at the New York Historical Society (May 1986), 27.

4. Philip C. Dolce, "Faces of Immigration: The Cubans of New Jersey," paper presented at the Immigration Studies Curriculum Conference (Jersey City State College, June 1986), 9–10; *Record*, 9 June 1985.

5. Eleanor Meyer Rogg and Rosemary Santana Cooney, *Adaptions and Adjustments of Cubans in West New York, New Jersey* (Bronx, N.Y.: Hispanic Research Center, Fordham University, 1980), 11–12; *Jersey Journal*, 28 December, 1984; *Dispatch*, 5 January 1984.

6. Dolce, "Faces of Immigration," 10; Susan Brait, "The Cubans of Union City," *New Jersey Monthly* 5 (1981): 67; Yolanda Prieto, "Reinterpreting an Immigration Success Story: Cuban Women, Work and Change in the New Jersey Community" (Ph.D. diss., Rutgers University, 1984), 100–104, 230–31; *New York Times*, 24 November 1970.

7. *Record*, 17 June 1985; *New York Times*, 22 November 1981.

8. Philip C. Dolce, "The McCarran-Walter Act and the Conflict over Immigration Policy during the Truman Administration," in Frank J. Coppa and Thomas J. Curran, eds., *The Immigrant Experience in America* (Boston: Twayne, 1976), 215–32; John Scanlon and Gilbert Loecher, "U.S. Foreign Policy, 1959–1980: Impact on Refugee Flow from Cuba," *Annals of the American Academy of Political and Social Science* 467 (1983): 116, 131–32; Norman Zucker, "Refugee Resettlement in the United States: Policy and Problems," *Annals of the American Academy of Political and Social Science* 467 (1983): 174–75.

9. Ibid., 153; George McKenna, *A Guide to the Constitution: The Delicate Balance* (New York, Random House, 1984), 346–47.

10. Ibid., 347–49.

11. *Record*, 22 October 1986.

12. Zucker, "Refugee Resettlement," 185; *Time*, 6 October 1986, 66–67; Earl E. Huyck and Leon F. Bouvier, "The Demography of Refugees," *Annals of the American Academy of Political and Social Science* 467 (1983): 41.

13. *New York Times*, 12 October 1986.

14. Ibid., 21, 26 May 1985, 19 October 1986; *Record*, 17 June 1986.

15. Ibid., 13 October 1986.

5

Immigration through the Port of New Orleans

JOSEPH LOGSDON

New Orleans has often puzzled visitors and commentators alike: The city stirs immediate curiosity but usually defies easy understanding. Familiarity with other American cities seldom helps either the casual tourist or the experienced traveler to resolve the enigma; instead, most initial observers too simply explain the exotic ambiance of New Orleans by labeling it a European city. In a sense, these observers are right—New Orleans has an unusual character. It resembles neither southern cities, such as Atlanta and Charleston nor such northern ones as Boston and Chicago. The unique architecture of its nineteenth-century neighborhoods—most still intact—quickly evokes a special sense of place, and a more prolonged stay uncovers a way of life that is neither southern nor northern. To be sure, southern visitors might find some similiarity in the climate, the pace of life, and the visible presence of blacks, just as northern visitors might recognize signs of ethnic diversity among the city's white population—Italian fruit stands, a German brewery, Irish politicians, Catholic churches, Latino music, and Jewish synagogues. Yet, for the casual visitor or trained observer, something usually remains strange or foreign about New Orleans.

Serious scholars have not surpassed casual observers in unraveling the enigma of New Orleans. Few urban experts have tried to place New Orleans in the ranks of American cities; in fact, except in the field of midnineteenth-century race relations, social scientists have generally ignored its development.[1] Ever since the early twentieth century when sociologists and historians began studying the modern city, they have turned elsewhere—normally to Chicago, New York, and Boston—to find their models for measuring social trends or discerning reality in urban America.

For the most part, pioneers in the field of urban studies were correct in this approach. As they knew it, urban America had been concentrated in a great manufacturing swath that ran from northeastern coastal cities

Immigrants at New Orleans Immigration Station, ca. 1913. *(Courtesy of the Historic New Orleans Collection.)*

to the western transportation terminals of St. Louis, Chicago, and Mil-waukee. It was no coincidence that in 1900 all but two of the fifteen largest cities lay within that band, for the region contained the heartland of urban, industrial America.[2] Chicago and New York, the dominant economic centers of urban America, quite appropriately also became our chief academic laboratories. By any standard, these were the ele-mental urban, immigrant centers of the United States.

Of the two largest cities outside this formative urban-industrial belt, New Orleans was more neglected by academic inquiry than its fellow misfit, San Francisco. Even if far removed from the center of the nation's industrial nexus, San Francisco developed in a way that better matched the normal patterns of urban America. From its original position as the primary Pacific entrepôt, San Francisco moved into manufacturing and finance and simultaneously sent out a railroad network to draw smaller towns into its metropolitan orbit. That transportation network also tied San Francisco into the major east-west trunk lines that connected it directly to the New York-Chicago axis over which flowed a steady supply of goods, labor, capital, and management.

Not so New Orleans. Its peculiarity, however, provides us with a potentially illuminating counterpoint, for New Orleans can give meaning to a study of American cities by offering some important contrasts. As C. Vann Woodward has frequently suggested, the miscreant and abnormal South offers scholars an easily available body of data for comparative analysis.[3] Whatever the merits may be of placing New Orleans in the southern category, a sharper and clearer picture may emerge when the unusual city of New Orleans is used for comparisons and contrasts in urban studies. In the areas of immigration and acculturation—classic themes for students of ethnicity and the city—New Orleans can help us understand other immigrant ports in the United States.

New Orleans entered the nineteenth century while still beyond both the physical boundaries of the United States and the historical boundaries of the Anglo-American experience. For many years after its founding in 1718, New Orleans languished amid the swamps of the lower Mississippi, never meeting the grandiose expectations of its French and Spanish colonial rulers. Even at the opening of the nineteenth century, its moderate growth to almost eight thousand left it a relatively backward outpost of the European empires in the Americas.[4] But almost at that moment, in 1802, the new president, Thomas Jefferson, having dispatched a minister to France to purchase New Orleans, was imagining another destiny for the city:

> There is on the globe one single spot the possessor of which is our natural and habitual enemy. It is New Orleans, through which the produce of three-eighths of our territory must pass to market, and from its fertility it will ere long yield more than half of our whole produce and contain more than half of our inhabitants.[5]

Because the city's location near the mouth of the Mississippi River gave it a commanding hold over the western interior of the United States, New Orleans was the key to Jefferson's entire program of economic growth and development. Within his own lifetime, flatboats and river schooners, laden with agricultural abundance, crowded the city's docks. And by 1817, after steamboats had penetrated the inland waterways as far upstream as Louisville, New Orleans became the major gateway to opportunity in the western interior of North America. The promise of cheap, fertile land drew vast numbers of not only Americans but also European immigrants on their way to the Mississippi valley, reshaping the backwater colonial outpost of New Orleans into one of the world's leading commercial and cosmopolitan centers.

The key period for immigration to New Orleans took place before the Civil War, in the booming decades from 1820 to 1860. The 550,000 immigrants who streamed through the port during those years made the city, by 1837, the nation's second leading port of entry. The flow was particularly heavy from 1847 to 1857, when over 350,000 immigrants jammed the docks and residential facilities of New Orleans. To be sure, no city ever threatened New York's dominance as a port of entry; the antebellum influx into New Orleans amounted to only 10 percent of all those who came to the United States from abroad and just 14 percent of the number who entered New York. Still, in most years, New Orleans surpassed Boston, Philadelphia, and Baltimore.[6]

The sudden decline of New Orleans as a port of entry was almost as dramatic as its rise. Although it was reopened to immigration following its blockade during the Civil War, the annual arrival of immigrants never again exceeded ten thousand and usually hovered closer to three thousand each year. In time, New Orleans fell behind not only its old Atlantic rivals Boston, Baltimore, and Philadelphia but also some new upstarts, including Galveston and Key West on the Gulf of Mexico, as well as San Francisco and Honolulu on the Pacific.[7]

Without question, trade always shaped the volume and character of immigration into New Orleans. In the antebellum years, a vast outflow of American agricultural surplus catapulted New Orleans to a commercial positon that closely rivaled that of New York and, on occasion, even surpassed it. During the four decades before the Civil War, New Orleans shipped over $1.5 billion worth of exports, just a half-billion dollars less than New York's total and almost a quarter of the entire nation's exports for that era.[8] In fact, by 1846, New Orleans was the fourth leading commercial center in the world. The foreign trade of New Orleans, however, was grossly imbalanced: Far less cargo returned to New Orleans from its foreign trading partners; its imports for the comparable period from 1821 to 1860 barely exceeded a value of $400 million. While New York attracted more than half of the nation's $6 billion worth of imports, New Orleans was low on the list when compared to other American coastal cities.[9] New Orleans' trade was also very seasonal, overwhelmingly concentrated during the seven-month period from October to April.

Captains of cotton ships that traveled from New Orleans to destinations in Liverpool, Le Harve, Bremen, and Hamburg had to search for return cargo during the busy harvest season when bales piled up in the warehouses of New Orleans waiting for delivery. Some returned via Atlantic ports, while others decided the one-way traffic was lucrative enough to bring back only large cobblestones or cheap French wine. But most ship captains turned their attention to more profitable human cargo. Consequently Irish, German, and French immigrants soon discovered a buyers' market for ocean passage to New Orleans. True, the voyage from northern Europe to New Orleans was much longer than the journey to one of the Atlantic ports in the United States, but it was often cheaper.[10]

For those who wished to travel to the American frontier, there was yet another inducement: River steamboats shared the same problem as the cotton ships. After descending the interior rivers to New Orleans laden with agricultural produce, these inland vessels found little cargo to carry upstream. River steamers thus not only offered cheaper fares to the western interior than did overland modes of transportation from the eastern ports, but they were also faster and more dependable.[11]

Most of the half-million immigrants entering New Orleans before 1860 hastened beyond the city to the western interior of the country. Because New Orleans and its rural environs offered few employment opportunities for poor laborers, who made up the bulk of foreign passengers arriving at its wharves, most immigrants stayed in the region only long enough to secure inland passage on a steamer going upriver beyond the deep South.[12]

Fear undoubtedly fueled immigrants' sense of urgency, for surrounded by swamps and devoid of even rudimentary sanitation, New Orleans had earned a frightening notoriety. It was swept by regular outbreaks of disease, particularly yellow fever, which soon became known as the newcomers', or immigrants', disease. Since yellow fever usually struck during the tropical heat that lasted from May until October, immigrant guidebooks and foreign consuls warned travelers to avoid New Orleans during that period.[13]

Still, thousands of stranded immigrants filled the city's hospitals and cemeteries. Local leaders generally ignored the problem because the business elite wanted a wide-open port. After public officials developed some half-hearted health measures for incoming vessels between 1818 and 1820, they not only abandoned their efforts but turned over all management of the port to private lessees. The city's resulting reputation was not wholly unattractive, however, because immigrant guidebooks directed to New Orleans all who had reason to fear that customs regulations or personal handicaps might exclude them from the United States.[14]

Only the terrible scourge of yellow fever from 1853 to 1854, which killed about eight thousand people in New Orleans and effectively closed the port, finally convinced business and governmental leaders to act. They secured state legislation to set up quarantine stations outside the city and forced most ships, especially those from tropical ports, to stop for health inspection during the long summer season. Nevertheless, leaders delayed construction of on-shore facilities for that purpose until 1859, just as the heyday of immigration to New Orleans was coming to an end.[15]

The Civil War abruptly terminated New Orleans's career as a leading port of entry, although immigration had already begun to wane in 1857. In that year, favorable conditions foreseen by Jefferson for the city's commercial dominance of the great Mississippi valley were undermined when railroads from the East reached St. Louis and the Mississippi River.[16] Almost immediately, immigration agents and guidebooks took note and urged Europeans headed for the American frontier to land at an Atlantic port, preferably New York, where they could secure swift, dependable railroad passage to the interior.[17]

Almost simultaneously with the completion of the east-west railroad network, steamship lines gained sway over the immigrant trade and fashioned close corporate ties with New York merchants and their railroad interests.[18] New Orleans was left out, for the large steam vessels could not pass the sandbars at the mouth of the Mississippi River. In fact, not until 1879, when the new Eads jetties directed the flow of the river in such a way that the resulting current dug out a thirty-foot channel, could the new ships enter. By then, however, it was too late: New immigrants from eastern and southern Europe were taking more direct routes to industrial jobs in northern cities. For those newcomers, New Orleans held little attraction, since it had the fewest number of manufacturing jobs of any major American city.

As massive immigration to the United States was reaching annual totals of one million or more in the early twentieth century, Justin F. Denechaud, Louisiana's energetic secretary of immigration and labor, lobbied in Louisiana and Washington, trying to break New York's virtual monopoly of the immigrant traffic. In 1911, he participated in a conference organized by the federal Bureau of Immigration to find ways of diverting immigration to other ports, and he persuaded the bureau to locate in New Orleans one of several new immigration stations, an attractive facility that opened in March 1913.[19] But these considerable efforts had such little impact that just twenty-one years later, the bureau closed its New Orleans station for lack of any substantial activity.[20]

There is, however, much more to the story of New Orleans as an immigrant port than its rapid rise and fall. Such a limited story would neither record the effect of immigration on the city nor explain the unusual way of life that emerged from the very complicated social and cultural commingling that took place in the Crescent City. The comparative value of the New Orleans immigration story rests more on its cultural and social dynamics than its gross economic and population statistics.

The unique New Orleans way of life stems largely from the unusual mix of people who settled the city. First of all, Anglo-Americans did not establish New Orleans. By the time they arrived in any significant numbers, New Orleans was already an exotic place in the American republic. During its first four decades or so, it was part of a French colony (1718– 63), and for the next four (1763–1802), it belonged to the Spanish empire. This colonial experience meant that English was not the prevailing language, Protestantism was scorned, public education was unheralded, and democratic government untried. New Orleans ws not like the rest of the United States; in fact, it was the first urban area where federal authorities tried to impose their own values and institutions on an essentially foreign society.[21]

If New Orleans were clearly not American, what was it? Positive description is more difficult. It was, of course, a Catholic city, but its ethnic makeup was less obvious. The French had never been able to create a new France as the English had created a new England. Almost from the beginning, France had accepted anyone who was willing to settle in its forsaken outpost at the mouth of the Mississippi: French, Germans, Italians, Indians, and the involuntary influx of Africans who made up the city's majority until the late 1830s. Well before the waves of nineteenth-century immigration began to diversify other American cities, New Orleans already had a century-old mélange of population that experienced travelers could compare to only such crossroads of the world as Venice and Vienna.

As late as 1834, John Latrobe found New Orleans totally different from his native Baltimore. New Orleans, he wrote, was "a place after its own fashion." Although he must have seen some ethnic diversity in east coast cities, that of New Orleans ("a continued stream of people of all ages, nations, and colours") intrigued him. He was disturbed, however, by the clashing Sunday morning sounds of Catholic church bells, vendors' cries, and the rollicking in bawdy cafes and barrooms. "French," he noted, "was the language that met my ear. Sometimes Spanish and rarely English."[22]

Latrobe was not alone in his reaction to sui generis New Orleans. Ever since Americans had begun to arrive at Jefferson's new settlement, they had been viewed almost as immigrants and interlopers. At the time of Louisiana's statehood in 1812, those who had been born elsewhere in the United States still made up a decided minority of the urban population of New Orleans. The French-speaking colonial population viewed them with suspicion and often hostility and tried very hard to retain economic and political control of both the city and the state of Louisiana.[23]

In the face of the steady stream of Americans entering the new state, the colonial population, or Creoles, looked for support from French immigrants who continued to arrive in surprisingly large numbers throughout the nineteenth century. Some came directly from France, while others arrived as refugees from Haiti and Cuba along with thousands of French-speaking slaves and free people of African decent. No other urban area in the United States drew such regular and substantial numbers of French-speaking immigrants during the nineteenth century. By 1860, there were 10,564 French-born residents in New Orleans, almost all living in the old Creole neighborhoods.[24] Because traditional shipping and trading patterns with France were never severed, many New Orleanians—black and white—also maintained regular contacts with France and its tributaries.[25]

The cleavage that developed between the city's two charter or ruling populations—Creole and Anglo-American—ultimately led in 1836 to an unusual division of the city into three separate municipalities. Each had its own governing body: an Anglo-American sector, the second municipality, on the up-river side of Canal Street, where English normally prevailed; and the two Creole sectors, the first and third municipalities, on the down-river side of Canal Street, where newspapers, businesses, theaters, publishers, schools, and churches used French.[26] This division within the boundaries of New Orleans fostered a bilingual and bicultural division similar to contemporary divisions within Canada and Belgium. The fissure was never complete, but few speaking French settled in the uptown Anglo-American sector, and only a small percentage of those speaking English took up residence in the downtown Creole communities.[27]

When larger waves of immigrants sailed into New Orleans during the 1840s and 1850s, they entered a city that was not just ethnically diverse but also seriously and legally divided. Acculturation, as a result, was more complicated than in most other American cities. New immigrants who were neither French nor Anglo-American had two models of behavior to guide them toward assimilation into the life of the city.

The largest flow of the new immigrants came from Germany. Although most of them passed through the city quickly on their way to Missouri and other states of the interior, by the time the massive surge of Germans came between 1847 and 1857, they had already set up religious and social institutions in New Orleans and developed a leadership class to give substantial assistance to their fellow countrymen. Most important was the Deutsche Gesellschaft, or German society, formed in June 1847 to protect German immigrants from unscrupulous "runners" who often lured newcomers into buying bogus or inferior accommodations and travel arrangements. The German society's agents tried to find local employment, health care, or financial aid for those who were stranded in the city, but they usually tried to move the Germans as quickly as possible to up-river destinations away from Louisiana.[28]

Many Germans, however, continued to settle in New Orleans. By 1850, there were 19,752 Germans listed in the census for the city and

24,614 for the entire state.[29] Diverse in their religious backgrounds, they organized Protestant, Catholic, and Jewish congregations, as well as lodges, gymnastic groups (the Turnvereine), and musical societies, such as the Sängerbund. Occupationally, they included architects, builders, and skilled workmen who fashioned many of the city's finer buildings and truck farmers, dairymen, and florists who helped adorn the city's famous gardens and kitchens with their bounty. Even before the Civil War, German leaders had begun to move into the political arena by founding German newspapers and winning political office.[30]

By most nineteenth-century accounts, it was not the presence of Germans but rather the sudden influx or Irish immigrants that raised a storm of antiimmigrant sentiment among Know-Nothings in New Orleans during the 1850s. Irish immigrants had always trickled into the new American city; some had even come during the colonial era. For these early Irish settlers, New Orleans seemed a rather tolerant Catholic city that offered Irish businessmen and professionals considerable opportunity and reward. In fact, the community held celebrations in honor of St. Patrick as early as 1809 and founded the city's second Catholic parish, St. Patrick's, in 1834.[31]

The welcome ended abruptly when the potato famine in Ireland drove the country's poorest elements to New Orleans and other American ports. For those desperate immigrants who swelled the number of Irish in New Orleans to 24,398 by 1860,[32] there was no organized support or assistance. Few of the Irish had money to move to farms in the West. Instead, most crowded into the city's riverfront neighborhoods and often fell victim to disease, crime, and unemployment. Their desperation also drove them into bitter competition with free blacks and slaves for the city's most dangerous and exploitive jobs.

Hostility to the Irish and other immigrants became particularly acute after 1852, when Anglo-Americans garnered enough votes in the state legislature to consolidate the three municipalities and the uptown suburb of Lafayette under a single urban government that they expected to dominate. But when the Irish and Germans joined the Creoles to defeat the Anglo-Americans' candidates the political reaction among the losers turned into an outburst of fury against all foreign elements but especially against the Irish. In succeeding elections, nativists formed the Know-Nothing party and used armed violence at the polls to gain control of the city. As both sides armed themselves within their old municipalities for further confrontation, only the threatened intervention of state authorities kept the city from erupting into a minor civil war.[33]

The violence left a deep mark on the city and drove many of the immigrants to long-standing antagonism toward the Anglo-Protestant elite who eventually won effective political and economic control of the city. Even today, the uptown neighborhoods of Germans and Irish have a greater cultural and social affinity with the downtown Creole sectors of New Orleans than with the adjacent and parallel neighborhoods of the wealthier Anglo-Americans.

Although the French, Germans, and Irish dominated the massive flow of immigration into the city in the years before the Civil War, an amazingly diverse group of immigrants came to New Orleans both before and after the war. True, New Orleans would receive few of the eastern European immigrants who made up so much of the wave of immigration that began in the 1880s, but immigrants who came to New Orleans had strains seldom seen elsewhere. Throughout the nineteenth century, for example, New Orleans was one of the few American cities to draw any substantial number of people from Spain and Latin America. In those categories, New Orleans remained either first or second until the mid-1890s, sometimes even surpassing New York.[34]

Regular shipping lanes to Cuba and the Caribbean rim probably explain this flow of immigration, since most Spanish entrants also came to the city after an intermediate stop in Cuba or a former Spanish colony. Even today, when airlines have replaced ship passenger service, New Orleans remains a major center in the United States for immigration from Nicaragua, Honduras, Guatemala, and Belize.

Immigration from Asia continued despite increasing federal restrictions against Asians. After 1882, the Chinese found that the haphazard enforcement of immigration law in New Orleans made it easier to enter there illegally than the more hostile west coast ports. Because they were part of the American empire after 1899, Filipinos escaped quota or exclusionary laws until 1934. By the early twentieth century, they formed a community of more than two thousand.[35] In recent years, Vietnamese and Vietnamese Chinese have refreshed this Asian presence and added to the diversity of New Orleans.

From the earliest years, various Mediterranean groups also moved toward New Orleans in considerable numbers. Greeks were numerous enough by 1864 to found the nation's first Orthodox church; Dalmatians (Croats) from the area around Trieste came in the 1850s to cultivate oysters in the Mississippi delta and to market them in New Orleans; northern Italian refugees from various periods of the risorgimento established such anticlerical institutions as Dante's Masonic Lodge in 1865 and published tracts against the papacy's political activities.[36]

The largest group from the Mediterranean basin, however, came from Sicily. By 1850, Sicilians had made New Orleans their primary link to the United States and helped make New Orleans the largest Italian settlement in the United States. Merchants from Palermo had designated New Orleans as the key depot for citrus fruit from the Mediterranean and once settled in the city, used their expertise in fruit handling and merchandising to expand their operations to Central America, where they found different tropical fruits, such as bananas, to market in both the United States and Europe.

To handle delicate fruit, Sicilian merchants of New Orleans recruited experienced laborers from Sicily during the 1870s and 1880s. By the early twentieth century, labor recuitment had become an independent business as sugar planters in southwest Louisiana sought to replace striking black and white workers in their cane fields.[37] From 1890 to 1910, more then fifty thousand Sicilians entered New Orleans despite the lynching of eleven of their compatriots during a wave of nativist violence in 1890 to 1891.[38] Although the outburst failed to slow the stream of Sicilians into New Orleans, about that time, Sicily began to send even larger numbers of immigrants to northern industrial cities in the United States. Meanwhile, most of the Sicilians who had come to Louisiana to work on sugar plantations drifted back to the New Orleans area to create a food empire that dominated the city's truck-farming, food-wholesaling, and retail grocery businesses.[39] By 1920, almost half of the grocery stores in the city were owned by Sicilians.[40]

More than its extraordinarily diverse immigration helped create the unusual way of life that today distinguishes New Orleans from its American counterparts. Somehow, a new common culture evolved from this diversity—a result quite different from the more typical deculturation and assimilation processes that have taken place in other large American cities.

In New Orleans, acculturation resulted in something of inestimable value—a new public culture related to place and tradition. New Orleanians have created an original cuisine that has drawn elements from the culinary traditions of the major groups that have come to the city. New Orleanians have also produced a unique architectural style that promotes a sense of pride and belonging; from the French Quarter to countless residential neighborhoods, one sees a vista that resembles no other place in the world. And who can ignore the music? New Orleanians created the art form of jazz, which still spawns new musical styles and their practitioners. Finally, New Orleanians have fashioned new forms of festival that include not only the exuberant weeks of Mardi Gras but numerous other public celebrations that delight the senses.[41]

It is not easy to explain why New Orleans has evolved this unique cultural tradition. The well-established French and Spanish tolerance of cultural differences helped set a model of acculturation quite different from that in the nation's more Anglo-Saxon cities. From the very beginning, the city's inhabitants became accustomed to diversity and difference. They were not afraid of the exotic but, indeed, were drawn to it.

U.S. Immigration Station, New Orleans, ca. 1913. *(Courtesy of the Historic New Orleans Collection.)*

Sometimes, white settlers even applauded the African culture of the slaves and free blacks who made up such a large proportion of the city's inhabitants in its first century of existence. As a result, West African dancing, festivals, and music as well as cuisine and decoration survived openly without the relentless cultural oppression that had occurred in British America. Nowhere else in North America had European and African cultures blended so fruitfully as in New Orleans.[42]

The setting and climate, no doubt, played a part in encouraging the city's early cultural interchange. Geography made New Orleans a virtual island surrounded by swamps and open water.[43] Limited space confined the population to narrow strips of land and forced it into greater physical intimacy than Americans were accustomed to in the more open sites of the Atlantic coast or interior plains and prairies. The mild climate also encouraged residents to go out-of-doors and participate in the street life on which the city's public culture has thrived.

The failure of New Orleans to develop an industrial economy with its own laws of land use for vast plants and working-class concentration undoubtedly enabled preindustrial cheek-by-jowl residential patterns to continue well into the nineteenth and twentieth centuries. Indeed, until better drainage methods opened large tracts of land in the twentieth century, many immigrant groups, especially Germans and Sicilians, continued to operate within city boundaries such old world pastoral pursuits as truck farms, nurseries, and dairies.

Whatever its impulse, widespread commingling became the key to the cultural development of New Orleans. Once the process began, it was difficult to stop, and each new wave of immigrants found itself drawn into the open, inviting, and evolving way of life. Leaders of neither dominant groups nor new immigrants could stop the process. Even Jewish rabbis, trained by old-world experience to protect special traditions, threw up their hands as their coreligionists reveled in shellfish delights and Mardi Gras festivities.[44] The city's rulers, who were sometimes alarmed by the commingling, could do no better, although they attempted to constrain the festive and sensuous celebrations that encouraged the mixing of bodies and cultures. The French tried to close the rowdy, unrestrained dance halls; the Spanish tried to restrict the cabaret gatherings of black slaves and free citizens; and the American authorities, in turn, enacted laws to establish color lines between blacks and whites in the city. But, in the long run, all measures designed to stop the social and cultural blending failed.[45]

For the most part, the main creative process took place within the ranks of ordinary people: Public culture was not a gift from the city's leaders. The first American newspaper, the *Picayune*, scorned Mardi Gras as a "miserable annual celebration," dismissed the costumes of the revelers as "outlandish and grotesque," and frowned on the "riffraff" who followed in the wake of the parades. Unable to stop the Mardi Gras celebrations, Anglo-American leaders eventually resorted to seizing control of the celebration and turning their membership in exclusive carnival organizations into a badge of social prestige in the city. Willy-nilly, they, too, joined in the fun and became "Creolized." Without realizing what was happening, the leaders repeated a half-century later the same process of rejection and then adoption of the city's music.[46] At the opening of the century, the *Picayune* condemned "jass," which had emerged from the musical tastes of black Creoles, American Negroes, Germans, and Sicilians, but today, the uptown set has made the celebrated brass bands an essential part of its own entertainment.

Anglo-Americans were never able to control the unusual process of acculturation in New Orleans. Ordinary people fashioned the way of life by drawing on what they found and adding to it something of their own—not just from such diverse European homelands as Ireland, Germany, Italy, France, and Spain but also from such places as Senegal, Angola, China, Haiti, the Philippines, Belize, Cuba, Virginia, and South Carolina.

Already by the 1880s, commentators had begun to discuss and examine this new public culture. Coming to New Orleans for the 1884 to 1886 World's Industrial and Cotton Centennial Exposition, a number of writers and journalists began to explore the city's peculiar ways in order to explain them to tourists who would attend the centennial. Emil Deckert, a German commentator who came to the fair, was one of the most perceptive visitors. Noting the quick deterioration of old-world German culture among his compatriots who lived in the city, he tried to explain the process of acculturation at work in New Orleans:

> Exceedingly interesting is the mixture of nationalities, because more heterogeneous elements meet and try to integrate here than in other cities . . . Negroes, mulattoes, quadroons, Choctaw Indians, Chinese, Spaniards, French, Italians, Irish, Germans, Anglo-Saxons—all are represented and mingle colorfully on the streets and in the markets, understand each other, haggle with each other, yet hold tenaciously fast to part of their uniqueness.

After a two-month stay, he concluded that in the behavior of New Orleanians, "there are delight and abandon to a much greater degree than one [is] accustomed to in Yankee cities."[47]

An even more gifted observer, Lafcadio Hearn, focused on the city's already famous cuisine. Hearn was trained by experience to explore the exotic and question the weaknesses of prevailing Anglo-American ways, for he was a permanent outsider. Born to a Greek mother and an Anglo-Irish father, he never felt accepted among his paternal kinfolk in Dublin. Fleeing to the United States in 1869 in search of personal identity, he eventually ended up in New Orleans for a ten-year stay. Still later, he explored the French West Indies and finally stopped his searching in Japan, where he became an honorary Japanese and brilliantly explained that nation's culture to the Western world.[48]

While in New Orleans, Hearn reveled in the delights of New Orleans and tried to explain the mysteries of the city's cuisine to native and tourist alike: "La Cuisine Creole (Creole Cookery) partakes of the nature of its birthplace—New Orleans—which is cosmopolitan in its nature, blending the characteristics of the American, French, Spanish, Italian, West Indian and Mexican."[49]

Somewhat later, outsiders and natives began to note other flowerings of the local culture, particularly its music and architecture. The best explanations of those traditions have usually recognized what Deckert and Hearn had observed earlier: Out of a varied population, there had emerged in New Orleans a new way of daily life that has given its inhabitants their powerful sense of local identity.[50]

This public culture provides more, however, than just a sense of identity and belonging. It constitutes the fabric of daily life for many people, evoking pleasure and building bonds of commonality among a mélange of inhabitants who can trace their backgrounds to almost every part of the globe. These inhabitants now share a culture related to time and place that celebrates ancestral memory and at the same time welcomes new and exotic elements.

In other American cities, no similar common culture has yet emerged. We may celebrate the mosaic of cultures that still exist in other cities and even wonder at the diversity that is possible in American pluralism. But we have also learned that old-world cultures seldom survive intact beyond two or three generations. It is simply impossible to sustain old-world habits away from the original setting that gave birth to them.

Unfortunately, no new way of life seems to have emerged from the mosaic of American pluralism to provide common ground for Bostonians, New Yorkers, or Chicagoans. Instead, those cities have created a collection of interests that reflect only weakly old-world backgrounds and now seem to portend a terrible specter of polarized racial identity. John Higham has already warned us that we need to find some commonality in our multiethnic societies without producing any forced rejection of ancestral origins. But he has not been able to find a model for his theoretical conception of "pluralistic integration," which he hoped would somehow "uphold the validity of a common culture, to which all individuals have access, while sustaining the efforts of minorities to preserve and enhance their own integrity."[51]

Moving beyond speculation, Higham has suggested that American intellectuals should search for answers by freeing themselves from "the narrowly American framework" and studying the problem in a broader international context. He has also encompassed an aesthetic vision of the architectural critic Robert Venturi: "I like elements which are hybrid rather than 'pure'. . . . A valid architecture . . . must embody the difficult unity of inclusion rather than the easy unity of exclusion."[52]

The creation of a common public culture in New Orleans offers no easy prescription for other cities. Besides, one could suggest that the cultural inclinations of New Orleanians have also restrained the city's economic development, slowed its citizens' social mobility, and deepened their terrible poverty. Nonetheless, studying such a new-world culture can help us understand the forces that have thwarted similar outcome elsewhere and can enable us to encourage some of the tolerance, openness, sensuality, and joyfulness that have allowed the public culture of New Orleans to flourish.

Perhaps if historians and social scientists are willing to explore contrasting cultural developments in multiethnic cities, we can help extend

American sensibilities to include the artistic vision of Sherwood Anderson, who visited New Orleans in 1925 and reported to his circle of fellow writers:

> I stick to my pronouncement that culture means first of all the enjoyment of life, leisure and a sense of leisure. It means time for play of the imagination over the facts of life, it means time and vitality to be serious about really serious things and a background of joy in life in which to refresh the tired spirits.
>
> In a civilization where the fact becomes dominant, submerging the imaginative life, you will have what is dominant in the cities of Pittsburgh and Chicago today.
>
> When the fact is made secondary to the desire to live, to love, and to understand life, it may be that we will have in more American cities a charm of place such as one finds in the older parts of New Orleans now.[53]

Notes

1. Alone among the largest cities of the United States, New Orleans has failed to elicit a modern urban biography. In 1967, Bayard Still noted this fact in an unpublished speech during ceremonies dedicating an urban studies institute at the University of New Orleans (in possession of author). The only urban biography of New Orleans was published in the 1920s by a former editor of the New Orleans *Times-Picayune*. See John S. Kendall, *History of New Orleans*, 3 vols, (Chicago, 1922). The work on comparative race relations is legion. The best includes Richard C. Wade, *Slavery in the Cities* (New York, 1964); Ira Berlin, *Slaves without Masters* (New York, 1974); and Leonard Curry, *The Free Black in Urban America* (Chicago, 1981).

2. Department of Commerce, Bureau of the Census, *Census, 1900.* Stephan Thernstrom perceptively described the industrial belt of cities in *A History of the American People* (New York, 1984) but noted only San Francisco, not New Orleans, as lying outside its perimeters (410).

3. C. Vann Woodward, *The Burden of Southern History* (Baton Rouge, 1960), see especially the chapter entitled "The Irony of Southern History." Woodward has recently modified some of his views in *Thinking Back: The Perils of Writing History* (Baton Rouge, 1986). In his edited work, *The Comparative Approach to American History* (New York, 1968), Woodward noted the inviting subject of immigration and acculturation in the United States (351): "While this [the impressive ethnic diversity] helps explain much of the variety in American culture, the very diversity of nationalities, religions, languages, and cultures among immigrants paradoxically accounts for an overwhelming pressure for uniformity. The necessities of assimilation to override ethnic, class, and cultural distinctions have contributed mightily to the shaping of an urban mass culture unfriendly to variety" (351).

4. The population in 1805 was 8,475. Of that number, 3,105 were slaves and 1,556 free blacks. See *New Orleans in 1805: A Directory and a Census* (New Orleans, 1936), 11.

5. Thomas Jefferson to Robert R. Livingston, 18 April 1802, in Paul Lester Ford, ed., *Writings of Thomas Jefferson*, vol. 8, 143–47.

6. Two excellent studies cover antebellum immigration to New Orleans: Alan A. Conway, "New Orleans as a Port of Immigration, 1820–1860" (M.A. thesis, University of London, 1949) and Frederick Marcel Spletstoser, "Back Door to the Land of Plenty: New Orleans as an Immigrant Port, 1820–1860," 2 vols. (Ph.D. diss., Louisiana State University, 1978).

7. This information is drawn from annual reports of various federal agencies charged with maintaining immigration totals for all American ports—first the Department of State (1860–70); the Treasury Department (1870–94); the Commerce and the Labor Department (1892–1912), and the Department of Labor (1913–20).

8. Spletstoser, "Back Door to the Land of Plenty," 215.

9. U.S. Bureau of Statistics. *Report on U.S. Commerce and Navigation* (1881) "New Orleans," appendix, xxi.

10. Conway, "New Orleans, 20–27.

11. Ibid., 41; Spletstoser, "Back Door to the Land of Plenty," 124–25. When all traveling expenses were added including food, Spletstoser notes it was slightly more expensive to travel to New Orleans but agrees that cheap steamboat fares made the overall journey to the interior via New Orleans a better bargain. Before the completion of railroad lines in 1857, overland travel from New York to St. Louis took about two weeks. See Philip Taylor, *Distant Magnet, European Emigration to the United States* (New York, 1971), 11.

12. The recent work by Gavin Wright, *Old South, New South: Revolutions in the Southern Economy Since the Civil War* (New York, 1986), probably best explains the inability of the rural South to attract many European immigrants in the nineteenth century. For a treatment of immigration to Louisiana outside of New Orleans, see William Francis Lawrence, "European Immigration Trends of Northeast Louisiana, 1880–1900," *Louisiana History* 26 (1985):41–52.

13. Conway, "New Orleans," 58.

14. Ibid., 92–93.

15. Ibid., 158–59.

16. Ibid., 204–6. The Jefferson quote from a letter to W. C. C. Claiborne was used in U.S. Congress, "Report on Internal Commerce," House Documents, 50th Congress, 1st session no. 6, part II, 185.

17. Taylor, *Distant Magnet*, 76–80.

18. Ibid., 94–95.

19. Department of Commerce and Labor, Bureau of Immigration and Naturalization, *Distribution of Admitted Aliens and Other Residents*, "Proceedings of the Conference of State Immigration, Land and Labor Officials, with Representatives of the Division of Information, Bureau of Immigration and Naturalization, Department of Commerce and Labor, Held in Washington, D.C., November 16 & 17, 1911" (Washington, D.C., 1912), 33–35, 92–93. Department of Labor, *Report of the Commissioner-General of Immigration* (1913), 287–88.

20. New Orleans *Times-Picayune*, 1 March 1934.

21. George Washington Cable, "New Orleans, Historical Sketch," in *Report on the Social Statistics of Cities, United States Bureau of Census, 1880*, XIX, 257. New Orleans very clearly does not fit the general pattern of eighteenth-century immigration that was noted by John Higham in *Send These to Me* (New York, 1975): "The First Immigration [1680s to 1803] had been entirely white and predominantly English speaking . . . very largely Protestant" (21).

22. Copy of MS. journal of John H. B. Latrobe at Historic New Orleans

Collection; original is part of the Latrobe Papers at the Maryland Historical Society.

23. Joseph G. Tregle, "Political Reinforcement of Ethnic Dominance in Louisiana, 1812–1845," in Lucius Ellsworth, ed., *The Americanization of the Gulf Coast, 1803–1850* (Pensacola, Fla., 1972), 79.

24. Paul F. LaChance, "The Politics of Fear: French Louisianians and the Slave Trade, 1786–1809," *Plantation Society in the Americas* 1 (1979): 162–97. U.S. Census, 1860.

25. Many French-speaking, black New Orleanians were involved in this cross-Atlantic, cultural interchange. See Rodolphe L. Desdunes, *Our People and Our History* (Baton Rouge, 1973; translation of original French work published in Montreal in 1911 under the title, *Nos hommes et notre histoire*. The interchange was on significant levels of achievement. Edmond Dédé, a New Orleanian of pure African ancestry, entered the Paris Conservatory of Music in 1857 and later was the conductor of Bordeaux's L'Acazar Theater Orchestra for twenty-seven years. See Marcus Christian, "Edmond Dédé," *Dictionary of American Negro Biography*, edited by Rayford W. Logan and Michael R. Winston (New York, 1982), 168–69. The interchange continued after the Civil War. In 1896, for example, a famous French-speaking black chef, Nellie Murray, went to Paris. On her way, she stopped in England, where she found cooking that was "simply horrid, horrid, horrid," but she reveled in the cuisine of France,

> Ah, that is grand. In my opinion Paris can do anything in the world for a person except bringing the dead to life. . . . My mouth waters every time I think of Paris and her kitchens. I could see New Orleans and her people in everything that was said and done—and cooked. Especially cooked. In Paris the people know how to live. I am in love with Paris and her dishes. . . . Of course, I learned to prepare many new dishes, for I had my eyes open. (New Orleans *Picayune*, 4 December 1986).

26. Leon C. Soulé, *The Know-Nothing Party in Louisiana: A Reappraisal* (New Orleans, 1961); Nathanial C. Curtis, *New Orleans; Its Old Houses, Shops, and Public Buildings* (Philadelphia, 1933), 118; for a contemporary observation, see Charles Lyell, *A Second Visit to the United States of North America* (London, 1849), II, 156–57.

27. Victor Hugo Treat, "Migration into Louisiana, 1834–1880: (Ph.D. diss., University of Texas, 1967), 328–32. For a corrective to the overexaggeration of the cleavage, see Joseph G. Tregle, "Early New Orleans Society: A Reappraisal," *Journal of Southern History*, 17 (1976): 245–82.

28. Conway, "New Orleans," 100–104.

29. U.S. Census, 1860.

30. John F. Nau, *The German People of New Orleans, 1850–1900* (Leiden, 1958). See also two M.A. theses at the University of New Orleans: Hilary Somerville Irvin, "The Impact of German Immigration on New Orleans Architecture" (1984), and Raimund Berchtold, "The Decline of German Ethnicity in New Orleans" (1984).

31. Earl Niehaus, *The Irish in New Orleans, 1800–1860* (New York, 1976), 12, 113–15. See also Dennis C. Rousey, "'Hibernian Leatherheads': Irish Cops in New Orleans, 1830–1880," *Journal of Urban History* 10 (1983): 61–84.

32. U.S. Census, 1860.

33. Soulé, *Know Nothing Party*, 47–119.

34. Annual federal reports of immigration placed New Orleans first or sec-

ond, almost always second behind New York, in the number of Spanish immigrants entering the United States from 1870 to 1892.

35. See John Cooke, ed., *Perspectives on Ethnicity in New Orleans* (New Orleans, 1979), 33–41; (New Orleans, 1980), 53–78; (New Orleans, 1981), 84–87.

36. Theodore Saloutos, "Greeks," in the *Harvard Encyclopedia of American Ethnic Groups*, (Cambridge, Mass., 1980) 433; Milos M. Vujnovich, *Yugoslavs in Louisiana*, "published on the occasion of the United Slavonian Benevolent Association Centennial 1874–1974" (Gretna, LA, 1974); Russell M. Magnaghi, "Louisiana's Italian Immigrants Prior to 1870," *Louisiana History* 27 (1986): 43–68.

37. Jean Ann Scarpaci, "Italian Immigrants in Louisiana's Sugar Parishes: Recruitment, Labor Conditions, and Community Relations, 1880–1910" (Ph.D. diss., Rutgers University, 1972).

38. Richard Gambino, *Vendetta* (Garden City, N.Y., 1977).

39. John V. Baimonte, Jr., "Immigrants in Rural America: A Study of the Italians of Tangipahoa Parish, Louisiana" (Ph.D. diss., Mississippi State University, 1972).

40. Anthony V. Margavio and Jerome J. Salomone, "The Passage, Settlement, and Occupational Characteristics of Louisiana's Italian Immigrants," *Sociological Spectrum* 1 (1981): 345–59. In part, because of their dispersal as shopkeepers, New Orleans Italians were less likely to live in segregated neighborhoods than Italians in other large American cities. See Anthony V. Margavio and J. Lambert Molyneaux, "Residential Segregation of Italians in New Orleans and Selected American Cities," *Louisiana Studies* 12 (1973): 639–45.

41. Joseph Logsdon, "The Surprise of the Melting Pot: We Can All Become New Orleanians," in John Cooke, ed., *Perspectives on Ethnicity*, (New Orleans, 1979), 5–10.

42. Thomas Marc Fiehrer, "The African Presence in Colonial Louisiana: An Essay on the Continuity of Caribbean Culture," in *Louisiana's Black Heritage* (New Orleans, 1979), 3–31. Fiehrer is the first to place the early cultural development of New Orleans within the tradition of acculturation found in French and Spanish colonies in the Caribbean. Others have developed comparisons between Anglo-American patterns and those of Latin Europeans but have not attempted to place New Orleans in this framework. See particularly Louis Hartz, *The Founding of New Societies* (New York, 1964); and Harry Hoetink, *Slavery and Race Relations in the Americas* (New York, 1973), 106–15. Without drawing a sharp comparative framework, several scholars have provided considerable evidence of the syncretism of New Orleans and its environs. See Henry A. Kmen, "Singing and Dancing in New Orleans, 1791–1841" (Ph.D. diss., Tulane University, 1961); Dena J. Epstein, *Sinful Tunes and Spirituals, Black Folk Music to the Civil War* (Urbana, Ill., 1977), 84–87, 90–98, 132–36. Another scholar has challenged the applicability of this approach to New Orleans and Louisiana, see David C. Rankin, "The Tennenbaum Thesis Reconsidered: Slavery and Race Relations in Antebellum Louisiana," *Southern Studies* 18 (1979): 5–31.

43. Peirce F. Lewis, *New Orleans: The Making of an Urban Landscape* (Cambridge, Mass., 1976), 1–45.

44. Henry Illoway, *Sefer Milchamoth Elohim: Being the Controversial Letters and Causuistic Decisions of the Late Bernard Illoway, Ph.D.* (Berlin, 1914), 15, 21–32, 189–92. For an elaboration of Jewish acculturation in New Orleans during the nineteenth century, see Harriet Kohn Stern, "Origins of Reform Judaism in New Orleans," (M.A. thesis, University of New Orleans, 1977).

45. Fiehrer, *The African Presence*, 25–30. The relationship between white immigrants and black New Orleanians remains a virtually unexplored topic.

Hostile job competition and color line laws did not act as complete racial barriers. For some initial exploration of the topic, see Randall M. Miller, "The Enemy within: Some Effects of Foreign Immigration on Antebellum Southern Cities," *Southern Studies* 24 (1985): 30–53; Ira Berlin and Herbert Gutman, "Natives and Immigrants, Free Men and Slaves: Urban Workingmen in the Antebellum South," *American Historical Review* 88 (1983): 1175–200. For Reconstruction and the late nineteenth century, see Ted Tunnell, *Crucible of Reconstruction: War, Radicalism, and Race in Louisiana, 1862–1877.* (Baton Rouge, 1984), 162–63; David Paul Bennetts, "Black and White Workers: New Orleans 1880–1900" (Ph.D. diss., University of Illinois at Urbana-Champaign, 1972), 313–92; George E. Cunningham, "The Italian, a Hindrance to White Solidarity in Louisiana, 1877–1898," *Journal of Negro History* 50 (1965): 22–36. The unadorned simplicity in the autobiography of Louis Armstrong, *Satchmo, My Life in New Orleans* (New York, 1954), may be the most accurate treatment of the complicated—sometimes friendly, sometimes hostile—relationship between immigrants and black New Orleanians. However severe the conflict, considerable cultural interchange took place. The important history of Italian-black interaction, for example, in the development of jazz remains to be explored.

46. D. Clive Hardy, *The World's Industrial and Cotton Centennial* (New Orleans, 1978).

47. Frederick Trautman, "New Orleans, the Mississippi, and the Delta through a German's Eyes: The Travels of Emil Deckert, 1885–1886," *Louisiana History* 25 (1984): 79–98 and passim.

48. Lafcadio Hearn, *Writings from Japan* (Middlesex, Eng., 1984). The introduction to this collection by Francis King provides a revealing portrait of Hearn's ability to understand the culture of exotic societies (7–16).

49. Lafcadio Hearn, *La cuisine creole* (Baton Rouge, 1967, reprint of original New York, 1885 ed.), v. Although Hearn did not give any credit to African traditions in this quote from the preface to the cookbook, he was aware of the African roots of New Orleans culture. In a book he had published in the same year, *Gombo Zherbes* (New York, 1885), Hearn spoke of the black "Creole *cuisinières*" and noted that they called their French patois Congo. In describing black proverbs in this book, he discussed not only African roots of the folklore but discerned elements in the local Creole dialect from the Ivory and Gold coasts, the Congo, Angola, and the lands of the "Eboes and Mandingoes" (3–4).

50. The New Orleans Chapter of the American Institute of Architects, *A Guide to New Orleans Architecture* (New Orleans, 1974); Marcelle Peret, "L'architecture en Louisiane au XIXe siècle," *Comptes rendus de l'athénée louisianais* (November 1952), 5; Henry A. Kmen, *Music in New Orleans: The Formative Years, 1791–1841* (Baton Rouge, 1966); Al Rose and Edmond Sanchon, *New Orleans Jazz, a Family Album* (Baton Rouge, 1967); and William J. Schafer, with assistance from Richard B. Allen, *Brass Bands and New Orleans Jazz* (Baton Rouge, 1977); Donald M. Marquis, *In Search of Buddy Bolden, First Man of Jazz* (Baton Rouge, 1978). Although Mardi Gras has not received such sophisticated treatment, a very provacative study has begun the exploration, Michael P. Smith, *Spirit World, Pattern in the Expressive Folk Culture of Afro-American New Orleans* (New Orleans, 1984).

51. Higham, *Send These to Me*, 242.

52. Ibid., 246.

53. William Faulkner, *New Orleans Sketches*, edited by Carvel Collins (New York, 1958), xvii–xviii.

"Immigration through the Port of New Orleans": A Comment

Randall M. Miller

"You might leave New Orleans, but New Orleans never leaves you." The conceit of that New Orleans maxim speaks volumes on the city's sense of its charms, and of its corruptions, which insinuate themselves into even the most resistant visitors. It also implies that the city's public culture, as manifested in its architecture, cuisine, and festivals, embodies the private values of its people. Perhaps. Finding that private New Orleans—the culture expressed in the daily rhythms of life and social relations—requires looking beyond the public gaiety and postures. In the daylight, Bourbon Street looks very different than it does at night. Blanche DuBois understood that.

Even for native New Orleanians, the city has many poses. Consider the case of Ignatius Reilly, the protagonist in *A Confederacy of Dunces*, the late John Kennedy Toole's unveiling of ethnic (and largely Catholic) New Orleans. For Reilly, the Crescent City is the best of all possible worlds because it is a "comfortable metropolis, which has a certain apathy and stagnation." But Reilly cannot escape the city's harder edges, as he learns in Levy's sweatshop and perambulations throughout New Orleans neighborhoods, where working people bear such names as Palumbo, Mancuso, and Gonzales. In the novel, Toole focuses on none of the city's vaunted "public culture," only on the contrasts within New Orleans. Indeed, at one point, Reilly even sells hot dogs (that most American of foods) in the French Quarter.[1]

New Orleans does not submit to easy classification, as another example makes clear. A. J. Liebling, a correspondent for the *New Yorker,* traveled to south Louisiana in 1960 to compile a foreign political bestiary that included such exotic types as Earl Long and Leander H. Perez. In the course of Liebling's travels, he came to appreciate the local culture of New Orleans but still struggled to define it. He discovered, for example, a city accent "associated with downtown New Orleans, particularly with the German and Irish Third Ward, that is hard to distinguish from the accent of Hoboken, Jersey City, and Astoria, Long Island, where the Al Smith inflection, extinct in Manhattan, has taken refuge." The reason, he surmised, was that "the same stocks that brought the accent to Manhattan imposed it on New Orleans."

Nevertheless, on hearing a native New Orleanian describe the city's culture as Mediterranean, Liebling later added, "New Orleans resembles Genoa or Marseilles, or Beirut or the Egyptian Alexandria more than it does New York, although all seaports resemble one another more than they resemble any place in the interior." He continued, "Like Havana and Port-au-Prince, New Orleans is within the orbit of a Hellenistic world that never touched the North Atlantic. The Mediterranean, Caribbean, and Gulf of Mexico form a homogeneous, though interrupted, sea. New York and Cherbourg and Bergen are in a separate thalassic system."[2]

What then of Irish and German accents? Liebling's two views of New Orleans—one placing the city within the nation's North Atlantic culture, the other outside it—further suggest the elusiveness of the real New Orleans.

The complexity and contradictions inherent in Toole's, Liebling's, and so many others' descriptions of the city and its culture(s) suggest the impossibility of finding a single New Orleans. Common to all such descriptions, however, is a recognition that ethnicity somehow works to give the city its peculiar shape and dynamic. Joseph Logsdon appreciates all this, and by suggesting how New Orleans's many immigrant and ethnic strands have been (and still are being) woven into a public culture, he offers a fresh look at the city and the process of acculturation.

Even so, some aspects of the public culture that Logsdon identifies as the product and embodiment of acculturation are rather recent developments in New Orleans; this is especially true of the public festivals, which in the past tended to be more ethnically exclusive, as, for example, the celebration of St. Joseph's Day largely remains. In the nineteenth century, much of the public culture was created by, and directed toward, New Orleans's own values and tastes. By contrast, the public culture that has emerged in the twentieth century is the expression of second- and third-generation immigrants and descendants of the deeply rooted Creole populations, all of whom are now more inclined to cater to the tourist trade in their restaurants and public festivals.

Logsdon is on firmer historical ground when he argues that New Orleans, sui generis, can serve as a counterpoint to traditional views of ethnicity and the American city that emphasize the interplay between industrialization, urbanization, and immigration. The New Orleans experience, he says, suggests another way, for New Orleans has remained an ethnically diverse immigrant city that never industrialized and thus diverged from the basic pattern of late nineteenth- and early twentieth-century American urban growth. By appreciating the uniqueness of New Orleans as a city, Logsdon concludes, it is possible to develop a new model of acculturation that is based on a public culture rooted in a "powerful sense of local identity."

The uniqueness of New Orleans derives from its history as a foreign, specifically a Latin city annexed by the United States but never successfully absorbed by Americans. For over two centuries, American settlers have attempted to impose an Anglo-American culture on the city, but even in our day of mass consumption and mass communication, New Orleans holds tenaciously to its particular heritage and habits, using the mass media to export rather than import a lifestyle. All their commercial corruption notwithstanding, Mardi Gras and other public festivals continue to celebrate the city's defiance of American manners and propriety; they exalt the city's own patron deities (and devils) as more beneficent and worthy in their caprice than any product or principle of modern society.

The city denies its American connection in other obvious and subtle ways. Its courts admit Roman law, and its citizens subscribe to a political morality at odds with the national standards of public responsibility and propriety. For example, in a celebrated federal trial that turned on the question of local versus federal perceptions of public trust, a jury in New Orleans recently acquitted the state's governor and his codefendants of using office for private gain. Moreover, although waiters at restaurants in the Vieux Carré and artists on Jackson Square obviously affect a French patois for the benefit of tourists, French remains quite literally the lingua franca of social and commercial intercourse among some of the residents of New Orleans. So, too, as Logsdon reminds us, evidence of the uniqueness of New Orleans abounds in the look, smells, sounds, and tastes of the city and its environs—all of which defy comparison with those of any other American city. Americans may have expropriated New Orleans jazz, and judging from the proliferation of Creole or Cajun cookbooks and restaurants, they now threaten to claim its cuisine as well, but the totality of New Orleans culture, its private as well as its public dimensions, is not available for export.

Immigration broadened the foreign character of New Orleans. As a major port, the city attracted a diverse population to work in the seasonal trades associated with moving goods associated with river and gulf commerce. It also became the funnel through which hundreds of thousands of immigrants passed during the nineteenth century, with over 550,000 entering its portals between 1820 and 1860. In the late antebellum period, New Orleans was the nation's second leading port of entry for immigrants, many of whom arrived in the steerage of otherwise under-

loaded ships sent to pick up bales of cotton for transport back to Europe.
In addition, New Orleans provided access to the midwest region, which
was easily and inexpensively reached by steamboat. Transportation,
then, played a large role in drawing and directing the immigrant flow.[3]

To understand the process of acculturation over time, it is important
to recognize that different immigrant groups established a critical mass
that gave each group the numbers sufficient to build and maintain its
own ethnic associations and exercise cultural influence on the city's other
populations. It is equally important to draw precise profiles of each
critical mass. In the case of New Orleans, the more balanced sex ratio
among midnineteenth-century immigrant populations, as compared
with heavily male immigrant populations of the late nineteenth century,
made possible the maintenance of ethnic boundaries. It also made a very
great difference for patterns of acculturation, adaptation, and assimilation that immigrants constituted (in rounded numbers) about 40 percent
of the total population of New Orleans in 1860, 19 percent in 1880, 10
percent in 1900, and less than 7 percent in 1920.[4]

If, as social scientists insist, ethnicity is in part a group's response to
others' perceiving it as separate, a sufficient mass was necessary to define
group identities. A group had to have enough people within an area to
be noticed. Asians did not seem to matter much in nineteenth-century
New Orleans, nor elsewhere in the urban South, because they were too
few to be noticed or even develop a large array of ethnic institutions. In
1880, for example, New Orleans had only eighty Orientals, the largest
concentration in any southern city. Even the two thousand or so Asians
living in the city by 1900 did not constitute a critical mass because several
very different, and sometimes mutually hostile, Asian groups made up
the total; no unified Asian community existed then or later. Asians
matter more in New Orleans today because their numbers have increased and, too, because consciousness of ethnicity generally has increased in recent times. As early as 1880, however, the city's two
thousand Italians became visible enough to evoke comment and some
concern, in part no doubt because the population was growing. (Indeed,
in 1880, New Orleans had the largest Italian community in the United
States, proportionate to the total city population.)[5]

Critical masses of French and Anglo-American immigrants and migrants settled in New Orleans during the nineteenth century, but neither
group achieved cultural dominance. Instead, their presence tended to
accentuate ethnic and political divisions within the city. French immigrants readily adopted the native French culture, thereby strengthening
it, but like the Creoles, the French insulated themselves physically and
socially from the larger population. Anglo-Protestant American new-

comers also kept to themselves socially even as they tried to make New Orleans into an American city in law, politics, and commerce.[6]

During the nineteenth century, the Irish and Germans provided the largest numbers of immigrants and gave the city its immigrant cast. The Irish and Germans differed, however, in their ethnic cohesiveness and interactions with the host culture(s).

German immigrants, whose influence Logsdon implies was significant, lacked sufficient cultural and social unity to impose a single powerful German imprint on the city. They were widely dispersed throughout the Second and Third Municipalities, and in Carrollton and Lafayette, and they were fragmented by differences in religion, region of origin, and class. The proliferation of German clubs, associations, and institutions bespoke the Germans' numerical significance in the city, but it also attested to their divisions, for such organizations tended to cater to very specific groups rather than bind the various German strands together. To be sure, distinct concentrations of Germans existed in various parts of the city, wherein various German cultural values survived and influenced the culture of non-Germans in their midst, and German *Gemütlichkeit* was easily accommodated in the city's genial public culture. But, overall, Germans were too diverse and divided to dominate the city.[7]

Not so the Irish, whose presence exceeded that of all other immigrant groups in influence before the Civil War and perhaps after it as well. By 1860, one out of five residents was Irish, and the Irish by force of numbers exercised social, cultural, and political muscle in the city. Irish immigrants had greater cohesion and wider influence than the Germans. In the great waves of late antebellum immigration, the vast majority of Irish immigrants entering New Orleans came from a few select counties in Ireland. They shared a common faith, poverty, and national identity. The Irish population was dispersed throughout New Orleans, although such identifiable Irish sections as the Irish Channel existed. The Irish often settled among blacks in poorer sections—a residential pattern born of common poverty but fraught with as yet unstudied possibilities for black and Irish cultural interaction. New Orleans was small enough so that dispersal did not diminish Irish power; in fact, Irish immigrants everywhere shared so many common cultural and class interests that dispersion served to broaden Irish influence on the city's culture.[8]

The Irish learned quickly enough how to function in an urban world. Irish priests, nuns, and parishioners and Irish devotional discipline gained the upper hand in the Catholic church, and Irish politicians and voters mastered the vagaries of New Orleans politics. In imposing a public order, the Irish literally policed the city—as priests in the parishes and police officers in the streets. To the extent that acculturation in nineteenth-century New Orleans responded to a powerful and (save perhaps in the French Quarter and the American district) pervasive Irish presence, it paralleled the experiences of several other American cities.[9]

In his attempt to delineate the uniqueness of the New Orleans experience as an immigrant depot and the patterns of acculturation occurring therein, Logsdon slights two very obvious distinctions New Orleans had among all the principal ports of entry. New Orleans was a Catholic city, in fact the only large American city with a predominantly Catholic tradition and culture, and it was a southern city.

Understanding the New Orleans Catholic culture is especially important, given the peculiarly unsettled, transient nature of the New Orleans immigrant population. Because so many immigrants looked on New Orleans as merely a way station to better fortune elsewhere, large numbers of them were reluctant to form any social ties with the city. Outside of work and the home, the church was the only agency of social association and cultural contact for many immigrants. Consequently, the fact that it had a special role and character in New Orleans helped shape the distinctive pattern of acculturation there.

The New Orleans Catholic jambalaya defies easy summary. By the 1860s, throughout the United States, Irish hegemony in the church was being challenged by other ethnic groups, all seeking cultural autonomy and control over their own parish life. In New Orleans, by contrast, the Irish were newcomers, struggling to suppress an existing tradition of French Creole latitudinarianism. Clashes over ethnicity and lay trusteeship figured prominently in the city's Catholic dynamic and, no doubt, patterns of acculturation.[10]

The city's Catholic culture and traditions provided both a canopy under which different immigrant groups might come together and a boundary separating Creoles and most nineteenth-century immigrants from the Anglo-Protestant culture of the Americans. The church functioned as an acculturating agent in its own right, providing a common religious language and institutional life for Creoles and the German, Irish, and later, Italian and other Catholic immigrants. The rapid rise of Irish influence in the church's institutional structure had far-reaching effects on immigrant adaptation. Unlike the insular, exclusive French, the Irish established schools, orphan asylums, and benevolent associations that they opened to all Catholics. Through its parochial schools, religious societies, and social services, the church sought to impose a common discipline on the city's diverse Catholic population. Given the disproportionate number of Irish priests and nuns running the schools, asylums, and all, by the end of the nineteenth century, many immigrant Catholics and their children had been "Irishized" on their way to becoming Americanized. In that way, though, some of the uniqueness of New Orleans as a Catholic city was eroded, for similar patterns of ethnic rivalry and eventual Irish institutional dominance occurred elsewhere.[11]

Logsdon's neglect of the religious dimension weakens but does not dispel his contention that New Orleans is a city like no other in the United States in its patterns of acculturation. While one might quarrel with such an argument on its face alone—for what city is not unique?—Logsdon's challenge to conventional models of American acculturation warrants consideration.

Certain characteristics of the New Orleans experience resemble cultural interactions elsewhere—especially in Hawaii, where Anglo settlers were themselves immigrant outsiders called *haole,* meaning foreigner or outsider.[12] In general, it appears looking at experiences away from the northeastern United States provides a new approach to questions of social interaction and cultural evolution. Thus, just as Gilberto Freyre and other Brazilian writers have done, Logsdon advances a cultural dialectic that, in his formulation, suggests a whole new people emerged from the process. Unfortunately, however, Logsdon simply assumes that the dialectic has operated continuously from the early nineteenth century to the present.

Without summarily rejecting Logsdon's argument, let me posit another theory—one that looks for continuities and convergences as well as divergences in the history of immigrant cities and focuses on the mid-nineteenth century when most immigrants arrived in New Orleans. Though Logsdon might deny it, a model of acculturation in New Orleans should apply to more than one locality and experience. The proper comparative framework is not just New Orleans and the rest of the world, but New Orleans within a regional matrix. Mobile and Charleston, for instance, at various times between 1800 and 1860 had patterns of immigration and settlement similar to those in New Orleans. In several ways, what Logsdon describes is a southern, or regional, pattern of immigrant acculturation based on southerners' own traditional attachment to place over time. To be sure, the volume of its immigration made New Orleans an aberration in a region that was nonimmigrant and nonurban, but regarding the role of its black population and the impact of its climate on public health, New Orleans was (and is) southern.[13]

The presence of blacks was the single most important element influencing the size and nature of particular immigrant communities—a fact that should have directed Logsdon to more than just passing reference to black and white interaction. Cities with high percentages of blacks in their total populations had low percentages of foreign born and vice versa. (The large number of blacks in southern cities was the most striking difference between southern and northern urban population profiles in the nineteenth century.)

In the antebellum period, the number of free and enslaved blacks in southern cities fluctuated in response to labor demands in the agricultural sector and the seasonal nature of much urban employment. White workers, including many immigrants, lobbied against allowing black slaves to hire their own time in cities and sometimes used violence to drive blacks away. Bitter competition between black and white urban laborers and craftsmen marked every southern city and defined local political agendas in Charleston, Savannah, and New Orleans. Where immigrants arrived in great numbers, blacks were not so necessary to urban economies, but interior towns that attracted few immigrants increasingly drew blacks to fill skilled and unskilled trades. Port cities had an elastic labor supply in immigrants, and in this regard, New Orleans led the way.[14]

Thousands of immigrants who arrived in New Orleans remained in the city—some by choice, many by necessity because they had no money to leave. German and Irish famine immigrants especially were forced by circumstance to stay in New Orleans after their arrival in the 1840s and 1850s. They displaced blacks in almost every occupation. As a consequence, the slave population of New Orleans actually fell from 17,300 to 14,000 between 1850 and 1860, while the free black population rose only slightly from 9,900 to 10,700 in the same period.[15]

After the Civil War, the population profile of New Orleans changed. Blacks migrated toward it and other southern cities in increasing numbers, as throughout the South blacks began to comprise a larger share of urban populations. Blacks who settled in New Orleans and other southern ports competed vigorously with native- and foreign-born whites for jobs. Because that competition kept wages down, southern cities were less attractive than northern ones for prospective immigrants. Promoters of the New South (like so many sunbelt boosters today) played up the low wages and abundant labor in the region as inducements for northern industrialists to relocate there, but those same conditions go far in explaining the South's failure to keep pace with midwestern communities in attracting immigrants after the Civil War or at any time well into the twentieth century. Those immigrants who did end up in New Orleans, or elsewhere in the South, were too few to redirect the population flow, and because late nineteenth-century immigrants included many southern Italians and Asians, were too poor, dark, and foreign for whites to embrace as their own.[16] In the hothouse of Reconstruction, the urban influx of blacks bred a politics of race that required people to line up as either white or black, and for almost a century thereafter, race superseded ethnicity in defining status and interest in public life.

Although ultimately conforming in many ways to the broader regional pattern, the interplay between "blacks" and immigrants in New Orleans at first reflected the special features of the city's antebellum "colored" population. French-speaking *gens de couleur libre* occupied a distinct cultural and social place in the city's tripartite Latin racial order. Among the *gens de couleur libre* were wealthy, well-educated slaveholders who moved comfortably among French Creoles in church and society and prided themselves on their French culture and attainments. They resisted attempts to classify them in any way with enslaved blacks, whom they despised for their Protestantism, their condition, and in a few instances, for their color. Even after emancipation had ended official distinctions between free and enslaved "colored" people, many colored Creoles refused to acknowledge any common bonds with former black slaves. In time, political necessity would force a marriage of convenience between black groups in New Orleans, and eventually, policies of segregation would destroy the colored Creoles' claims to special status, for they became lumped together with blacks, irrespective of previous circumstance or condition. But throughout the nineteenth century, the insularity of colored Creoles meant that their interactions with immigrants were qualitatively different from those of Afro-Protestant black slaves or freedmen who competed directly with immigrants for jobs, lived among them in poor neighborhoods, and mingled with them in the same taverns and groceries.[17]

The prevalence of disease in New Orleans, and the South in general, strongly influenced the nature and flow of immigration. Cholera and yellow fever epidemics were regular occurrences in southern cities. While northern cities also suffered from periodic outbreaks of cholera in the nineteenth century, yellow fever was largely a southern affliction. No city suffered more health problems than New Orleans. Regarding yellow fever alone, the city experienced epidemics in 1817, 1832, 1835, 1837, 1839, 1841, 1847, 1853 (during which year roughly nine thousand persons died), 1854, 1855, 1858, 1867, and 1878. A host of other endemic diseases added to the city's sorry history of seasonal scourges, as did poor health management, laissez-faire attitudes, and ignorance. The increasing number and virulence of epidemics in New Orleans after 1830, however, stemmed in part from increased immigration. As large numbers of nonimmune immigrants crowded into New Orleans, they became victims of south Louisiana's pestilences. Population growth fed and spread epidemics, which abated only when cold weather came and people left the city.[18]

More than any other southern city, New Orleans refused to adopt measures to prevent epidemics. In the interests of holding onto their trade, civic leaders and businessmen in New Orleans proclaimed their city a healthy place. When yellow fever did strike, they often suppressed the information until the outbreak had spread so far that it could not be disguised; then commerce ceased, and all who could afford to do so fled the city.

Rather than admit that the scourges were in any way endemic, which would have cast the city in a bad light, civic leaders and merchants blamed the problem on immigrants. A brand of "medical Know-Nothingism" emerged whereby immigrants were charged with introducing sickness into the city. Epidemics originated in immigrant wards and raged within them; consequently, opined the worthies of New Orleans, immigrants must be the cause of the disease. To be sure, the Howard Association, Charity Hospital, and various churches and individuals offered comfort and care to the poor, who suffered most during epidemics, but immigrants met indifference, even hostility, from many of the city's native-born (and so somewhat immune) population. The identification of immigrants with epidemic diseases was so often repeated and deeply ingrained that it became an article of faith, even among learned individuals, and persisted to the end of the century.[19]

The high incidence of sickness and death among the immigrants, especially new arrivals, affected the personal lives and social organization of immigrants in countless ways, as yet unexplored. While disease may have intensified some immigrants' sense of isolation and drawn them to their own institutions and social relationships, it may also have forced other immigrants outward, away from their immigrant contacts. In addition, the ravages of disease made immigrants more vulnerable to other afflictions, more likely to lose work, and probably more subject to depression and self-doubts than were members of the native-born or acclimated populations. At the same time, epidemics disorganized immigrant families, forcing large numbers of widows and orphans to seek relief, thereby placing themselves under some public or private authority. The need for companionship and support may have contributed to acculturation in other obvious ways, such as marriages and adoptions across ethnic boundaries. [20]

Epidemics also encouraged immigrants to leave the city, and the region, for seemingly healthier locales. Equally significant, the reputation as America's unhealthiest city caused many prospective immigrants to avoid New Orleans and the South as a whole. Those most likely to bypass New Orleans were literate and propertied immigrants—those with knowledge of conditions in America and sufficient resources to act on that knowledge. German immigrant guidebooks especially condemned the lower Mississippi area as unhealthy and pestilential and urged prospective immigrants to avoid the region if at all possible.[21]

Patterns of the cotton trade directed a disproportionate number of poor and poorly educated immigrants, mostly German and Irish, to New Orleans in the antebellum period because transatlantic fares were inexpensive. The city's reputation for disease and its tardy and inefficient quarantine policies, which did not include on-shore health inspection facilities until 1859, both had the same effect. Besides those immigrants who lacked the resources to make choices, New Orleans also received immigrants who were likely to have been rejected at ports with stricter admission policies. As a result, the size and character of the New Orleans immigrant population, and thus the process of ethnic acculturation, was in large part a product of the city's epidemiological environment.

Logsdon lists several other factors that explain the decline of New Orleans as an immigrant port in the nineteenth century. The city's economy hinged on a commerce it could not control. With the advent of railroads, the city lost ground to Great Lakes and eastern cities in the competition for midwestern products. Dependence on southern staples, which fell in value after the Civil War, also contributed to the city's flagging economic fortunes and lessened its need for workers. Natural geographic barriers, especially the long distance from Europe and the difficulty and expense of clearing mud and sand from the river, further limited economic and, thus, population growth. New Orleans also lacked viable local industry to compensate for commercial losses. And so on.

Once again, the timing of the decline of New Orleans as an immigrant port of entry fits into a larger regional pattern. The Civil War, that great divide in southern history, hurt southern immigrant cities less because of the physical damage they suffered, which could be repaired and rebuilt, than for the disruption of commercial connections and the destruction of the agricultural hinterlands serving them. Southern cities survived and recovered from the Civil War, and city building did not cease, but significant foreign immigration to southern cities did.[22]

After the Civil War, all southern states established immigration bureaus to induce immigrants to settle within their bounds. The bureaus, including Louisiana's especially active one, published guidebooks and other promotional materials extolling the physical, political, and social benefits awaiting immigrants. Bureaus sent representatives abroad to circulate information, and they supported private and local efforts to encourage immigration.[23]

Nevertheless, such endeavors came to little and affected cities least of all. The entire immigrant recruitment campaign was premised on agricultural needs. Cities played no part in its promises or prospects except perhaps as initial landing points and eventual markets for immigrant farmers. Postwar immigrant recruitment focused mainly on persuading farmers from northwestern Europe to settle in the South, but southern appeals generated scant interest among immigrants. The farmers that

southern states wanted were those least likely to find the region's de-
pleted soils and strange climate attractive, especially when more favorable agricultural and economic conditions beckoned in midwestern
states.[24]

Private schemes to foster immigration were more successful if only
because state-supported efforts reaped such a meager harvest. With
mixed success, after 1890, railroad companies sought immigrants to
settle their lands, and planters enlisted immigrants to replace or displace
black laborers. Failing to persuade German farmers to come, private
concerns in Louisiana engaged labor contractors to supply Chinese
workers and later, southern Italians to work in gangs on large sugar
plantations. The labor experiments failed. The Chinese and southern
Italians proved as intractable as blacks had been and either fled or were
pushed off the plantations.[25]

Those who remained in the lower Mississippi delta region drifted
toward the cities, especially New Orleans, where they made up a new
underclass of workers. Although some eventually moved into various
trades and small businesses, such as green groceries, many languished at
the economic bottom. Their poverty condemned them in white southerners' eyes; so, too, did their color and the circumstances of their arrival
in Louisiana and Mississippi. Foreign-born workers who came in the late
nineteenth century were clearly outsiders. They were dark Mediterra-
neans or Asians in a southern world acutely sensitive to color; they were
almost all males in a society distrustful of any unattached "colored" man.
They were sojourners in a culture rooted in a powerful sense of place
and suspicious of strangers. That such immigrants were hired to per-
form work traditionally associated with blacks reinforced native-born
white southerners' negative attitudes toward them.

Almost all young, single men, southern Italians found companionship
among themselves but also among blacks and colored Creoles in the
sugar parishes. Local stories circulated about dark Italians and black
women creating a new race of mixed blood. In public documents, the
state government referred to southern Italians and their progeny as
"Dagos," a term in folk parlance that became more generally applied to
"mixed-blood" fruiters and fishermen in Orleans, Jefferson, and
Plaquemines parishes. After 1876, "Dagos" were regarded by the state,
along with the former *gens de couleur libre*, as Negroes for purposes of
public identification. When southern Italians moved to New Orleans,
then, they carried a burden of racial identification that marked them as
undesirable in white eyes.[26]

In this light, anti-Italian feeling in late nineteenth-century New Orleans takes on new meaning. The lynching of eleven Italians in New
Orleans in 1891, ostensibly for murdering the Irish police chief, repre-

sented more than vigilantism against foreigners and an inevitable conclusion to several years of Irish-Italian rivalry and violence; the city, in fact, had been fairly tolerant of immigrants. The lynching represented rather the need of the white community (of which Irish Catholics were an integral part) to define social boundaries. Lynching, after all, was a method of social and political control whites usually reserved for "colored" people. Lynching southern Italians in New Orleans shows that acculturation there would be shaped by social and political contexts that moved from the Latin model of racial openness to the southern one of racial exclusiveness.[27]

A fuller appreciation of the New Orleans, or any southern city's, experience with immigration demands consideration of those peculiarly local conditions that discouraged as well as attracted immigration. In comparative terms, it is also useful to remember that discouragements fed on themselves, making the region increasingly less attractive to immigrants and as the immigrant influx to southern cities dwindled to almost nothing by 1900, making the region increasingly parochial and hostile to outsiders. New Orleans remained exceptional among southern cities in its ability to attract at least some new immigrants, but it had lost its earlier character. The violence against southern Italians in New Orleans illustrates how intolerant and uneasy with newcomers the once great immigrant port of entry had become.

The significance of New Orleans as an immigrant port was largely confined to the midnineteenth century. Despite efforts by civic promoters early in the twentieth century to revive immigrant traffic, New Orleans never regained its standing, although since the early 1970s, the city has reluctantly received an influx of Vietnamese refugees and immigrants from the Caribbean and Central and South America. The brevity of the city's importance as a major immigrant port of entry does not suggest that immigration has been inconsequential in continuing to influence the character of New Orleans, for an ethnic dialectic is at work today. Nor does it suggest that patterns of immigration to, and immigrant adaptation in, New Orleans may not be instructive. It does suggest, however, that understanding how New Orleanians, or any American people, came to be requires close attention to the particular circumstances of their arrival and adjustment in particular places over long periods of time and the need to cut into the veneer of any public culture.

Notes

My essay benefited from a critical reading by Paula Benkart and from research completed under an Albert Beveridge Travel Grant from the American Historical Association.

1. John Kennedy Toole, *A Confederacy of Dunces* (New York, 1981 ed.), 139 (quote) and passim.

2. A[bbott] J. Liebling, *The Earl of Louisiana* (Baton Rouge, 1970), 39 and 87 (quotes) and passim.

3. On immigration and migration to (and through) antebellum New Orleans, see A[lan] A. Conway, "New Orleans as a Port of Immigration, 1820–1860" (M.A. thesis, University of London, 1949); Frederick M. Spletstoser, "Back Door to the Land of Plenty: New Orleans as an Immigrant Port, 1820–1860," 2 vols. (Ph.D. diss., Louisiana State University, 1978); and Victor H. Treat, "Migration into Louisiana, 1834–1880" (Ph.D. diss., University of Texas at Austin, 1967). On population figures, see U.S. Bureau of Census, *Seventh Census of the United States, 1850* (Washington, D.C., 1853); and U.S. Bureau of Census, *Population of the United States in 1860* (Washington, D.C., 1864). To reconstruct patterns of emigration, immigration, and settlement, and profiles of immigrants, consult the New Orleans Passenger Lists, 1851–1860 (City Archives, New Orleans Public Library); and Naturalization Records of Orleans Parish, 1845–1899 (Tulane University). For an immigrant's personal narrative of traveling to New Orleans, with comparisons between the treatment of first-class and steerage passengers, see Ann (Raney) Thomas Coleman, "Reminiscences," 49–53 (Duke University).

4. These and all subsequent population figures are based on federal census figures.

5. On the size and characteristics of specific immigrant communities, see the indispensable collection of vital statistics in *Statistics of the Population of the United States,* vol. 1 (Washington, 1883), especially tables VI (416–25), IX (447–56), XV (536–37), and XVI (538–41); and George E. Waring, Jr., comp., "The Southern and Western States," *Report on the Social Statistics of Cities, Tenth Census of the United States, 1880,* vol. 9 (Washington, D.C., 1886), which includes a revealing fifty-four-page account of New Orleans by George W. Cable.

6. The dynamics between the French and Anglo-Americans need further study. A good brief introduction is Henry Blumenthal, *American and French Culture, 1800–1900: Interchanges in Art, Science, Literature, and Society* (Baton Rouge, 1975), 10–15 and passim. See also Marie S. Dunn, "A Comparative Study: Louisiana's French and Anglo-Saxon Cultures," *Louisiana Studies* 10 (1971): 131–69; Edward Larocque Tinker, *Creole City: Its Past and Its People* (New York, 1953); Selma Klein, "Social Interaction of Creoles and Anglo-Saxons in New Orleans, 1803–1860" (M.A. thesis, Tulane University, 1940); and Livingston DeLancey, "French Influence in New Orleans," *French Review* 13 (1940): 483–87. Separatism was maintained by building a network of French associations, such as mutual aid societies. For one example, see *Abrégé historique de la société française de bienfaisance mutuelle de la Nouvelle-Orléans* (New Orleans, 1903) and the society's "Register of Members," [1873–1898] Société Française de Bienfaisance et d'Assistance de la Nouvelle-Orléans Papers (Duke University). On the interplay between French, Anglo-American, and immigrants in New Orleans, see especially Roger Shugg, *Origins of Class Struggle in Louisiana: A Social History of White Farmers and Laborers during Slavery and After, 1840–1875* (Baton Rouge, 1972 ed.), chap. 2–3 and passim.

7. On the Germans, see J. Hanno Deiler, *Geschichte der Deutschen Gesellschaft von New Orleans. Mit einer Einteitung* (New Orleans, 1897); J. Hanno Deiler, *Geschichte der New Orleanser Deutschen Presse* (New Orleans, 1901); John F. Nau, *The German People of New Orleans, 1850–1900* (Leiden, The Netherlands, 1958); and Raimund Berchtold, "The Decline of German Ethnicity in New Orleans" (M.A. thesis, University of New Orleans, 1984).

8. On the Irish, see Earl F. Niehaus, *The Irish in New Orleans, 1800–1860* (Baton Rouge, 1965). My own research in federal census records, hospital and poor house records, city directories, tax and court records, and travelers' accounts suggests that the poorer Irish congregated in identifiable clusters, although the Irish did disperse generally throughout the city.

9. On the Irish in the church, see Niehaus, *The Irish in New Orleans*, 98–111; and Randall M. Miller, "A Church in Cultural Captivity: Some Speculations on Catholic Identity in the Old South," in Randall M. Miller and Jon L. Wakelyn, eds., *Catholics in the Old South: Essays on Church and Culture* (Macon, Ga., 1983), 29–37, for the interplay between the Irish and other Catholics; and Spletstoser, "Back Door to the Land of Plenty," 393–98. On the Irish in the police force, see Dennis C. Rousey, " 'Hibernian Leatherheads': Irish Cops in New Orleans, 1830–1880," *Journal of Urban History* 10 (1983): 61–84.

10. On the church in New Orleans, generally, see Roger Baudier, *The Catholic Church in Louisiana* (New Orleans, 1939); Shugg, *Origins of Class Struggle*, 62–63; Miller, "Church in Cultural Captivity," 29–37 and passim; and the rich and abundant correspondence of Bishop Antoine Blanc, New Orleans Papers (University of Notre Dame).

11. Ibid. See also New Orleans *Le Propagateur Catholique* for 1843–1844 regarding the trusteeism controversy.

12. For a useful introduction to the *haole* in Hawaii, see Elvi Whittaker, *The Mainland Haole: The White Experience in Hawaii* (New York, 1986). Whittaker shows that whites had to adapt to being identified as ethnic and no more than equal in a pluralistic society that was in a state of social and cultural flux.

13. No full treatment of immigration and ethnicity in the southern setting exists, but Jason Silverman's forthcoming book, *Beyond the Melting Pot in Dixie: Immigration and Ethnicity in Southern History*, will go far toward meeting the need. General surveys of immigration and its effects in antebellum southern cities include Ira Berlin and Herbert Gutman, "Natives and Immigrants, Free Men and Slaves: Urban Workingmen in the Antebellum South," *American Historical Review* 88 (1983): 1175–1200; Randall M. Miller, "The Enemy Within: Some Effects of Foreign Immigrants on Antebellum Southern Cities," *Southern Studies* 24 (1985): 30–53; and Herbert Weaver, "Foreigners in Ante-Bellum Towns of the Lower South," *Journal of Southern History* 13 (1947): 62–73. The literature on specific groups and on groups in particular southern states and locales is vast. For brief surveys, see Randall M. Miller, "Immigrants in the Old South," *Immigration History Newsletter* 10 (1978): 8–14; and Jason Silverman, "Writing Southern Ethnic History: An Historiographical Investigation," *Immigration History Newsletter* 19 (1987): 1–4. My reading of southern urban history from a regional perspective owes much to David R. Goldfield, *Cotton Fields and Skyscrapers: Southern City and Region, 1607–1980* (Baton Rouge, 1982).

14. Compare Richard Wade, *Slavery in the Cities: The South, 1820–1860* (New York, 1964); and Claudia Goldin, *Urban Slavery in the American South, 1820–1860: A Quantitative History* (Chicago, 1976).

15. Ibid; Spletstoser, "Back Door to the Land of Plenty," 292–300, 376–92; and Richard R. Tansey, "Economic Expansion and Urban Disorder in Antebellum New Orleans" (Ph.D. diss., University of Texas at Austin, 1981), 94–112, 119–36, and passim.

16. Good discussions of black movement and life in New Orleans include John W. Blassingame, *Black New Orleans, 1860–1880* (Chicago, 1973); Geraldine McTigue, "Forms of Racial Interaction in Louisiana, 1860–1880" (Ph.D. diss., Yale University, 1975); and Dale Somers, "Black and White in New Orleans: A

Study in Urban Race Relations, 1865–1900," *Journal of Southern History* 40 (1974):19–42.

17. On the special features and identities of the New Orleans "black" populations, see David C. Rankin, "The Forgotten People: Free People of Color in New Orleans, 1850–1870" (Ph.D. diss., Johns Hopkins University, 1976); Donald E. Everett, "Free Persons of Color in New Orleans, 1803–1865" (Ph.D. diss., Tulane University, 1952), especially 203–25; Rodolphe L. Desdunes, *Nos hommes et notre histoire; notices biographiques accompagnées de réflexions et de souvenirs personnels, hommage à la population créole, en souvenir des grands hommes qu'elle a produits et des bonnes choses qu'elle a accomplies* (Montreal, 1911); Charles B. Roussevé, *The Negro in Louisiana: Aspects of His History and His Literature* (New Orleans, 1937). On the persistence of colored Creole culture and attempts at social isolation, see Blassingame, *Black New Orleans*, 21–22; and Arthé Anthony, "The Negro Creole Community in New Orleans, 1880–1920: An Oral History" (Ph.D. diss., University of California, Irvine, 1978). On the confusion of racial and cultural definitions, see Virginia R. Dominguez, *White by Definition: Social Classification in Creole Louisiana* (New Brunswick, N.J., 1986). Relations between Catholic colored Creoles and Irish immigrants were sometimes cordial, as in the request of one Creole to marry an Irish woman who worked as his governess: Fr. E. Dupuy to Antoine Blanc, 13 June 1853, New Orleans Papers.

18. Jo Ann Carrigan, "Yellow Fever in New Orleans: Abstractions and Realities," *Journal of Southern History* 25 (1959):339–55; Jo Ann Carrigan, "Privilege, Prejudice, and Strangers' Disease in Nineteenth-Century New Orleans," *Journal of Southern History* 36 (1970):568–78; John H. Ellis, "Business and Public Health in the Urban South during the Nineteenth Century: New Orleans, Memphis, and Atlanta," *Bulletin of the History of Medicine* 44 (1970):197–212.

19. Ibid. See also Miller, "The Enemy Within," 45; and Shugg, *Origins of Class Struggle*, 51–56. The tendency to implicate immigrants as authors of epidemics persisted. As late as 1895, for example, the popular New Orleans author Grace King implied as much in her account of the antebellum scourges. See King, *New Orleans: The Place and the People* (New York, 1895), 283–89.

20. On the charitable responses to victims of diseases, see Shugg, *Origins of Class Struggle*, 56–58; and Spletstoser, "Back Door to the Land of Plenty," 300–320. The effects on the immigrants' lives remains unstudied. Data on immigrant admissions to hospitals, orphanages, and other service institutions can be gleaned from each institution's annual reports—thus, *Report of the Board of Administrators of the Charity Hospital . . .* for 1851–70. For examples of individual experiences, see Reports of the Asylum for the Relief of Destitute Orphan Boys [1839], 18–19 (Tulane University); John Page Diary, vol. I, 1836–38 (Tulane University); correspondence in Administration Papers (for example, box 1, folder 16; box 2, folders 14, 18; and box 3, folders 4, 8, 12), Poydras Home Collection (Tulane University); Mary Farney to Antoine Blanc, 30 January 1854, New Orleans Papers; New Orleans *The True Witness and South-Western Presbyterian*, 18 September 1858; *New Orleans Medical News and Hospital Gazette* 2 (1855–56):234; 6, part 2 (1859–60):902–8; [Joseph Jones], "Notes," Charity Hospital Cases, 1869–70, Joseph Jones Papers (Louisiana State University, Baton Rouge); Charity Hospital Case Record Book, 1883–84, Charity Hospital Papers (Louisiana State University, Baton Rouge).

21. See, for example, Traugott Bromme, *Hand- und Reisebuch für Auswanderer und Reisende nach Nord-Mittel- und Süd-Amerika* (Bamberg, 1853), 248–51.

22. A good description of postwar southern urban development, with some attention to immigration patterns, is Lawrence H. Larsen, *The Rise of the Urban*

South (Lexington, Ky., 1985). See also Goldfield, *Cotton Fields and Skyscrapers,* chap. 3.

23. On postwar efforts to recruit immigrants, see Rowland T. Berthoff, "Southern Attitudes Toward Immigration, 1865–1914," *Journal of Southern History* 16 (1951):328–60; Robert L. Brandfon, *Cotton Kingdom of the New South: A History of the Yazoo Mississippi Delta from Reconstruction to the Twentieth Century* (Cambridge, Mass., 1967), chap. 7; Bert J. Lowenberg, "Efforts of the South to Encourage Immigration, 1865–1900," *South Atlantic Quarterly* 33 (1934):363–85; and C. Vann Woodward, *Origins of the New South, 1877–1913* (Baton Rouge, 1951), 297–99. For an excellent analysis of the changing conditions that caused southern states to pursue immigration and fail in their efforts, see Gavin Wright, *Old South, New South: Revolutions in the Southern Economy since the Civil War* (New York, 1986), especially 51–80.

24. On Louisiana specifically, see E. Russ Williams, Jr., "Louisiana's Public and Private Immigration Endeavors: 1866–1893," *Louisiana History* 15 (1974):153–74; and Charles Shanabruch, "The Louisiana Immigration Movement, 1891–1907: An Analysis of Efforts, Attitudes, and Opportunities," *Louisiana History* 18 (1977):203–26. For examples of Louisiana's interests, see *Report of the Bureau of Immigration to the General Assembly of Louisiana* (New Orleans, 1867); J. C. Kathman, *Information for Immigrants into the State of Louisiana* (New Orleans, 1868); *Report of the Commissioners of Emigration to the General Assembly of Louisiana* (New Orleans, 1870); *New Orleans Weekly Louisianan,* 22 January 1871; T[homas] W. Poole, *Some Late Words about Louisiana* (New Orleans, 1889), 3–18, 25–31, and passim; and the Minutes (1877–91), Louisiana Sugar Planters' Association Papers (Louisiana State University, Baton Rouge). For examples of pamphlets directed toward European immigrant groups, see *La Louisiane. Ses grandes avantages attractifs pour les emigrants* ([New Orleans], 1866); and Louis Voss, *Louisianas Einladung an deutsche Landwirte und Kolonisten* (New Orleans, 1907). For a good contemporary assessment of why Louisiana failed to attract the "right" kind of immigrants, see *New Orleans Picayune,* 2 December 1908.

25. On the Chinese, see Lucy M. Cohen, *Chinese in the Post–Civil War South: A People Without a History* (Baton Rouge, 1984); Stephen Duncan to S. A. Davis, 4 October 1872, Duncan Papers (Louisiana State University, Baton Rouge); William Gay to Andrew Gay, 13 February, 20, 21, 22 March 1871, box 48, Edward Gay and Family Papers (Louisiana State University, Baton Rouge). On the Italians, see Jean Ann Scarpaci, "Italian Immigrants in Louisiana's Sugar Parishes: Recruitment, Labor Conditions, and Community Relations, 1880–1910" (Ph.D. diss., Rutgers University, 1972). For study of earlier Italian immigrants, see Russell M. Magnaghi, "Louisiana's Italian Immigrants Prior to 1870," *Louisiana History* 27 (1986):43–68. *Invito della Louisiana a coloni e agricoltori italiani* ([New Orleans], n.d.) is a promotional pamphlet. Letters in the Edward Gay and Family Papers for 1871 and the minutes (1877–91) and correspondence (1877–1905) in the Louisiana Sugar Planters' Association Papers are also very useful. From 1904 to 1905, the Italian ambassador to the United States visited lower Mississippi plantations on which Italians worked and later published an account of what he observed: Edmondo Mayor des Planches, *Attraverso gli stati uniti* (Torino, 1913).

26. Negative statements about southern Italians abound in personal correspondence and other documents. Three representative examples are May McDowell to Grace King, [4 April 1891], Grace King Collection (Louisiana State University, Baton Rouge); Alice Thrasher to Arthur Thrasher, 14 November 1896, Arthur Thrasher Papers (Louisiana State University, Baton Rouge); and

Michael La Sorte, *La Merica: Images of Italian Greenhorn Experience* (Philadelphia, 1985), 142. Southern Italians were burdened by the image of the Mafia, which even their supporters believed existed; see, for example, J. N. Pharr to D. Caffery and Son, 19 September 1902, Pharr Papers (Louisiana State University, Baton Rouge). Italians' association with crime existed in the public mind in New Orleans as early as 1869: Damon L. Barbat, "The Illegitimate Birth of the Mafia in New Orleans," *Southern Studies* 24 (1985):343–51. Conflict between Italians and Irish in New Orleans evoked commentary from many sources, including a Dane in New Orleans, who styled the Italians barbarians and clannish: letter of 3 November 1890, signed J. S., in *Den nye Verden,* 21 November 1890.

27. On the murder of Police Chief Hennessy, the subsequent lynching, and anti-Italian feelings, see Barbara Botein, "The Hennessy Case: An Episode in American Nativism, 1890" (Ph.D. diss., New York University, 1975); Richard Gambino, *Vendetta* (Garden City, N.Y., 1977); and Humbert Nelli, "The Hennessy Murder and the Mafia in New Orleans," *Italian Quarterly* 19 (1975):77–95. On conflicts and associations between blacks and Italians, see, for example, George E. Cunningham, "The Italian, a Hindrance to White Solidarity in Louisiana, 1890–1898," *Journal of Negro History* 50 (1965):22–36. Anti-Italian violence was not confined to New Orleans. For a discussion of the hanging of six Italians in Amite City, Louisiana, in 1924, see John V. Baiamonte, Jr., *Spirit of Vengeance: Nativism and Louisiana Justice, 1921–1924* (Baton Rouge, 1986).

6

Immigration through the Port of San Francisco

Charles Wollenberg

In his excellent article on New York in the Freedom's Doors exhibition catalog, Elliott Barkan makes little distinction between the concept of an immigrant city and an immigrant depot.[1] This is perfectly understandable, for in the history of New York, the two phenomena have been virtually synonymous. Such is not the case, however, for San Francisco. The Golden Gate metropolis has been a city of immigrants for more than 130 years but seldom if ever have the majority of foreign-born residents used the city as their original port of entry to the United States. The history of San Francisco as an immigrant depot has therefore been somewhat distinct from its history as an immigrant city.

Both histories, though, have common roots in the gold rush of 1849, which almost instantaneously transformed San Francisco into an urban center.[2] The lure of quick wealth attracted people of all races and nationalities to the city. French newspapers ran lotteries offering trips to California as prizes, and some of the winners may have eventually formed part of San Francisco's prestigious French colony. Gold seekers from Mexico, Peru, and Chile caused a dramatic increase in the Bay Area's Spanish-speaking population, and like the native-born "Californios," they were often victims of Anglo violence and oppression. Immigrants from Australia, New Zealand, and Hawaii pioneered transpacific routes, and significant numbers of Chinese began arriving in 1852. While many of the early immigrants soon returned home, others stayed, and the Gold Rush produced a cosmopolitan, multinational population mix that has characterized the Bay Area ever since.

In 1860, San Francisco had the highest proportion of foreign-born residents of any American city. By 1880, about 60 percent of San Francisco's population was of immigrant stock, people who were either foreign born themselves or children of foreign-born parents.[3] This was the highest such percentage of any American city at that time. And the impact of immigration was not limited to San Francisco alone; the entire

143

Passengers arriving from the Orient in San Francisco, ca. 1924. *(Courtesy of the National Archives.)*

Bay Area was affected. Immigrants and their children were found at every level of society, but primarily they were members of blue-collar families. The early history of the region's working class is to a large extent a history of immigrants and their children.

As in other U.S. metropolitan regions, Europeans accounted for the largest share of the Bay Area's foreign-born population. The great majority of these European immigrants originally entered the United States on the East Coast, coming west overland, often after some years of residence in America. Although direct passage from Europe to California was possible in the nineteenth century, it was not practical until after the completion of the Panama Canal in 1914.[4] By that time, World War I and the subsequent enactment of restrictive immigration legislation limited further European arrivals. Late nineteenth- and early twentieth-century San Francisco, then, was to a large extent a city of European immigrants but not an important port of entry for European immigration.

The Irish were the most numerous immigrant group by the 1880s, when they and their children made up nearly a third of San Francisco's entire population. The gold rush had occurred in the midst of the great migrations caused by Ireland's potato famine, and many of the new Irish Americans eventually made their way west. Residents of Irish descent included mining magnates, industrialists, and politicians of both corrupt and reformist persuasions. As in other cities, Irish political influence resulted in strong Irish representation in the municipal work force, particularly in police and fire departments. By the 1880s, the Irish also dominated the region's powerful Catholic clergy and its parochial schools.[5]

Despite the prominence of many nineteenth-century Irish Americans, most of San Francisco's Irish population belonged to the working class. It did much of the basic labor that transformed the Bay Area into a major metropolitan region, and several of the most important leaders of the thriving local labor movement were also of Irish descent. Such working-class neighborhoods as South of Market, were often predominantly Irish, though never exclusively so.[6]

The gold rush coincided not only with the potato famine, but also with economic changes and revolutionary upheavals in central Europe that contributed to significant immigration from Germany and the Austro-Hungarian Empire. One of the founders of the Bay Area's wine industry was a self-proclaimed Hungarian nobleman, and Germans were numerous in retail commerce and the region's skilled trades. Founders of a number of well-known Bay Area Bavarian Jewish families were also part of the larger German-speaking immigration. Scandinavian and British immigrants were important in the building trades and were also found in maritime occupations, serving not only as seamen but also as skilled boat and ship builders. Indeed, the Bay Area's great fleet of lumber schooners was called the Scandinavian navy because of the birthplace of most of the officers and crews.[7]

By the 1890s, the Bay Area, like other regions, began to feel the effects of the "new" immigration from southern and eastern Europe. Portuguese, particularly from the Azores, played a major role in Bay Area agriculture as orchardists, dairy farmers, and cannery workers. Greeks engaged in railroad labor and operated small stores and cafes. Social upheavals and persecution in tsarist Russia prompted migrations of Polish and Russian Jews, including a remarkable community of socialist chicken farmers in Petaluma, while the same upheavals also caused migrations of conservative Russian Christians, both Orthodox and Protestant.

Italians comprised by far the largest of the new immigrant groups. A few northern Italians had arrived during the gold rush, opening small businesses and restaurants. They and Dalmatian (Croat) immigrants from what is now Yugoslavia soon dominated San Francisco's fishing industry, introducing lateen sail fishing boats to the bay and establishing

Fisherman's Wharf. Beginning in the 1890s, the small Italian immigrant community was overwhelmed by a much larger Italian migration. While the bulk of Bay Area Italians continued to have roots in northern Italy, many of the newcomers immigrated from such southern regions as Sicily. As a result of new migrations, by 1920, Italians had replaced the Irish as California's most numerous foreign-born group.[8]

Like the Irish, Italians were found at every socioeconomic level of Bay Area life, including the financial sector where A. P. Giannini founded in 1904 what was to become the giant Bank of America. But also like the Irish, Italians were primarily working class. By the early twentieth century, they were in engaged in most blue-collar occupations, and many working-class neighborhoods were becoming increasingly, but not exclusively, Italian. In particular, San Francisco's North Beach, settled by Chileans in early gold rush days and then by Irish and Germans, had become predominantly Italian by the turn of the century.[9]

Although most Italian immigrants became city dwellers, some of the newcomers played a vital role in developing Bay Area agriculture. They labored as agricultural and cannery workers and operated truck farms and dairies, often on the edge of urban settlement. Italians contributed significantly to the growth of the region's wineries, established fine restaurants, and dominated the area's wholesale fruit, vegetable, and wine distribution networks. They were also active at the other end of the food chain, organizing scavenger companies that to this day dispose of garbage in both San Francisco and Oakland.[10]

Italians and other European immigrants experienced prejudice and discrimination at the hands of "native" Bay Area residents—who themselves had often arrived only a few years earlier. Sometimes antiimmigrant sentiment was combined with religious bigotry. Thus prominent Jewish businessmen in San Francisco founded their own social club in part because they were banned from many of the city's other men's clubs. Some business leaders who headed the 1856 Vigilance Committee displayed a not-too-subtle anti-Irish bias, and anti-Catholicism was behind some of the furious competition between public and parochial schools in late nineteenth-century San Francisco. By the beginning of the twentieth century, the large influx of Italians and other southern Europeans was raising new nativist fears.

What is surprising, however, is not that such prejudice existed in San Francisco but that it was less vehement and had less impact than in most other American metropolitan regions with very large and diverse foreign-born populations. Overt job discrimination against European immigrants was rare in the Bay Area. Moreover, multinational working-class districts, rather than exclusive ethnic neighborhoods, were the general rule. While eastern employers often exploited national and religious differences to break unions and strikes, the powerful Bay Area labor movement was largely the creation of immigrants from many nations who showed a remarkable ability to cooperate and maintain solidarity.[11]

The comparative lack of prejudice was due in part to the newness of the region. Even at the end of the nineteenth century, almost everyone was a fairly recent arrival, and rigid social structures had not had time to develop. Except for a few brief periods of severe depression, the economy was expanding, so that the success of one group did not necessarily come at the expense of another.

The region's immigrant experience was also affected by the fact that a large portion of Bay Area Europeans was not fresh off the boat. Having previously lived for some time in the East, many Bay Area European immigrants already had considerable American experience and knowledge of English. Consequently, they were probably less willing than east coast immigrants to work for very low wages and break strikes. They may also have felt less need to maintain very close-knit ethnic neighborhoods. Finally, they were usually more than willing to join with native-born whites in a common prejudice against the Chinese, whom labor historian Alexander Saxton has called the white working class's "indispensable enemy."[12]

The Bay Area's long heritage of anti-Asian discrimination goes back at least to 1852, the year of the first large-scale immigration from China to California (and thus to the United States). The pioneers of Asian immigration to America, coming from the troubled region around the city of Canton, hoped to "get rich quick" as did most others in gold rush California. But racial discrimination soon forced the Chinese to look for economic activities serving white miners instead of competing with them. Because there were few women in early gold rush California, many of the mostly male Chinese found a niche in what the nineteenth century considered women's work: laundry, cooking, and domestic service. Gangs of Chinese also worked otherwise unoccupied gold fields and took low-paying jobs avoided by whites. Thus, by the time construction began on the transcontinental railroad in 1862, the immigration route from Canton and the tradition of cheap Chinese labor were well established, to the great advantage of the Central Pacific Railroad and many other local employers who profited fully from the prevailing racial prejudice.[13]

For the Chinese, San Francisco became the major port of entry, with the Pacific Mail Steamship Company's wharf serving for many years as America's chief depot for incoming Asians. As a result, early in its history, the city established a strong transpacific connection that has never been severed. Until the 1870s, most California Chinese lived in the mountain counties where mining and railroad construction were centered. Even then, however, San Francisco, the primary port of entry, was the unofficial capital of Chinese America.

Wealthy Chinese merchants and labor contractors established stores, offices, and dormitories in San Francisco. The city was headquarters for regional associations, clan organizations, and secret societies (tongs) that were the institutional foundations of Chinese immigrant life in America. And it was in San Francisco, along DuPont Street (Grant Avenue) that the Bay Area's most famous ethnic neighborhood developed. Other California communities also had large Chinatowns, but none rivaled the size and importance of San Francisco's. Indeed, San Francisco's Chinatown may well be the nation's oldest urban immigrant community that has been continually occupied by the same ethnic group.[14]

The completion of the transcontinental railroad in 1869 forced the Chinese out of the mountain counties and into new occupational fields. They became an important component of California's agricultural labor force and often established small truck farms of their own. Chinese crewmen served on merchant ships and fishing vessels, and Asian immigrants also became a significant part of the urban work force.[15] The number of Bay Area Chinese steadily increased, and by 1880, they comprised about 10 percent of San Francisco's population. But since the great majority of Asian immigrants were young, unattached men, they made up far more of the city's work force.

Unfortunately, the rapid growth in the Chinese population coincided with the major economic depression of the late 1870s. As unemployment increased, white workers were willing to take jobs traditionally reserved for the Chinese. At the same time, companies that previously hired only whites were now tempted to employ cheaper Chinese labor. Direct economic competition between whites and Asians exacerbated American racial prejudices and poisoned the social and political atmosphere. The causes of the economic hard times were complex and poorly understood, but the Chinese made a perfect scapegoat.[16]

The chief political agent of anti-Asian sentiment during the late 1870s was the Workingman's Party, an organization started by San Francisco labor leaders. Under the demagogic control of Denis Kearney, the party abandoned its broad reform platform as anti-Chinese rhetoric came to the fore. Kearney, an Irish immigrant, as were many of the workers who attended his sandlot meetings, linked racism, ethnic rivalry, and economic competition in the simple slogan, "the Chinese must go." When prosperity finally returned in the 1880s, the Workingman's party disintegrated, and Denis Kearney became a conservative businessman. But anti-Asian sentiment had been established as an important ingredient of California politics and public policy, and so it remained for another sixty years. The San Francisco Board of Education, for example, excluded

Chinese children from public schools for nearly fifteen years. After the state supreme court ruled in 1885 that such exclusion was unconstitutional, the city operated a segregated elementary school for the Chinese until the 1930s.[17]

Nationally, the most important result of the rising tide of anti-Chinese politics was the passage by Congress of the Chinese Exclusion Act in 1882. The law marked an important turning point in American history, for it was the nation's first instance of substantial immigration restriction. As such, it has become an important symbol, of both the racist character of past American immigration policy and the difficulties overcome by past generations of Chinese Americans. Ironically, it went into effect just as the Statue of Liberty was being erected in New York Harbor. The act, which was renewed and amended several times, never fully stopped Chinese immigration. A few illegals continued to slip through, and the law allowed exemptions for government officials, students, and teachers. In addition, American-born children of Chinese parents were U.S. citizens and thus eligible to reenter the country.

Between 1910 and 1940, the federal government ran an interrogation and detention center on Angel Island in San Francisco Bay to investigate prospective Chinese immigrants and determine whether they were eligible for entry. Investigations were complicated because the 1906 earthquake and fire had destroyed San Francisco's birth records, making it difficult to prove whether or not a young Chinese applicant was in fact an American-born citizen as he or she claimed. Stays of three to six months in the prisonlike detention barracks were common, as the proceedings, including intensive interrogations, dragged on. Although the center was theoretically designed for immigrants of all nationalities, more than 90 percent of those detained were Chinese.[18]

Angel Island was therefore not the Ellis Island of the West, a receiving point for most west coast immigrants of all nationalities. Instead, it was a peculiar product of the Chinese Exclusion Act, whose primary purpose was to control and restrict Chinese immigration.

The Chinese immigrant population gradually declined after 1882. Since most Chinese in California were unattached men intending to return to their homeland, there was only a small number of second-generation Chinese Americans, and it took several decades for the Chinese population of the state to recover to its 1880 level. Anti-Chinese sentiment continued to be an important part of California life, and San Francisco's Chinatown, as a place of refuge for a harassed people, reflected a siege mentality. Of the other Bay Area Chinatowns, only Oakland's also survived the exclusion era.[19]

Meanwhile, the Japanese replaced the Chinese as California's most numerous Asian immigrant group, filling employers' demands for a new

Angel Island Immigration Station, San Francisco, ca. 1930. *(Courtesy of the National Archives.)*

source of cheap nonwhite labor. Although San Francisco was an important port of entry for new Japanese residents (many of whom came by way of Hawaii), Los Angeles eventually attracted the largest concentration of Japanese. The Chinese had come to California when San Francisco was the major urban center in the American West. By the time of large-scale Japanese immigration at the beginning of the twentieth century, however, Los Angeles had begun a period of dramatic population and economic growth.[20] In southern California's dynamic economy, the Japanese were able to occupy roles already filled in the Bay Area by other groups, particularly Chinese and Italians. The Bay Area did indeed have a substantial Japanese immigrant population, but while San Francisco's Japanese district was called little Osaka, that of Los Angeles was little Tokyo.

The Japanese had become California's chief target of anti-Asian prejudice by the time of the 1906 earthquake. Reinforced by long international rivalry between the United States and Japan, social conflict in California often caused or at least coincided with serious international incidents. Such was the case in 1906 when the San Francisco Board of Education attempted to force all Japanese children into the city's segregated Chinese school. After Japanese parents complained to Tokyo newspapers and the Japanese government, Japan regarded the matter as a national insult. President Theodore Roosevelt eventually forced the city to readmit Japanese children to the regular schools—the Chinese continued to be segregated—but the incident was one of many that left a bitter legacy on both sides of the Pacific. Later, California's Alien Land Act, which deprived Asian immigrants of their right to hold agricultural property, had similar repercussions.[21]

The tragic culmination of this interrelationship between international and domestic events came in the form of Executive Order 9066, issued by President Franklin Roosevelt in early 1942. The order required all people of Japanese descent living on the West Coast, immigrants and American citizens alike, to leave their homes to be interned in goverment camps for the duration of World War II. The action was justified as a wartime emergency measure, but it served no valid military or security purpose. Rather, it was the logical outcome of anti-Asian fears and stereotypes that had been developing in California and the nation at least since the initial arrival of the Chinese in 1852.[22]

By the time of World War II, Congress had, in effect, extended Chinese exclusion to Japanese immigration as well. The immigration laws of the 1920s instituted quotas that not only sharply reduced migrations from southern and eastern Europe but also banned most additional immigrants from Asia. However, quotas were not applied to the western hemisphere, and increasing numbers of Mexicans replaced earlier arrivals from Europe and Asia in the California labor market. Immigration from the Philippines, then an American possession exempted from Asian exclusion, also took up some of the slack. Although most Mexicans traveled overland to southern California and the San Joaquin valley, Filipinos often came by sea to San Francisco, making the Bay Area and central California's agricultural regions the chief centers of Filipino immigrant population.[23]

The 1930s Depression greatly reduced the demand for immigrant labor. Some local California authorities even forcefully repatriated Mexicans by cutting off relief benefits, and Congress placed severe restrictions on further Filipino immigration. But the labor needs of World War II's superheated economy produced vast new migrations to the Bay Area. The local black population soared as did the Hispanic segment, spurred by new immigration from Mexico and Central America. As a wartime ally, China could no longer be denied the right of legal immigration, and in 1943, Congress ended sixty years of exclusion, granting China a token annual quota of 105 arrivals. After the war, Japan and the newly independent Philippines also received similar small quotas.[24]

The great change in immigration policy, however, came in 1965 as a result of new racial attitudes formed in the war and postwar eras. Congress finally scrapped the quota system with its built-in national and racial bias favoring northwestern Europe, and for the first time since 1882, U.S. immigration laws gave Asia equal status with Europe.[25] In the Bay Area, the result has been vast new waves of Chinese and Filipino immigration that have dramatically changed the region's demography. At the same time, Indochinese refugee provisions have produced new communities of Vietnamese, Cambodians, and Laotians.

Asians in general have been the fastest growing segment of the Bay Area population, but the number of both legal and undocumented arrivals from Mexico and Central America have also substantially increased. In addition, recent immigrants from Europe, the Middle East, and the Indian subcontinent are significant components of San Francisco's population.[26] To the extent that the city remains an important immigrant port of entry, it is by way of the San Francisco International Airport. Since the Pan American Clipper inaugurated transpacific service in the 1930s, San Francisco has had major air links with the Far East. Nevertheless, today's airline routes often dictate that Asians arriving in the city must have already gone through immigration entry procedures in Los Angeles or Seattle.

As in the nineteenth century, the Bay Area's dynamic economy attracts most of today's new arrivals. Asian and Hispanic women, for example, do much of the assembly work in Silicon Valley, and immigrants are heavily represented in San Francisco's massive tourist and convention industries. The city's largest union, the hotel and restaurant workers, is predominantly non-white and heavily immigrant. Far Eastern immigrants, in particular, have also been attracted by the region's long heritage of Asian settlement and the resulting presence of large Asian-American communities.

In 1980 slightly over 28 percent of San Francisco's residents were foreign born—a higher percentage than that of either Los Angeles or New York. People of Asian descent alone comprise about a quarter of the city's population.[27] San Francisco's experience in this regard has been much like that of California as a whole. The state is now the destination of approximately one-quarter of all immigrants coming to the United States, and immigration may account for as much as one-half of California's total population increase between 1980 and the year 2000. By the early twenty-first century, the Bay Area's population and that of the state as a whole may well contain a "majority of minorities." Or, to put it more accurately, eventually there will be no majority group in the regional and state population.[28]

The Bay Area's multinational heritage, begun during the gold rush, is thus alive and well. San Francisco continues to be both an immigrant city and, to a lesser extent, an immigrant depot—an important destination and a port of entry for the vast multiethnic migrations that are changing the face of the nation.

Notes

Portions of this essay are based on the author's *Golden Gate Metropolis, Perspectives in Bay Area History* (Berkeley: Institute of Governmental Studies, University of California Press 1985).

1. Elliott Barkan, "New York City: Immigrant Depot, Immigrant City," in *Freedom's Doors, Immigrant Ports of Entry to the United States* (Philadelphia: The Balch Institute, 1986), 1–12.

2. Best sources for early gold rush San Francisco are Roger W. Lotchin, *San Francisco 1846–1856: From Hamlet to City* (New York: Oxford University Press, 1974); and Gunther Barth, *Instant Cities: Urbanization and the Rise of San Francisco and Denver* (New York: Oxford University Press, 1975).

3. For immigrant numbers and percentages, see William A. Bullough, *The Blind Boss and His City: Christopher Augustine Buckley and Nineteenth-Century San Francisco* (Berkeley: University of California Press, 1979); United States Bureau of the Census, *Population of Cities 1790–1900* (Washington, D.C., 1901), 430–32, and *Tenth Census of the United States, 1880; Statistics of Cities* (Washington, D. C., 1887), II, 769.

4. For a discussion of sea routes, see John H. Kemble, *San Francisco Bay: A Pictorial History* (New York: Bonanza Press, 1957); Oscar Lewis, *Sea Routes to the Gold Fields* (New York: Alfred A. Knopf, 1949); and Robert J. Schwendinger, *International Port of Call: An Illustrated History of the Golden Gate* (Woodland Hills, Calif. Windsor Press, 1985).

5. For Irish participation in the establishment, see Bullough, *Blind Boss;* and Richard Dillon, *Iron Men* (Point Richmond, Calif.: Candela Press, 1984).

6. For general coverage of the Irish, see R. A. Burchell, *The San Francisco Irish 1848–1880* (Berkeley: University of California Press, 1980); and James P. Walsh, ed., *The San Francisco Irish 1850–1976* (San Francisco: Irish Literary and Historical Society, 1978).

7. Schwendinger, *International Port of Call*, includes discussions of immigrants in the maritime labor force. Also see Irena Narell, *Our City: The Jews of San Francisco* (San Diego: Howell-North, 1981); and Fred Rosenbaum, *Free to Choose: The Making of a Jewish Community in the American West* (Berkeley: Western Jewish History Center, 1976).

8. Best sources on the Italians are Dino Cinel, *From Italy to San Francisco: The Immigrant Experience* (Stanford: Stanford University Press, 1982); Deanna P. Gumina, *The Italians of San Francisco 1850–1930* (New York: Center for Migration Studies, 1978); and Andrew Rolle, *The Immigrant Upraised* (Norman: University of Oklahoma Press, 1968).

9. Richard Dillon, *North Beach, The Italian Heart of San Francisco* (Novato, Calif.: Presidio Press, 1985).

10. Stewart E. Perry, *The San Francisco Scavangers* (Berkeley: University of California Press, 1978).

11. Immigrant participation in the labor movement is discussed in Ira B. Cross, *A History of the Labor Movement in California* (Berkeley: University of

California Press, 1935); and David Selvin, *The Sky Full of Storm* (San Francisco: California Historical Society, 1966).

12. Alexander Saxton, *The Indispensable Enemy: Labor and the Anti-Chinese Movement in California* (Berkeley: University of California Press, 1971).

13. For general coverage of Chinese immigration, see Jack Chen, *The Chinese of America* (San Francisco: Harper & Row, 1980); Stuart C. Miller, *The Unwelcome Immigrant: The American Image of the Chinese* (Berkeley: University of California Press, 1970); and Mary Roberts Coolidge, *Chinese Immigration* (New York: Holt, 1909).

14. Gunther Barth, *Bitter Strength: A History of the Chinese in the United States* (Berkeley: University of California Press, 1964); Sanford M. Lyman, *The Asian in the West* (Reno: University of Nevada Press, 1970).

15. Saxton, *Indispensable Enemy.*

16. A standard source for the anti-Chinese movement is Elmer C. Sandmeyer, *The Anti-Chinese Movement in California* (Urbana: University of Illinois Press, 1939). For a discussion of the Workingman's Party, see Neil L. Shumsky, "San Francisco Workingmen Respond to the Modern City," *California Historical Quarterly* 55, no. 1 (1976): 46–57.

17. Charles Wollenberg, *All Deliberate Speed: Segregation and Exclusion in California Schools 1855–1975* (Berkeley: University of California Press, 1976), 28–47.

18. Him Mark Lai et al., *Island: Poetry and History of Chinese Immigrants on Angel Island* (San Francisco: San Francisco Study Center, 1980); Francis Clauss, *Angel Island: Jewel of San Francisco Bay* (Menlo Park, Calif.: Briarcliff, 1982).

19. Among the sources for the twentieth-century Chinese immigrant experience are Maxine Hong Kingston, *China Men* (New York: Alfred A. Knopf, 1980), and *The Woman Warrior* (New York: Alfred A. Knopf, 1976). Also see Victor Nee and Brett De Bary Nee, *Long Time Californ': A Documentary Study of an American Chinatown* (New York: Pantheon, 1973).

20. General coverage of Japanese immigration is included in Bill Hosokowa and Robert A. Wilson, *East to America: A History of Japanese in the United States* (New York: Morrow, 1980); and Harry H. L. Kitano, *Japanese Americans: Evolution of a Subculture* (Englewood Cliffs, N.J.: Prentice-Hall, 1969).

21. Roger Daniels, *The Politics of Prejudice: The Anti-Japanese Movement in California and the Struggle for Japanese Exclusion* (Berkeley: University of California Press, 1978); Wollenberg, *All Deliberate Speed*, 48–81.

22. Among the many works on the relocation are Jacobus Ten Broek et al., *Prejudice, War, and the Constitution* (Berkeley: University of California Press, 1954); Roger Daniels, *Concentration Camps U.S.A.* (New York: Holt, Rinehart & Winston, 1971); and Yoshiko Uchida, *Desert Exile: The Uprooting of a Japanese American Family* (Seattle: University of Washington Press, 1982).

23. Good sources on Mexican immigration are Albert Camarillo, *Chicanos in California: A History of Mexican Americans in California* (San Francisco: Boyd & Fraser, 1984); and Rodolfo Acuna, *Occupied America: A History of Chicanos* (New York: Harper & Row, 1981). Coverage of Filipino immigration is included in H. Brett Melendy, *Asians in America: Filipinos, Koreans, and East Indians* (New York: Hippocrene, 1981).

24. David M. Reimers, *Still the Golden Door: The Third World Comes to America* (New York: Columbia University Press, 1985), 11–38.

25. Reimers, *Still the Golden Door*, 63–90; Thomas J. Archdeacon, *Becoming Americans: An Ethnic History* (New York: The Free Press, 1983), 202–36.

26. United States Bureau of the Census, *1980 Census of Population: Detailed*

Population Characteristics, California (Washington, D.C., 1983), 18–20.

27. United States Bureau of the Census, *1980 Census of Population: General Social and Economic Characteristics, California* (Washington, D.C., 1983), 49.

28. For a foreign perspective on California's demographic future, see *The Economist* (19–25 May 1984): 1–22 (survey section).

"Immigration through the Port of San Francisco": A Comment

Hilary Conroy

Charles Wollenberg's point that Angel Island in San Francisco Bay was very different from Ellis Island is well taken. It had no Statue of Liberty; it was no gateway to freedom. Instead, it was a detention center for Asian immigrants; a place for exclusion, suspicion, and deportation rather than a welcome mat for immigrants—at least up until World War II.

Given this point and the celebrative nature of the Freedom's Doors summer of 1986, it is not surprising that Professor Wollenberg's essay has almost as much to say about Europeans as Asians. Irish, Italian, and Jewish immigrants made up the majority of the city's foreign-born residents, although San Francisco was not generally their port of entry. Such street names as Kearney, Geary, Powell, Anza, Arguella, Fulton, and Eddy are certainly not Asian; indeed, it is Stockton Street that runs through Chinatown. Nor are other big names in San Francisco—Sutro, Giannini, Ghiradelli, Spreckels, Ruef, Rossi—Asian.[1]

Thus, I have no quarrel with Wollenberg's attention to the non-Asian immigrants, who, for the most part, came to San Francisco from Europe via east coast ports of entry. In addition, Wollenberg has done a good job with Chinese exclusion, the background and effect of the 1882 law that marked "a turning point in American history [as the] first instance of substantial immigration restriction."[2] Of course, this exclusion of the Chinese was to provide the rationale for subsequent exclusion in the Asiatic Exclusion Law of 1924 of the Japanese and other co-called orientals, including "high-cast Aryan" Hindus as nonassimilable aliens ineligible for citizenship.[3]

Nevertheless, there was a brighter side even in those dark days of Asian exclusion—Honolulu and Hawaii, generally. Honolulu, not San Francisco, was the real port of entry for Asians, or at least it was, as it became known in the era of Theodore Roosevelt, the main vestibule.[4] Moreover, although the situation in Hawaii was not without its problems,

156

there was much more of an "aloha" spirit than in California. A few remarks about Honolulu and Asian immigration seem appropriate, given Hawaii's importance for the early-stages of both Japanese and Korean immigration.[5]

In general, Asian immigration was sugar coated in Hawaii, with a double entendre intended. Asians were brought in to work the sugar (and later pineapple) plantations, but although their wages were low, work hours were long, and the sun was hot, Hawaii provided a great improvement over what these immigrants were used to at home. Furthermore, there was a concerted effort, especially after a minor fiasco with the importation of the first Japanese labor contingent in 1868, to keep everybody happy.[6] Hence, considerable sugar coating. This effort, however, did not include offering Asian immigrants a significant role in the political power structure, although the Japanese were told they had been excluded from membership in the newly created all white legislature inadvertently.[7]

Indeed, after the Japanese government investigated and complained about Hawaii's handling of the so-called first-year people (*Gannen mono*) immigrants of 1868, the American powers-that-were in Hawaii were very careful in handling Japan and the Japanese, which helped the cause of other Asians as well. Following King Kalakaua's visit to Japan in 1881, Robert W. Irwin, a well-connected American (descendant of Benjamin Franklin), managed to restart immigration. He continued to supervise it, keeping a very close watch to be sure the Japanese were inspected, respected, and happy until he was ousted by Sanford Dole and the annexationists in 1894 for being rather too pro Japanese.[8] Dole and Company found, however, that they could not even discriminate against saké in favor of California wine as they wished to do, and by the time of annexation (1898), Hawaii had settled into a spirit of at least semialoha with its Asian population. That spirit was soon enhanced by the possibility that Hawaii's Asians could now more easily depart for California if dissatisfaction set in. In fact, Honolulu proceeded to welcome Koreans and then Filipinos as a safety valve labor force as the Chinese and Japanese went on to higher things than contract labor in cane fields.[9] The planters were very skilled in keeping different ethnic groups from forming a fully interethnic labor movement, but they employed paternalism to keep the harvests coming, using benevolence and benevolent associations rather than cruel Kearney-ism and exclusionism as in California.

To make a long story short, Hawaii's early experience resulted in a significantly different handling of the Japanese minority during the Pacific war. In California during the 1940s, the negative heritage of exclusion prevailed, as alien Japanese and Japanese Americans were both rounded up and sent off to relocation centers.[10] In Hawaii, despite the trauma of Pearl Harbor, except for a few presumably dangerous individuals, the Japanese population was left undisturbed.[11] In more recent times, when such names as Inoue, Matsunaga, and Fong catalog the political leadership of the fiftieth state, it has become clear that its vestibule port of entry, Honolulu, was a freedom's door substitute for San Francisco insofar as Asians were concerned.[12]

Notes

1. In addition to works cited by Professor Wollenberg see Walton Bean, *Boss Ruef's San Francisco* (Berkeley: Univ. of California Press, 1952) for a fascinating study of that city's turn of the century politics. See also Stuart C. Miller, *The Unwelcome Immigrant* (Berkeley: Univ. of California Press, 1969) for a well-developed argument that the Chinese exclusion movement had strong advocacy in eastern states as well as on the West Coast. Jonathan Goldstein also discusses this issue from an analysis of archival materials located in Philadelphia and other east coast cities. Jonathan Goldstein, *Philadelphia and the China Trade* (College Park, Penn. Pennsylvania State University Press, 1978).

2. Early but still useful studies are Mary Roberts Coolidge, *Chinese Immigration* (New York: Henry Holt & Co., 1909) and Rodman W. Paul, "The Origin of the Chinese Exclusion Issue in California," *Mississippi Valley Historical Review* 25 (1938): 181–96. Francis L. K. Hsu's *Chinese and Americans: Passage to Differences* (Honolulu: University of Hawaii Press, 1981) throws much light on attitudinal problems. Shirley Hune, "The Politics of Chinese Exclusion: Legislative-Executive Conflict, 1876–1882," *Amerasia Journal* 9 (1982): 5–27 and H. Mark Lai, "The Chinese Exclusion Act: Observations of a Centennial," *Amerasia Journal* 9 (1982): 1–4 give recent perspectives. See also Roger Daniels, "American Historians and East Asian Immigrants," *Pacific Historical Review* 43 (1974): 449–72.

3. See Roger Daniels, *The Politics of Prejudice: The Anti-Japanese Movement in California and the Struggle for Japanese Exclusion* (Berkeley: University of California Press, 1962; 2d ed. 1977) for the standard study of the problem. Yamato Ichihashi's *Japanese in the United States* (Stanford: Stanford University Press, 1932) was a remarkably objective earlier study coming just before the Japanese American antagonism leading to the Pacific war began to heat up. Key cases preceding the Exclusion Law of 1924 were *Takao Ozawa* v. *United States* (260 U.S. 173), *The Supreme Court Reporter*, vol. 43 (St. Paul, Minn.: West Publications Co., 1924), 65–69 and *United States* v. *Bhagat Singh Thind* (261 U.S. 204), SCR, 338–42. Ozawa was a well-assimilated, English-speaking Christian Japanese who had graduated from high school in Berkeley, California. His petition for naturalization was denied on the grounds that he was neither Caucasian nor of African descent. Thind, a high-caste Hindu, claimed that he *was* Caucasian, but the court held that the racial background of Caucasians from India was probably mixed and even if it were not, Thind could not be considered white in the United States. See also, Jeff H. Lesser, "Always 'Outsiders': Asians, Naturalization, and the Supreme Court," *Amerasia Journal* 12 (1985–86): 83–100.

4. A. Whitney Grisold in his now classic *The Far Eastern Policy of the United States* (New York: Harcourt Brace & Co., 1938) gives an early analysis of the "vestibule" problem in Chap. 9, 333–79. See also Thomas A. Bailey, *Theodore Roosevelt and the Japanese-American Crisis* (Stanford, Calif. Stanford University

Press, 1934). In their fine recent study, Robert A. Wilson and Bill Hosokawa refer to Japanese immigration from Hawaii, Mexico, and Canada as intermediary or secondary immigration that President Roosevelt was empowered to prevent by the Immigration Act of 20 February 1907. *East To America: A History of the Japanese in the United States*, (New York: Quill, 1982), especially chap. 8, 124–25.

5. See Hilary Conroy, *The Japanese Frontier in Hawaii, 1868–1898* (Berkeley: University of California Press, 1953); reprinted as *The Japanese Expansion into Hawaii, 1868–1898* (San Francisco: R and E Research Associates, 1973); and Wayne Patterson, "The Korean Frontier in America," 2 vols. (Ph.D. diss., University of Pennsylvania, 1977). Patterson's study is scheduled for publication by the University of Hawaii Press.

6. The "fiasco" of 1868 in which 147 Japanese laborers came to Hawaii delayed the beginning of the big immigration push by seventeen years, but even it ended happily for most of the immigrants. See the detailed study from archival sources by Masaji Marumoto entitled "'First-Year' Immigrants to Hawaii and Eugene Van Reed," in Hilary Conroy and T. Scott Miyakawa; eds., *East across the Pacific: Historical and Sociological Studies of Japanese Immigration and Assimilation* (Santa Barbara, Calif.: ABC-CLIO Press, 1972), 5–39. The fiasco resulted in an investigation and the suspension of immigration by the Japanese government. It was mainly due to poor preparation and hasty mismanagement by Hawaii's American agent in Japan, Van Reed. The second beginning in 1885 was much more carefully arranged—to maximize satisfaction on both sides—with Robert W. Irwin, Hawaii's new representative in Japan, watching the details. See Yukiko Irwin and Hilary Conroy, "R. W. Irwin and Systematic Immigration to Hawaii," in Conroy and Miyakawa, eds., *East Across the Pacific*, 40–55.

7. Documents on the constitution matter are contained in Japanese Foreign Office (Gaimushō), *Nihon Gailō Bunsho* (Foreign Affairs Documents) 21 (1888):424, 443–64, 459–64 especially. See also Conroy, *The Japanese Frontier in Hawaii*, 96–99.

8. On Kalakaua's visit to Japan, see William N. Armstrong, *Around the World with a King* (New York: F. A. Stokes, 1904). The Irwin system, which was worked out between R. W. Irwin as Hawaii's representative in Japan and Irwin's great Japanese friend in high places, Count Inoue Kaoru, required health certification, interpreters, doctors, and inspectors to see that work and workers fared well on the plantations. A Japanese consul general was also to keep watch on conditions of the workers in Hawaii; wives (up to some 20 percent of the total number of immigrants—5,487 out of 28,691—until 1894 were women) were allowed to come, and Buddhist clergy were given equal rights with Christian missionaries to organize and proselytize. See chap. 7, "The Convention-Contract System," and chap. 9, "Japanese Society Comes to Hawaii," in Conroy, *The Japanese Frontier*. Irwin's ouster in 1894 is explained by Yukiko Irwin, in Conroy and Miyakawa, 51–53. Wilson and Hosokawa entitle their chapter on Hawaii "Hawaiian Success Story," *East to America*, (chap. 10).

9. While awaiting annexation by the United States, the Republic of Hawaii (1894–98) under President Dole indulged in discrimination against the Japanese in various ways. One of the most offensive was to put a high import duty on saké by classifying it as a grain alcohol rather than a wine. When self-styled Japanese merchants and businessmen of Hawaii protested, Dole vetoed the measure, and he and his foreign minister were very much on the defensive. See *Pacific Commercial Advertiser*, 16 June 1896; Merchants to Dole, 13 June 1896, Archives of Hawaii, Foreign Office and Executive, President file. The politically dominant haoles (whites) of Hawaii, who had become very tense and defensive about the

growing Asian immigrant population during the Republic of Hawaii period, relaxed greatly after annexation in August 1898. Instead of seeking ways of curtailing further Asian immigration, as had been their purpose since the end of R. W. Irwin's government-sponsored convention contract system in 1894, they now encouraged more workers to come, and private immigration companies, which had been trying to promote such now had an open sesame, of which they took full advantage. See Alan Takeo Moriyama, *Imingaisha: Japanese Emigration Companies and Hawaii* (Honolulu: University Hawaii Press, 1985), especially 144–49. Ronald Takaki discusses the transition from mainly Japanese to Korean and Filipino immigration to Hawaii in *Pau Hana: Plantation Life and Labor in Hawaii, 1835–1920* (Honolulu: University of Hawaii Press, 1983), especially 46–56. Also Miriam Sharma, "Pinoy in Paradise," *Amerasia Journal* 7 (1980): 91–117.

10. Among the many books on the wartime relocation of Japanese see especially Roger Daniels, *The Decision to Relocate the Japanese* (Philadelphia: Lippincott, 1975), and his *Concentration Camps USA* (New York: Holt, Rinehart & Winston, 1972); Peter Irons, *Justice at War: The Story of the Japanese American Internment Cases* (New York: Oxford University Press, 1983).

11. In Hawaii, evacuating the Japanese population was considered unnecessary and unfeasible and they were "allowed as much freedom as the rest of the civilian population"; see Audrie Gardner and Ann Loftis, *The Great Betrayal: The Evacuation of the Japanese-Americans during World War II* (London: Collier-MacMillan, 1969), especially 20–21. Dillon S. Meyer, director of the War Relocation Authority, says in his memoir of the evacuation that "the Western Defense Command pressed strongly for the evacuation of several thousand Issei and Nisei from Hawaii. Fortunately, Admiral Nimitz and General Emmons did not agree," and very few were evacuated to the mainland, although some of the few who were proved to be "hardnosed toughs"; see Meyer, *Uprooted Americans: The Japanese Americans and the War Relocation Authority during World War II* (Tuscon: University of Arizona Press, 1971), 243–44. See also, "The United Japanese Society of Hawaii," James H. Okahata, *A History of the Japanese in Hawaii* (Honolulu: UJSH, 1971), especially chap. 30, entitled "Enemy Aliens." In 1949, while memories were still fresh, the author interviewed Mr. Soga Yasutaro, editor of Hawaii's largest Japanese newspaper of prewar days. He had been singled out as a dangerous alien and sent to an Arizona relocation center. "I learned to play softball there," he said.

12. Of course, it is possible to take a more jaundiced view of race relations in Hawaii, as do Theon Wright, *The Disenchanted Isles* (New York: Dial Press, 1972); Paul Jacobs and Saul Landau, *To Serve the Devil* (New York: Random House, 1971), vol. 2; John Reinecke, *Feigned Necessity* (San Francisco: Chinese Materials Center, 1979); Lawrence Fuchs, *Hawaii Pono* (New York: Harcourt & Brace, 1961); and to a certain extent the works of Takaki, Moriyama, and indeed Conroy, cited in notes 5, 6, and 9. But a recent (summer 1986) visit to Hawaii after some years of absence reminded me just how far ahead of most of the world race relations are in Hawaii and that Sidney Gulick's old *Mixing the Races in Hawaii* (Honolulu: Hawaiian Mission Board, 1937) might have been more on target in its optimism than seemed ever possible at the time.

7

Immigration through the Port of Los Angeles

Elliott Barkan

In June 1983, *Time* magazine ran a cover story entitled "The New Ellis Island."[1] Its theme was that Los Angeles is being invaded. Writer Kurt Andersen added that even "in San Diego, nearly 2,500 Mexicans, Salvadorans, and Guatemalans are waved through each month." An invasion? Waved through? Twenty-five hundred per month *there*? A new Ellis Island in Los Angeles? Firt of all, immigrants are *not* waved through, and in San Diego 617 immigrants legally entered the country during that month, only 6,659 during that entire fiscal year. Even at San Ysidro, which had ranked fourth in the nation as a port of entry during the early 1970s but had slipped to seventh in 1983, only fifteen hundred newcomers were processed that June, and its average for the year was under twelve hundred per month.[2] What, then, about the invasion theme and the new title of Los Angeles? Has that city really been experiencing such an onslaught? Are Rand Corporation demographer Kevin McCarthy and others correct in comparing it to New York's famed portal of portals? And, finally, what about the claim in Andersen's article that in 1982 alone ninety thousand immigrants settled in Los Angeles and two million since 1970?

These questions can best be placed in perspective by noting that prior to 1929 Los Angeles was so insignificant a port of entry that the government kept no separate records for it. During the next quarter-century, it received .5 percent of the nation's immigrants (15,177), whereas San Francisco processed nearly 2 percent—and New York, 59 percent of the total.[3] In all of 1955 Los Angeles received 1,411 immigrant admissions; approximately another quarter-century later, in 1982 (no data exist for 1980 and 1981), it was greeting an average of nearly 8,000 immigrants each month (95,864 that year),[4] compared to about 9,300 for New York City. Does that warrant a new title for the City of Angels? More importantly, why did that city not play a more significant role earlier, and how and why did it become prominent when it did—after 1955?

Filipinos arriving at Los Angeles airport, ca. 1950. *(Courtesy of Visual Communications, Asian American Studies Center, Inc.)*

Early Immigration

When the pueblo of Los Angeles was founded in 1781, it was a Spanish outpost more easily reached overland from Mexico than by sea. Aside from Spanish friars, no Europeans made an effort to settle there, and early Angelenos made little use of the bay at San Pedro over 20 miles to the south. In fact, prior to Mexican independence in 1822, few ships stopped in that bay or anywhere else in California.

During the twenty-six years of Mexican rule, San Pedro was busier, and many ships sailed into San Pedro and waited for the "lighters"—flat bottomed boats—to carry passengers and cargo near shore. Often, people and goods had to be carried part way to dry land. Newcomers could then take the Sepulveda family's stagecoach line northward from the bay to Los Angeles. When that pueblo was incorporated as an American city in April 1850, its population had risen to a mere 1,610 (out of 92,500 statewide). San Francisco, though far better situated, had not done much better until gold altered the balance.[5]

Los Angeles in 1850 had no significant harbor and no convenient avenue to the interior as had New York and San Francisco. But it was in California, and as would prove even more important for its ultimate destiny, California stretched along most of the nation's Pacific rim, drawing people from many parts of the world in search of wealth. By the time New York's forerunner of Ellis Island, Castle Garden, opened in 1855, it was San Francisco that had become the western portal to America. As newcomers came mostly by sea or, after 1869, by train to, or through, San Francisco, the state's population quadrupled in the 1850s to 380,000, rose nearly 50 percent in the sixties, over 50 percent in the seventies, and 40 percent in the eighties.

By 1890, fully 30 percent of California's 1.2 million people were foreign born, nearly one-third of them Chinese and one-third German or Irish. Just a few hundred Chinese and small clusters of other groups, including some four hundred Mexicans and forty Japanese, were in Los Angeles even though it had been estimated that approximately 200,000 people may have passed through it during the 1880s as a result of the railroad fare war. Only 50,400 persons were counted in that city in 1890, but it was, nevertheless, at the threshold of rapid growth.[6]

The man who took the first step toward making Los Angeles rather than San Francisco California's candidate for the Ellis Island of the Pacific Coast was Phineas Banning, who chose to dig for gold not in the Sierras but in the mud flats of San Pedro. In 1854, two years after opening a stagecoach line to Los Angeles, he bought 2,400 acres of marsh land, drained them, and established New San Pedro, subsequently renamed Wilmington, six miles closer to Los Angeles and better protected.[7] Throughout the next half-century additional improvements to the harbor, a railroad link with Los Angeles, and finally the Southern Pacific Railroad all prepared the way for incorporating Wilmington and San Pedro into Los Angeles in 1909.[8]

The completion in 1911 of federal improvements to the harbor still did not transform Los Angeles into a significant port of entry for immigrants. It did, however, accelerate the economic development of the region, which then provided a basis for its ultimate success as a gateway to America half a century later. Meanwhile, until the 1930s at least, most immigrants in Los Angeles had lived somewhere else in the United States before settling there.[9]

Most early Mexicans in the city came from nearby Sonora, but Mexican-born people comprised only one in six residents in 1860 and one in twenty-five twenty years later (438 people). Two hundred Chinese lived near the old plaza by 1871, most apparently having moved in from the north. During the 1880s, Italians, Norwegians, Jews, and Japanese began trickling in, and, by the turn of the century, the ethnic composition of Los Angeles had become quite a bit more diverse. Nevertheless, the "ethnic" numbers were still small in 1900 compared to the total population of over 102,000. Most Angelenos were native born Americans, but the Chinese community by·the plaza had already attracted much attention: The Japanese were beginning to coalesce south of San Pedro and First streets in what would soon become Little Tokyo; Japanese farm laborers were more evident in the county; Mexicans were visible on Boyle Heights but drifting eastward as Jews moved in; and Japanese, Italian, and Scandinavian fishermen and seamen were a more common sight in and around the harbor. Greeks, Croats, Dalmatians, and others would soon be, too. Over 800 Mexicans, 2,100 Chinese, and 150 Japanese appeared in the 1900 census of the city.

A decade later, the population of Los Angeles had tripled and included over 4,000 foreign-born Japanese, almost 2,000 Chinese, and over 5,600 Mexicans, as well as 3,800 Italians and over 4,000 Russian-born persons. The census of 1920 found the Chinese population only somewhat more numerous, whereas the Japanese had more than doubled (their children had increased tenfold). Nonetheless, the 2,561 Chinese and 19,911 Japanese made up a tiny fraction, just 2.4 percent, of the county's population. The number of Mexican-born, most fleeing from the revolution, quadruped to nearly 22,000. Still, foreign-born whites made up nearly 18 percent of the county's 936,500 people, and over half of them lived in the city itself (91,722 out of 166,579). Of those 91,722, nearly 16 percent were German, 10 percent Scandinavian, and 9 percent Italian; more than 6 percent spoke Yiddish, and well over a third were British. In addition, hundreds of Arabs, Armenians, Serbs, Croats, Slovenes, and Slovaks reflected the changing sources of American immigration. However, as few of these newcomers had entered the county directly via the harbor, the city was still a destination point rather than a significant port of entry.[10]

Later Immigration

When Los Angeles did at last become a mecca for immigrants, it did so for a variety of reasons similar to and very dissimilar from those that influenced its famous sister port in the East. First, just as economic and political developments in Europe and the United States in the nineteenth century had focused attention and migration activities on the Atlantic region, to the benefit of ports on the Atlantic rim, in the twentieth century the political, military, and economic emergence of the Pacific region and the western United States enhanced the roles of west coast ports. Second, the industrial development that had made the mid-Atlantic section of the country an ideal place for immigrants seeking employment was mirrored after 1880 by Southern California's agricultural development; the discovery of oil and the advent of petroleum processing firms in and around Los Angeles during the next decade; and the growth of other diverse industries, as well as fishing and coastal shipping operations in the early 1900s.

By that time, too, just as the Erie Canal and the steam railroad had extended New York's impact beyond the valley of the Hudson River, Los Angeles had knit together the Los Angeles basin with a network of interurban electric railways and, later, highways. Within twenty years, the city itself had grown to over four hundred square miles and was the crucial nexus of that network. Somewhat amusingly, but probably accurately, the city was depicted by Andrew Rolle as replicating itself over and over—one hundred "midwestern towns that each numbered a population of ten thousand persons."

The irresistible lure of golden California was also heightened by two advantages New Yorkers could only envy. If the letters and stories that circulated from those already in California were not enough to whet the taste of others (along with all the remittances the immigrants were sending home), the promotional campaigns of the railroads, citrus growers, water districts, and new communities depicted most alluringly the "Mediterranean" climate, the lush landscaping, abundant water supply for lawns and swimming pools, and the generally inviting conditions of Southern California, "the golden land of the orange and spring eternal." This appealing climate, and the way of life it conjured up, would prove invaluable in attracting to Los Angeles millions from throughout the Pacific and Latin American regions (as well as from all parts of the nation). At the same time, Hollywood's emerging movie industry soon provided Los Angeles with the worldwide publicity that eventually cinched the city's place in the history of American immigration.[11]

During the 1920s, Los Angeles grew at a dramatic pace. The county's population jumped by 136 percent during the decade and by 1930 had reached 2.21 million people. Moreover, revised data for 1930, published in the 1940 census, indicated that the number of foreign-born whites had risen even faster (167 percent). That figure was one-and-a-half times greater than the state's overall rate, illustrating that a further shift to the south was underway.

Such growth of the foreign-born population was almost as pronounced in the city as in the county, and there is no doubt that the huge influx of Mexicans was a major factor. It is not surprising, then, that while one-fifth of the state's foreign born had entered the United States during the 1920s, 29 percent had in Los Angeles.[12] By 1930, the number of British and Armenians had doubled and that of the Jews had expanded two-and-a-half times. From Albanians to Ukrainians, from Flemish to Polish, across the board their numbers increased. Syrians, Greeks, Italians, and German and Russian Jews were now familiar Angelenos. Many were peddlers or operated grocery stores, produce markets, and many other businesses. In addition, while the Chinese population had risen by one-third, the Japanese community had grown by 80 percent to 35,400 in the county and 21,000 in the city. Furthermore, even allowing for the known confusion of the 1930 census with respect to Mexicans, at least 45 percent of the state's Mexican-born population (175,600 out of 388,138) resided in Los Angeles County. However, many Mexicans and Mexican Americans were being forced east within the city and into the county by the growing commercialization of the downtown area and were experiencing a "barrioization" that was creating a "Mexican city . . . within the heart of Los Angeles."[13]

By 1930, approximately 11.2 percent of the county's people were either nonwhites of foreign extraction or Latinos (including, I estimate, several thousand Filipinos). Another 12.8 percent were foreign-born, non-Mexican whites, and 20.3 percent were second-generation white Americans. Taken together in 1930, nearly 43 percent of Los Angeles County's population was of foreign stock, but only 2 percent were Blacks.[14] Perhaps as significant, during the 1920s, the total growth in Los Angeles was proportionally over four times greater than San Francisco's, and the rate of its foreign-population growth was over ten times that of San Francisco's. Foreigners did make up a considerably larger percentage of San Francisco's population (61.5 percent), and San Francisco was still the chief port of entry in the West, but Los Angeles had clearly taken a commanding lead as the West's principal destination for natives and foreigners. The stage was set for its full leadership role in California's—and America's—immigration history.[15]

Immigration Stations

In the early years, when few immigrants came directly to Los Angeles, no effort was made to record even their numbers, let alone how they were processed. Most were apparently first checked on board ship, and those with disease, or subject to delay for other reasons, were placed in the local jail. The rest most likely went to the customs building near Timm's Landing or, after 1900, to the second floor of the A. P. Ferl Building at Beacon and Seventh streets in San Pedro. Around 1920, by which time one-quarter of all immigrants arriving by sea were landing on the West Coast, the federal government decided that the time had come for an immigrant station in the Los Angeles harbor. As the project

Los Angeles Immigration Station, 1926. *(Courtesy of Los Angeles Department of Harbors.)*

moved ahead, the probable impact of impending quota laws was obviously either overlooked or ignored.

The building was constructed by the Los Angeles Harbor Department at the end of San Pedro's Twenty-second Street, on the west side of the harbor channel, and ships were to dock quite near this simple but imposing two-story, stone structure. On the first floor, running half the length of the building, was the inspection area, with medical and detention rooms on one side and a baggage room and railroad ticket office at the other end. Upstairs, two large rooms were set aside for those staying overnight. Two smaller rooms were designated for first-class passengers and two others for those found to have diseases. An adjacent dining room completed the main floor plan. It cost $80,000 to build and was nearly finished by spring 1922.

A dispute over the rent delayed its opening, but city officials hoped it would become a major transit point for immigrants and particularly Chinese workers crossing to the Caribbean. On 28 November 1922, the *San Pedro Daily News* carried a large banner headline, "Immigration Station Now in Use." "Nineteen Hindoos and one Japanese" had been detained there after arriving on the *Rakuyo Maru*. They had been denied entry to Mexico because they lacked the five thousand *pesos* (or equivalent) that all immigrants were required to possess, and they were kept at the station for ten days, although it was "not as yet properly fitted up for immigrants."

The building did open the following year, but the government kept no separate immigration statistics for Los Angeles until fiscal year 1929. If the 75 percent drop in immigration recorded in San Francisco was any indication of the impact on Los Angeles of the immigration laws of 1921 and 1924, not many were processed in the new station. In fact, beginning in 1928, the U.S. Post Office began to use substantial parts of the building; quota laws and then the Depression kept San Pedro from ever becoming a significant port of entry. In fiscal year 1929, the first with recorded immigration data for the port, 2,340 persons were admitted there, but the number fell to 1,607 in 1930 and, during the remaining eight years of its use, only about 3,500 immigrants were processed at that Twenty-second Street station. Most newcomers still came to Los Angeles after having initially arrived elsewhere.

Nonetheless, despite the dwindling numbers, the federal government decided to construct its own building on property it held directly across the channel entrance way on the southern end of Terminal Island. There, by early 1938, the immigration service was operating in its new three-story processing center. It received only nine thousand or so immigrants in the next seventeen years and was even pressed into service as a detention center for enemy aliens during World War II. San Francisco remained the chief western port of entry, especially for military spouses arriving after the war.[16]

Migration Streams

Momentum can be a powerful factor. Migration streams, once begun, etch lines that subsequent shiploads of immigrants eagerly follow. In the nineteenth century, as the forces of war, civil war, overpopulation, political change, religious persecution, and economic upheaval rolled across Europe, greater and greater numbers fled, many to South America and Canada but most to the United States. After 1891, two-thirds of this country's immigrants came through the open doors of Ellis Island until all of the doors to the United States were nearly closed in the 1920s. When the immigrant portals were pried slightly open two decades later, Americans found that the Second World War throughout the Pacific and America's involvement in virtually every one of its arenas had altered the balance of migration push forces and created new migration streams and channels. All the desperation and urgency that had driven (and would again drive) immigrants and refugees from Europe to the Ellis Island of the East now began unburdening even greater numbers from the densely populated lands of Asia and the South Pacific and later from

Central and South America. The Korean War increased the pressure, and American intervention in more recent wars in Southeast Asia unleashed waves of refugees to the United States, far exceeding in number those who had come from Europe.

Refugees, however, account for only part of the transformation of our immigrant population. Political unrest and uncertainty in Korea, Taiwan, the Philippines, Argentina, and Chile; civil wars in El Salvador, Guatemala, and Nicaragua; revolution in Cuba and Iran; overcrowding in Hong Kong and fear of the aftermath of Hong Kong's transfer to Chinese jurisdiction; the inability of the economies of India, Korea, and the Philippines to absorb their rising numbers of university graduates, especially in medical and engineering fields; serious underemployment and unemployment in Mexico, Ecuador, Peru, and Colombia; a general lack of opportunities in England and (along with military pressures) Thailand, Israel, and Egypt; religious and political discontent in the Soviet Union; and the desire for family reunification among Chinese, Japanese, Koreans, and Filipinos are only some of the forces in some countries that have brought ever-growing numbers of people here during the past two decades. To those throngs, of course, we must add everyone from Austria to Zambia who simply saw in America more hope than at home and the thousands of spouses and children of American military personnel stationed in many parts of Europe and Asia.[17]

As is well known, the overhaul of our immigration laws in 1965 removed discriminatory quota barriers that had contained the flow of many Asian and Pacific peoples to a small rivulet. Less than 7 percent of all America's newcomers between 1950 and 1965 were from the Asian and Pacific regions of the world. Legislative reforms were made without accurate forecast of their impact with respect to nations on the Pacific rim, but after 1965 all the forces we have just enumerated came into play. The Asian and Pacific rivulet quickly became the new human tidal wave bound for America.[18] The only remaining question was where the "Ellis Island of the West" would emerge.

Mines Field, a small airport in the former Rancho Aguaje de la Centinela, carved out of wheat, barley, and bean fields, became the official Los Angeles municipal airport in July 1928. Thirteen years later, it was Los Angeles Airport. In December 1946, when Pan American Airways began the first international flights into Los Angeles Airport, the immigration service opened its offices there. A short time later, Mexicana Airlines became the first foreign carrier to bring in newcomers. Just as the timely opening of Ellis Island had anticipated the huge influx that followed, so, too, did this new portal to America open just in time to receive the next great tide of future Americans. As it turned out, Los Angeles did not benefit so much as a port of entry for immigrant-laden ships of the sea but from its new Ellis Island for ships of the air.

The city had welcomed newcomers by land and sometimes by sea, but its destiny as an immigrant-receiving city was to be linked largely to its airport. Forces of political and social change that had irreversibly shifted our sources of immigration to the Pacific would focus attention on the West Coast and forces of technological change would make Los Angeles the most accessible of the west coast cities. By the late 1970s, it would stand out as the principal west coast port of entry and within the next decade would far surpass Honolulu, which had been the leading Pacific processing center since the mid-1960s.[19]

The emergence of Los Angeles as a major port of entry had taken decades, accelerating particularly during the 1950s. It is unlikely that even ten thousand persons had passed through the original Twenty-second Street immigration station, while perhaps nine thousand more were processed in the new Terminal Island building before it was converted to the Immigration and Naturalization Service's (INS's) regional center in 1955. While overall annual immigration fluctuated between a quarter and almost a third of a million during the 1950s, the number entering through Los Angeles began climbing steadily from 280 in 1950 to 2,500 in 1956. In the following year, Los Angeles at last surpassed San Francisco in the number of immigrants processed (3,895 to 2,984), and by 1960, Los Angeles had 8,582 immigrants—double San Francisco's total.[20]

The census of 1960 found Los Angeles at an interesting juncture—still reflecting its past immigrant patterns, yet revealing the threads of change. Obviously, quota laws, the Depression, the repatriation of Mexicans in the early 1930s, Operation Wetback (directed against undocumented Mexicans between 1952 and 1954), and just plain aging had all taken a toll of the foreign born at the same time that the city and county were benefiting immensely from the two recent wars and the concomitant economic growth. Since 1930, the city's total population had doubled (to 2.48 million), but the number of foreign born had risen by only about one-fourth (to 312,663). I estimate that the entire foreign stock in the county had increased by three-quarters (to 1,654,791, of whom 34.8 percent—576,380—were foreign-born). Yet the white ethnic distribution was quite similar to that in 1930: 12 percent British, 6 percent Scandinavian, 11 percent German or Austrian, 7 percent Italian, 8 percent Russian, over 10 percent other eastern and southern European, and nearly 11 percent Canadian.

At the same time, figures for three other groups foreshadowed new trends for Los Angeles as the destination of new waves of immigrants. In

1930, the Mexican population had equaled less than 8 percent of the county's foreign-stock population; it was now over 18 percent (299,509). Central and South Americans, who had made up a mere .1 percent earlier, were now almost 2 percent—not significant in percentage terms but 12.7 times greater numerically (31,413). Finally, all Asians represented probably 2 percent of the foreign-stock population as the Depression got under way; in 1960, they comprised 7.2 percent of that population in Los Angeles County (118,360). All told, two out of five first- and second-generation Californians resided in Los Angeles County in 1960.[21]

Western Portal to America

More complete data from the INS are available for the period since 1955, and the INS public-use computer tapes for the 1970s and 1980s in particular enable us to see the city's role with greater clarity. During the quarter-century from 1955 to 1979, almost one-fourth of all immigrants arriving or being adjusted to permanent resident status on the Pacific Coast were processed in Los Angeles, compared with 18 percent in San Francisco. On the Pacific Rim, with the exception of 1964 and 1965, only Honolulu annually surpassed Los Angeles in legal immigrants, for 7.46 percent went through Honolulu versus 3.97 percent through Los Angeles during that twenty-five-year period.

Between 1955 and 1965, a total of 83,218 people entered or had their status adjusted in Los Angeles, an average of 7,565 per year. Under the revised laws, 271,810 people were admitted there between 1966 and 1979, resulting in an increase of 157 percent in the yearly Los Angeles average to 19,415. In fact, however, annual admissions reached 45,387 in 1978 and 42,774 in 1979. In those two years, one-third of the one million new immigrants recorded by the United States were persons already in this country whose legal status was adjusted to that of permanent resident; 32 percent of that number were Southeast Asian refugees, nearly nine-tenths of them from Vietnam. Thirteen percent of these Vietnamese were processed in Los Angeles, making them the leading group admitted in Los Angeles—one in six of all those entering there in 1978 to 1979. Unquestionably, the many legislative and administrative changes between 1952 and 1978 combined with crises and pressures in the sending nations to augment the flow of Asian, Pacific, Mexican, and Central and South American immigrants—and, with them, the role of Los Angeles.[22]

But, most significantly, Los Angeles had become a port of entry in the broadest sense. It was an increasingly important gateway for the nation and California as well as a major destination for immigrants. During the period analyzed in depth, 1972 to 1979, Los Angeles certainly did not come close to matching New York City, but it was also vastly different from the leading western port of entry, Honolulu. Of the 3.6 million immigrants admitted or adjusted during these years, 28.5 percent came through New York City, 11 percent through Honolulu, and 5.45 percent via Los Angeles. Nevertheless, only 59 percent of those processed in New York City were planning to live in New York state, and only 15.2 percent of those processed in Honolulu wanted to stay in Hawaii, but 91.7 percent of the newcomers in Los Angeles intended to remain in California. Furthermore, although New York City did continue to be the foremost mecca, with nearly 18 percent of all immigrants going to or remaining there, compared with only 4.7 percent to the city of Los Angeles, no other city was a closer second, not even Miami (4.02 percent).

In three other ways, aside from the very different composition of the people admitted, the pattern developing in Los Angeles—and by extension, for the whole West Coast—was different from that of New York. First, four-fifths of all new immigrants who were bound for New York state were admitted in New York City, whereas only a little more than one-fifth of new Californians came through Los Angeles. Second, 83 percent of all immigrants who were going to New York City arrived or were processed there, but only 33 percent of those intending to reside in Los Angeles were processed there. (For example, 27.5 percent of those headed for Los Angeles entered via Honolulu.) Finally, of all those arriving or processed in New York, 52 percent planned to stay in that city, while just 38 percent of those processed in Los Angeles intended to remain in the Los Angeles area.[23]

Even so, the shift to Los Angeles continued. In the early 1980s, Los Angeles became the leading western portal to America, overtaking San Ysidro and Honolulu. This new leadership role on the Pacific rim was as solidly rooted in historical and environmental factors as New York's on the Atlantic, but those historical, environmental, and geographical variables were significantly different in the West, and it is therefore less likely that Los Angeles will ever monopolize immigration into the West as New York has in the East. North of Florida, immigration to the East Coast has long been tantamount to entering through New York City, so greatly has it dominated that region. By contrast, because of geography and the way immigration patterns to the West developed, California-Mexico border stations and the cities of San Francisco, Honolulu, Seattle, and possibly even San Diego will continue to be important. Nonetheless, by the mid-1980s Los Angeles stood second only to New York City and had come closer than any other port during the past 160 years to equaling its volume of immigrants.[24]

Exactly when in the half-century or so after 1930 did Los Angeles rise from obscurity as a port of entry to second place? Although the data for 1980 and 1981 are missing, we do know that the relative importance of Miami, Honolulu, and even San Ysidro declined for a time after 1979. Furthermore, between 1977—a peak year with 601,442 newcomers— and 1982, another peak year, with 594,131, New York City's share of all immigration slipped from 23.4 to 18.7 percent, while that of Los Angeles more than doubled from 7.5 to 16.1 percent (95,864) persons). Although New York recovered its dominant position, processing one-fourth of all those admitted in 1984 and 1985, Los Angeles remained firmly in second place: Between 1982 and 1985, Miami processed 7.4 percent and Honolulu 3.9 percent of the 2.27 million immigrants admitted. Los Angeles recorded 13.72 percent of the total—311,176 people— compared to New York's share of 22.6 percent for that entire four-year period.

The adjustment of Southeast Asian refugees to permanent resident status, which had become a major factor in the immigration picture in 1978 and 1979, was an especially important component in the spectacular 1982 Los Angeles figure of nearly 96,000 newcomers processed. That record number marked the city's ascent to second place as a port of entry and drew considerable media attention, notably the *Time* cover story we began with. Of the 45,600 Southeast Asian refugees who received immigrant resident status in California in 1982, three-fourths acquired it in Los Angeles, and they constituted more than one out of three in the Los Angeles district total that year. In fact, during the period from 1982 to 1985 (the last four years of available data), not only was one in five persons admitted in Los Angeles a Southeast Asian refugee, but the most numerous group of all was Vietnamese, as had been the case in 1978 and 1979, too. Yet, we must add that while these refugees clearly bolstered the district's number of people processed, so broad had been the diversity of immigrants admitted there that its second-place position would have remained secure without any refugees. Nonetheless, together the preference of so many immigrants and refugees for Southern California certainly reenforced the image by the early 1980s of Los Angeles as the new Ellis Island.[25]

Major Immigrant Groups

The diversity among those who have been arriving in Los Angeles has been as great as that of those entering New York, albeit involving quite

Rank Orders of Immigrants Admitted in Los Angeles and of Those Going to
the Los Angeles Area via Los Angeles and of All Immigrants Going to the City
of Los Angeles, 1972–79

Admitted/Adjusted in Los Angeles		Designating Los Angeles Area		Designating Los Angeles City	
1. Chinese	9.39%[a]	1. Cubans	9.88%	1. Mexicans	32.19%
2. Mexicans	9.17[a]	2. Vietnamse	9.25	2. Filipinos	11.21
3. Cubans	9.07[a]	3. Mexicans	8.60	3. Koreans	11.17
4. Vietnamse	8.04[a]	4. Chinese	8.00	4. Chinese	6.51
5. Salvadrns	4.96[a]	5. Salvadrns	6.46	5. Salvadrns	4.00
6. Filipnos	4.62[a]	6. Filipinos	5.15	6. Cubans	3.50
7. British	4.36[a]	7. Koreans	4.44	7. Vietnamse	2.64
8. Koreans	3.82[a]	8. Guatmlans	3.32	8. Guatmlans	2.21
9. Iranians	2.77[a]	9. Iranians	2.92	9. Japanese	1.53
10. Indians	2.71[a]	10. British	2.87	10. Iranians	1.39
11. Japanese	2.48[a]	11. Japanese	2.82	11. British	1.20

[a] One of the top ten immigrant groups in terms of number admitted.

different groups. In volume and variety, these new Americans have
certainly made Los Angeles the West's New York, and the Los Angeles
International Airport that city's Ellis Island. Consequently, Los Angeles
has played a critical role in California's progress toward becoming the
state with the greatest total population (1964), the highest number of
resident aliens (1960), the most new immigrants arriving (1976), and the
largest foreign-born population (1980).

The major groups represented by the 190,000 who entered through,
or were adjusted in, Los Angeles between 1972 and 1979 included eight
of the top ten groups nationwide (see the table that follows) but only four
among New York's top ten. And other differences abound; for example,
Iranians ranked ninth in Los Angeles but twenty-first in New York.
Salvadorans, Guatemalans, and Nicaraguans, who ranked fifth, twelfth,
and seventeenth, respectively, were more prominent in Los Angeles
than they were either nationally or in New York, while Dominicans,
Ecuadorans, Haitians, and Guyanese comprised unusually large percentages among the immigrants in New York City. These groups reflect
not just proximity and available airline connections but also long-existing
and well-known migration patterns that both legal and undocumented
migrants have followed. If we include the Japanese, the eleven leading
groups in Los Angeles contributed over 61 percent of all those processed
in Los Angeles, significantly more than New York's leading eleven (50.4
percent).

As the table indicates, four groups clearly dominated the Los Angeles
immigration scene during the 1970s: Chinese, Mexicans, Cubans, and
Vietnamese. They and Salvadorans and Filipinos were the same leading

groups both processed there and foremost in designating the Los Angeles basin as their intended or current home. Together with Koreans, the seven groups comprised a majority of all those admitted in as well as those who indicated they were remaining in the Los Angeles area. Moreover, the fact that just three groups made up a majority of all newcomers nationwide designating the City of Los Angeles reinforces the extent to which, even with the broad overall diversity of the immigrant population, a handful of groups actually dominated the profile of new foreign-born residents in the Los Angeles area. By contrast, in New York City the top three groups comprised only 28 percent, and the top seven, 46 percent.

The sizable differences between the percentages of total admissions and those designating the city of Los Angeles as their residence among Mexicans, Filipinos, and Koreans reflects the extent to which these groups were entering via such other ports as Honolulu or the California-Mexican border and heading toward the Los Angeles basin. On the other hand, for fourteen of the fifteen leading groups the percentage designating the Los Angeles area corresponds much more closely to their proportions among those admitted via Los Angeles, a strong indication that those entering or being adjusted in Los Angeles have been developing ethnic communities in smaller cities and neighborhoods adjacent to the central city, such as in Norwalk, Artesia, Glendale, Palos Verdes, Wilmington, Long Beach, Westminster, Hawthorne, and Monterey Park. Finally, highlighting the dramatically distinctive role of Los Angeles, six of the top ten groups processed in Los Angeles were Asian/Pacific/Middle Eastern; three were Latino, and one was European.[26]

These immigrant groups entering via Los Angeles stand out among all United States immigrants in several ways. For example, compared with all newcomers, somewhat more immigrants arriving in Los Angeles were female (54.2 percent versus 53 percent) and more were married (56.7 percent versus 52.3 percent). Significantly, more Mexicans and Filipinos arriving in Los Angeles were females when compared with the whole group admitted nationwide, while Korean, Japanese, Guatemalan, and German males were proportionally more prominent than among the entire group admitted nationwide. Even though slightly more women, in percentage terms, said they were housewives only and gave no other occupation, far fewer children aged fourteen and under came through compared with all immigrants (17.4 percent versus 22.4 percent). In addition, beginning in 1977, a very noticeable jump occurred in the number of older, retired people admitted in Los Angeles, which was in large measure a consequence of changes in the immigration laws and the eagerness of new citizens to bring in their parents. Furthermore, in three occupational categories, foreigners processed in Los Angeles were appreciably different from the national profile of immigrants during those eight years: Far more people there claimed managerial or clerical positions, and far fewer listed themselves as nonfarm laborers.

All these observations, however, to some degree obscure the extraordinary increases experienced by most of the nationality groups entering through Los Angeles in the 1970s. Overall, the number arrving or being processed went from 11,271 in 1972 to 29,573 in 1977 and, as noted, to 45,387 the following year and 42,774 in 1979. During the 1970s, we have observed, the first wave of Southeast Asian refugees received immigrant status, and a flood of Mexicans entered or converted their status prior to legislative changes phasing in a uniform, worldwide United States immigration policy.[27] There were also more newcomers from the Americas and substantially greater numbers of Chinese, Koreans, and Iranians. Indeed, nearly every group sampled experienced striking growth at this time. It was commonplace for the number entering Los Angeles to double between 1972 and 1979, but there was actually a sixfold increase in Iranians and East Asian Indians, a tenfold jump in Chinese, and a vast leap in Vietnamese from 57 to 8,312 in 1978 and 6,091 in 1979. Over eight thousand Laotians and Cambodians were recorded in 1978, too, and five thousand more the next year. Of course, these statistics reflect changes in status as well as new arrivals, for between 1972 and 1979, 23.6 percent of all immigrants were already in the country, and 11.8 percent were refugees.

Despite these many outstanding changes, Los Angeles was monopolizing neither the entry of any group nor even the total admissions to the western United States. None of the twenty-one groups sampled had even 40 percent of its immigrants entering through Los Angeles, although seven groups had 55 to 75 percent of all their people processed in New York City.

Finally, the 1982 to 1985 data reveal that a significant reordering of the list of leading immigrant groups processed in Los Angeles has occurred, although nine of the top eleven in the table were still the same. The most notable changes were the prominence of Southeast Asian refugees (Vietnamese ranked first, Kampucheans/Cambodians seventh, and Laotians twelfth), the rise of Koreans to second place, and the near disappearance of Cubans (from 9 percent of the total in the 1970s to less than 1 percent in the 1980s) due to the fact that few of the Cuban refugees who arrived in 1980 (the Marielitos) made their way to California.[28]

With the Los Angeles district (which is almost tantamount to Los Angeles International Airport) processing nearly 14 percent of all newcomers to America and the Los Angeles Basin remaining an important destination for close to 10 percent of them, including large numbers of

Southeast Asians, Mexicans, Koreans, Filipinos, and many Middle Eastern and Central American people, its leadership is undeniably real. But,
for reasons already discussed, that leadership will not be as pervasive as
New York's, for Los Angeles, I have suggested, is not likely to monopolize west coast immigration. Its Ellis Island will, therefore, differ from
the original not only in the whole format of proceedings but in the very
magnitude of its role. Nonetheless, data certainly indicate that Los Angeles is gathering strength and prestige in other ways than just as a port
of entry. Recent proposals by Los Angeles Mayor Tom Bradley to construct a west coast Statue of Liberty there may be part promotion and
will come to nought, but the idea does symbolize that the importance of
Los Angeles for many new Americans is not just as their portal to
America but as their destination for a life in America.[29]

New-Citizens

One critical measure of the impact of immigration patterns is the
extent to which groups persist in an area, integrate, and seek citizenship.[30] Of course, any analysis of naturalization records for the 1972
to 1980 period will include only a limited percentage of those who were
admitted during the 1970s, although after 1975 a growing proportion of
newly naturalized citizens had been admitted in the 1970s. For example,
in Los Angeles, in fiscal year 1976, 26 percent of those naturalized had
come in the 1970s; just four years later 64.5 percent had.[31] The proportion of recent immigrants naturalized in Los Angeles was at least twice
that in New York. Consequently, 5.45 percent of all immigrants went
through Los Angeles from 1972 to 1979, whereas nearly 10 percent of
all new citizens were sworn in there.

These one-in-ten new Americans who were naturalized in Los Angeles
and made up over 52 percent of California's new citizens[32] (even though
only about a fourth of the state's newcomers had gone there) provide a
profile that can help us better understand who our new Americans are.
For example, the sex ratio among these people was nearly identical to
figures for all new citizens and thus was slightly more balanced than that
of the immigrants. The percentages of those married and those divorced
were higher than nationally and considerably greater than among immigrants who were admitted. Thus, not only were many immigrants mar-
rying after arrival but many others were also paying the price of
separation and divorce for their adjustment experience.[33]

In terms of occupation, proportionally fewer of those naturalized in
Los Angeles than nationally cited no occupation (33.1 percent versus
35.8 percent). With respect to net percentages in each occupational

category, new citizens in Los Angeles held more white-collar positions and had smaller percentages in every blue-collar category: 58.2 percent versus 50.6 percent were white-collar workers, with nearly half of that group holding professional, technical, and kindred positions (27.2 percent versus 32.7 percent nationally). Finally, given that 34.7 percent of the women listed no outside occupation (housewives) but 72.8 percent indicated a married status, it is safe to assume that at least one-third of the women were married and also working outside the home at the time they applied for citizenship.

During the early 1970s, far more soldiers and veterans applied for citizenship in Los Angeles, most of them Filipinos. That persisted until 1977, by which time the end of the Vietnam war and the prominence of the newest wave of immigrants were clearly apparent. We then also see a further drop in the number of spouses and children of citizens qualifying and a jump to 89 percent (versus 82 percent nationally) of those naturalized under the general provisions that required a five-year waiting time. In 1980, the percentage of those naturalized under the general provisions in Los Angeles already exceeded that of the nation as a whole by ten points, for the city had only half the national proportion of spouses of citizens and merely one-fourth the total percentage of children of citizens. These new citizens were truly new Americans, planting new family roots here.

Even though there was only a partial overlap between new immigrants and new citizens, there was a remarkably close parallel in origins between the two groups. Five of the top six groups designating Los Angeles as their intended/current residence (Mexicans, Filipinos, Koreans, Chinese, and Cubans) were the five leading groups naturalized there. They constituted 64.6 percent of all Los Angeles immigrants but only 49.5 percent of its new citizens because many of the Asians arrived later in the decade and were not yet eligible for citizenship by 1980 and the Mexicans, who equaled nearly one-third of all newcomers bound for Los Angeles, did not apply as rapidly as did other groups.[34]

Three other points are worth making: Seven percent of those going to Los Angeles were either Salvadoran (4 percent), Guatemalan (2.2 percent), or Nicaraguan (.8 percent), a measure of the growing unrest in Central America. Some ten thousand of them came to California between 1972 and 1976, yet only about 2,500 to 2,600 were naturalized there between 1981 to 1983, suggesting that their recency of arrival may have combined with a reluctance to switch nationalities and possibly even the hope of returning home.[35] Second, in contrast, once the Vietnamese who were admitted or adjusted in the late 1970s became eligible in the early 1980s, they seized the opportunity for citizenship; nationwide, 32,850 became citizens from 1981 to 1983, and nearly 32 percent of them were naturalized in California. Finally, the small but steady numbers of arriving Argentinians, Egyptians, and (prior to 1977) Iranians do not stand out numerically among the immigrant population but do appear more prominently among new citizens in the 1980s.[36]

All in all, naturalization patterns in the 1970s and early 1980s closely mirrored the entry of a particular number of prominent groups: Filipinos, Mexicans, Chinese, Koreans, Cubans, and, most recently, Vietnamese. The number of new Cuban citizens will level off in the absence of further significant refugee admissions, and the same will likely be true for Vietnamese in the not-too-distant future. No decline in the arrival of the others is immediately foreseen, and they will continue to dominate the immigration and naturalization processes, especially in Los Angeles and California.

Impact of the New Immigrants

One last measure of the impact of the new immigration emerges from the censuses of 1970 and 1980. To put it most succinctly, while the city's population was rising merely 5.4 percent during the decade (due, in large measure, to significant out-migration by the native born), the net number of foreigners jumped 95.7 percent. True, in the basin—the Los Angeles-Long Beach urbanized area—the population rose 13.5 percent, but the number of foreign born more than doubled (up 121 percent). Only 183,619 immigrants had designated Los Angeles city as their residence when they were legally admitted between July 1969 and October 1979, yet the actual increase in foreign born was more than twice that (not adjusting for the last half of 1969—the half-year before the 1970 census was taken—or emigration, deaths, undercount, uncounted, undocumented immigrants, and so on). Although it appears from Passel's work and Muller's estimates that some of the difference does include undocumented aliens appearing for the first time in the 1980 census count, I would suggest that even if adjustments were made for the factors already noted, it is clear from data on specific groups that Los Angeles has been an important secondary destination for many immigrants.[37]

In both 1970 and 1980, there were proportionally more foreign born in the city than in the larger basin, and the ratio has been increasing (in 1970, 19.2 percent versus 17.2 percent; in 1980, 27.1 percent versus 20.4 percent). In 1980, there was also in the city a somewhat greater percentage of people of Spanish origin (27.5 percent versus 25.2 percent)[38] and of Asian and Pacific racial background (7 percent versus 5.8 percent) in Los Angeles. On the other hand, the seven major single

European ancestry groups were more dispersed, comprising 16.3 percent of the city population and 18.5 percent of that in the basin. The six principal multiple European ancestry groups included in the 1980 census made up 27.7 percent of the city's total population but a much more significant 40.2 percent of the population in the Los Angeles-Long Beach region.[39] Findings indicate, then, that Asians and recently arrived non-Mexican Latinos were more concentrated in the city, but persons of European extraction and Mexicans were more predominant in the surrounding communities as well as in the city. Not all measures are readily available for comparisons between the two census years, but the data undoubtedly strengthen the conclusion that Los Angeles has indeed become the portal for many of the newest waves of immigrants and the mecca for even more.

In an average year, immigrants from nearly 140 nations have been seeking admission in Los Angeles. Just as Koreans have transformed Olympic Boulevard and the neighborhoods of Monterey Park, Cerritos, Hollywood, and Hawthorne; Chinese from Taiwan, Hong Kong, Mainland China, and Vietnam have revitalized Chinatown; and ethnic Vietnamese have altered Westminster and made Bolsa Avenue synonymous with their own familiar sights, sounds, and tastes. Samoans can be found most prominently in the southern part of the county (especially in Carson), while Arabs and Armenians are present in the north (particularly Glendale); the English are quite noticeable in Santa Monica and Iranians in Beverly Hills—except on Sundays, when they fill the parks, strolling and socializing along Ocean Boulevard in Santa Monica. Central and South Americans have made the central and downtown areas of the city truly Latino, and Mexicans continue to make their way to Boyle Heights, El Monte, and East Los Angeles. Filipinos wend their paths to the central city, West Covina, and Wilmington; Thai entrepreneurs draw more and more of their compatriots to the Hollywood and Melrose districts, transforming Sunset Boulevard and Melrose Avenue; and Cambodians concentrate in Long Beach and, most recently, in Echo Park.[40]

Other groups may be more scattered, such as the Japanese and Chinese in Culver City, Gardena, Palos Verdes, and Monterey Park; Soviet Jews and Israelis in many parts of the San Fernando Valley; and East Asian Indians in Palms and Artesia. But annual holidays, parades, and special events make it clear that Los Angeles is a city every bit as ethnically rich as New York though with considerably different ingredients.

The city of Los Angeles may not receive quite the number of immigrants that some ascribe to it (at least with respect to legal ones) and Los

Angeles International Airport may not quite constitute a new Ellis Island, for it is not likely to represent to the West Coast what New York's Ellis Island was to the East Coast. But on the West Coast, Los Angeles is now the leading port of entry and the single foremost destination of newcomers; it is creating its own version of the Ellis Island–New York experience and, in a sense, is going beyond the loosely used label of a new Ellis Island. Los Angeles may truly be the prototype of the twenty-first-century city or region in the United States: not one center nor one city, not one dominant group nor one identity, but a spellbinding diversity most truly representative of what the nation is today and will become tomorrow.[41]

While these new waves of immigrants will probably be no more successful than prior ones in altering the fundamental norms of American society, they will, in all likelihood, contribute substantially to the general social, cultural, and political milieus. Thus, as political affairs writer Kevin Phillips recently observed, "It may be that 21st Century California candidates *will* find it political to eat dim sum and develop a taste for serrano chiles before they pitch the electorate in greater Los Angeles."[42]

Notes

1. Kurt Andersen, "The New Ellis Island," *Time* 13 June 1983, 13–25. See also the excellent special issue of *Time*, "Immigrants. The Changing Face of America," 8 July 1985.

2. U.S. Department of Justice, *Annual Report of the Immigration and Naturalization Service, 1970–1979*, table 5, and unpublished tables for 1982 to 1984, furnished by the statistics section of INS,—with many thanks to Margaret Sullivan and Michael Hoefler.

3. Unpublished tables from the INS. At least as far back as 1937, published tables included Los Angeles in the ports of entry data. From 1945 to 1979, they were labeled table 5. None are available for 1980 to 1981, and, since then, they have been IMM 5.1 in the INS's *Statistical Yearbook*s. However, beginning in 1984, that table includes only new immigrants and not the total number processed and given permanent resident status in each port.

4. About twice that number of nonimmigrants also entered through Los Angeles in 1982 (*Statistical Yearbook*, 1982, 197). In the most recent report available, for 1985, 76,011 were admitted through Los Angeles versus 140,796 via New York (INS public use tape).

5. Andrew Rolle, *Los Angeles. from Pueblo to City of the Future* (San Francisco: Boyd and Fraser, 1981), 8–21; Lynn Bowman, *Los Angeles: Epic of a City* (Berkeley: Howell North, 1974), 328–38; and Oliver Vickery, *Harbor Heritage* (Mountain View, Calif.: Morgan Press, 1979), 25, 33, 84.

6. Allyn C. Loosely, "Foreign-Born Population in California, 1848–1920" (M.A. thesis, University of California, 1927), 21, 32; Andrew Rolle, *Los Angeles*, 30, 37; John Modell, *The Economics and Politics of Racial Accommodation. The Japanese of Los Angeles, 1900–1942* (Urbana: University of Illinois Press, 1977),

17, 24; and William Mason and John A. McKinley, *The Japanese of Los Angeles* (Los Angeles: County Museum of Natural History, paper no. 1, 1969), 1–5.

7. Harris Newmark, *Sixty Years in Southern California, 1853–1913*, 4th ed. rev. (Los Angeles: Zeitlin and Ver Brugge, 1970), 23; Vickery, *Harbor Heritage*, 7–8; Rolle, *Los Angeles*, 24–25; and Merry Thompson, "The Miracle of a Muddy Tideflat" (Los Angeles: Junior League, 1980). The latter is provided to people visiting the General Phineas Banning Residence Museum in Wilmington and is a good short history of the harbor, accompanying an excellent photo display on San Pedro's history.

8. Vickery, *Harbor Heritage*, 106, 137, 142; Rolle, *Los Angeles*, 30, 42, 52; and Thompson, "The Miracle,: 9, 21.

9. Robert Weinstein, a well-known local expert on the history of shipping, remarked to the author that there was "no great reason [for immigrants] to come to San Pedro" until the 1920s. Telephone interview, 26 April 1985. See, too, Modell, *Japanese of Los Angeles*, 20.

10. Richard Griswold de Castillo reported that there were 242 foreign-born Mexicans in Los Angeles in 1850 out of 1215 Spanish-speaking people; in 1860, 640 out of 2,069; and in 1880, 438 out of 2,166; see *Los Angeles Barrio, 1850–1890. A Social History* (Berkeley: University of California Press, 1979), 40. Albert Camarillo estimates the whole Mexican population in 1900 as between three thousand and five thousand; at least double that in 1910; and well over thirty thousand in 1920; see *Chicanos in a Changing Society* (Cambridge: Harvard University Press, 1979), 20. Ricardo Romo gave the 1920 figure as 33,644 in *East Los Angeles. History of a Barrio* (Austin: University of Texas Press, 1983), 80. See Mason, *The Japanese*, 3–4 and 6, for the other figures.

The 1930 census indicated that there were 36,248 Chinese and 41,356 Japanese in California in 1910; thus, Los Angeles was yet to draw them heavily, although between 2,000 and 3,000 Japanese moved there following the 1906 earthquake (Mason, *The Japanese*, 16). In 1920, Los Angeles County's 2,561 Chinese were 9 percent of the state's 28,812 Chinese, and the 19,911 Japanese in the county equaled 28 percent of the 71,952 in California. While two-thirds of the nation's Chinese were in the state, over 88 percent of mainland Japanese were; see U.S. Bureau of Census, *Fifteenth Census of the United States: 1930. Population*, vol. 2, *General Report*, tables 9 and 11; and vol. 3, part 1, *Alabama–Missouri*, California tables 13 and 17.

In September and October 1975, Emanuel Parker wrote a six-part series for the *San Pedro News Pilot* on ethnic groups that had settled in San Pedro. The first, on 15 September, was entitled "The Melting Pot—1. Croatians gave San Pedro their skills as fishermen." The next day, "The Melting Pot—2. Filipino descendants form viable part of harbor life" appeared; 18 September, "25,000 Yugoslavs live in area; credited with early development"; 22 October, "First Norwegian settlers arrive in San Pedro in 1883." Later came "San Pedro fishing industry owes a lot to early Italian settlers" and "The Melting Pot—6. Greek immigrants among early pioneers in building San Pedro" (courtesy, San Pedro Historical Society; no dates on the last two). See, too, Munson Kwok's lengthy letter regarding the Los Angeles Chinatown, in *Asian Week*, 5 October 1984.

11. See Rolle, *Los Angeles*, 34, 55–57, 92, 97; Modell, *Japanese of Los Angeles*, 24; Willis Miller, "The Port of Los Angeles–Long Beach in 1929 and 1979: A Comparison," *Southern California Quarterly* 65, no. 4 (1983): 341–75; Walter Bean and James Rawls, *California, an Interpretive History*, 4th ed. (New York: McGraw Hill, 1983), 319–21 and chap. 25; Warren Beck and David Williams, *California. A History of the Golden State* (Garden City, N.Y.: Doubleday, 1972), chap. 17; and the

San Pedro Daily News, 3 October 1922. The lush images of the city and reference to it as the Chicago of the west can be found in the 1981 television documentary "The Thirsty City," narrated by Eddie Albert.

12. The sources for the data include Camarillo, *Chicanos,* 20; Romo, *East Los Angeles,* 80; *1930 Census, Population,* vol. 2, part 1, *General Report,* 369 and 380; and vol. 3, part 1, *Alabama—Missouri,* California tables 13, 17–19; Bureau of Census, *Sixteenth Census of the United States: 1940. Population. Nativity and Parentage of the White Population. General Characteristics,* table 3, 12, table 6, 52–53; and *Mother Tongue,* table 4, 34.

The 1940 census reclassified most 1930 Mexicans as whites. We say most because the original 1930 total was 388,138, and the revised Mexican white foreign stock total was given as 358,138. The state total went up 191,346, or 7819 fewer than the 199,165 foreign-born white Mexicans listed in 1940, which is close to the original report that had already included 8,648 foreign-born white Mexicans. While no data are given for the county, the net increase in foreign-born whites of 51,026 is quite close to the revised total of Spanish-speaking persons (56,304), less all persons from Spain and Central and South America who were enumerated in the original report (5,453). Romo gave the figure of 97,116 for all Mexicans in the city (p. 80), but, in citing 167,000 for the county, he overlooked those counted as whites. Note that these revisions do not alter the overall proportion of foreign-stock people in Los Angeles in 1930. Nonetheless, even the revised figures are not without problems, because Table 16 in 1930 had given a full foreign-born count for the city of 247,135. The revised figure of 232,874 foreign-born whites, leaving a net number of other foreigners of only 14,261, does not reasonably allow for the large number of foreign-born Asians. Finally, the total foreign stock is rounded off to 950,000 to include Asians not separately enumerated.

13. Figures for white and nonwhite Mexicans were combined from California tables 17–19 for foreign born and second generation; thus, the actual total was higher because third and later generations are not included. See Camarillo, *Chicanos,* 220 and 225. The quote is his.

14. Calculation of nonwhites and Latinos totaled 246,866 and included 175,600 white, foreign-stock and nonwhite Mexicans, 30,000 Filipinos, 3,572 Chinese, 35,390 Japanese, and 2,314 persons of foreign stock from Central and South America. The total of 950,000 white and nonwhite foreign stock included all foreign-born whites (282,655); second-generation whites (448,979); 35,390 Japanese; 3,572 Chinese; 30,000 Filipinos; and 167,024 Mexicans (the remaining Mexicans having already been included in the foreign-born white total).

Peter Smith indicates that the Filipino population went from about 2,360 in 1910 to 21,000 in 1920, to 108,260 in 1930, of whom 40 percent were on the mainland. Lorraine Crouchett noted that 31,092 had gone there just between 1923 and 1929. Since Smith reports that 69 percent of mainland Filipinos were in California in 1940, I have simply estimated that at least 30,000 of the 43,000 he calculates were on the mainland in 1930 were in California. See Smith, "The Social Demography of Filipino Migrations Abroad," *International Migration Review* (hereafter *IMR*) 10, no. 3 (1976): 321–25; Crouchett, *Filipinos in California. From the Days of the Galleons to the Present* (El Cerrito, Calif.: Downey Place Publishing House, 1982), 33; and James P. Allen, "Recent Immigration from the Philippines and Filipino Communities in the United States," The *Geographical Review* 67, no. 2 (1977): 195–97.

15. Interestingly enough, Los Angeles City in 1930 had a total of 247,135 foreign born, of whom 181,848 were white and 65,287 nonwhite (26.4 percent);

San Francisco had 171,641, of whom 153,386 were white and 18,255 nonwhite (10.6 percent). Second, whereas 29.1 percent of Los Angeles' foreigners had arrived between 1920 and 1930, only 24.2 percent of San Francisco's had, further suggesting that the newer immigrants were now more often heading to Los Angeles. Finally, in terms of eight principal groupings, contrasts between the two cities in terms of the "new versus "old" dichotomy in 1930 are quite revealing:

1930 *Total Population*	*Los Angeles* *1,238,048*	*San Francisco* *634,394*
Foreign Born		
English	12.2%	7.2%
Irish	4.0	10.8
German/Austrian	12.1	13.8
Scandinavian	8.9	9.8
Russian	10.9	4.9
Italian	7.0	17.8
Other southern and eastern European[a]	10.3	7.6
Canadian	16.9	6.3
Second Generation		
English	11.8	7.9
Irish	9.7	20.7
German/Austrian	21.7	19.4
Scandinavian	10.1	7.5
Russian	8.2	3.1
Italian	6.2	14.9
Other southern and eastern European[a]	6.5	4.9
Canadian	17.8	5.7

[a] Polish, Czech-Slovak, Hungarian, Yugoslav, Greek, and Armenian.
SOURCE: See note 11, Tables 18–19.

In addition, in 1930, 43.6 percent of the state's Chinese and 6.4 percent of its Japanese were in San Francisco, compared with 9.3 percent and 36.3 percent, respectively, in Los Angeles.

16. This description of the port and buildings is based on the following interviews: with historian Robert Weinstein, 26 April 1985 (by telephone); Bill Olesen of the San Pedro Maritime Museum, 7 March 1985; Munson Kwok, president of the Chinese Historical Society of Southern California, 5 May 1985 (by telephone); Sherm Zinger and Joe Thomas, Los Angeles Harbor Department, San Pedro, 1, 19 March, 29 April 1985; Joe Flanders and Rose Pericich, INS Regional Headquarters, Terminal Island, 7 March 1985; and Jim Lesley, chief inspection officer, INS, San Pedro, 15 April 1985 (by telephone). The blueprints of the station are in Drawings File 1691-7A of the Harbor Department, San Pedro, but the complete records of its construction, use, and conversion are unavailable aside from notes on the original blueprints. Accounts from 1922 are in the *San Pedro Daily News*, 27 May, 19 June, and 28 November 1922. The figures for admissions appear in an unpublished table from the INS.

17. There are innumerable works dealing with this period, the worldwide changes, and their impact on our immigration patterns. See Elliott Barkan,

"Portal of Portals: Speaking of the United States 'as though it were New York'—and Vice Versa," paper presented at the New York Historical Society Annual Conference (17 May 1986); Elliott Barkan and Robert O'Brien, "Naturalization Trends among Selected Asian Immigrants, 1950–1976," *Ethnic Forum*, 4, nos. 1–2 (1984): 91–108; Elliott Barkan, "Whom Shall We Integrate? A Comparative Analysis of the Immigration and Naturalization Trends of Asians before and after the 1965 Immigration Act (1951–1978)," *Journal of American Ethnic History* 3, no. 1 (1983): 29–56; "New Origins, New Homelands: Immigration into Selected Sunbelt Cities," paper presented at the conference "The Sunbelt: A Region and Regionalism in the Making?" (Miami, 4 November 1985); and "Evermore the Golden Gate: Recent Immigration and Naturalization Patterns in California," paper presented at the American Studies Association (San Diego, 1 November 1985).

In addition, see David Reimers, *Still the Golden Door. The Third World Comes to America* (New York: Columbia, 1985); Robert Warren, "Volume and Composition of U.S. Immigration and Emigration," in Roy Simon Bryce-Laporte, ed., *Sourcebook on the New Immigration* (New Brunswick, N.J.: Transaction, 1980), 1–14; Robert W. Gardner, Bryant Robey, and Peter C. Smith, "Asian Americans: Growth, Change, and Diversity," *Population Bulletin* 40, no. 4 (1985); Peter C. Smith, cited in note 14; James Allen, cited in note 14; Ian R. H. Rockett, "Immigration Legislation and the Flow of Specialized Human Capital from South America to the United States," *IMR* 10, no. 1 (1976): 47–62; Ernesto Pernia, "The Question of Brain Drain from the Philippines," *IMR* 10, no. 1 (1976): 63–72; Alejandro Portes, "Determinants of Brain Drain," *IMR* 10, no. 4 (1976): 489–508; Hyung-chan Kim, "Some Aspects of a Social Demography of Korean Americans," *IMR* 8, no. 1 (1974): 23–42; Charles Keely, "Philippine Migration: Internal Movements and Emigration to the United States," *IMR* 7, no. 2 (1973): 177–88; Eui-Young Yu, "Korean Communities in America: Past, Present, and Future," *Amerasia Journal* 10, no. 2 (1983): 23–51; Leon Bouvier, "International Migration: Yesterday, Today, and Tomorrow," *Population Bulletin* (September 1977; updated August 1979); and citations in notes 27, 29, and 34.

18. David Reimers, "An Unintended Reform: The 1965 Immigration Act and Third-World Immigration to the United States," *Journal of American Ethnic History* 3, no. 1 (1983): 9–28.

19. The commencement of international flights to and from Los Angeles Airport across the Pacific in December 1946 (and directly to Europe over the pole in November 1954) confirmed the fact that San Pedro's time had passed as an immigrant portal to America. In January 1955, the station there became the Western Regional Headquarters of the Immigration and Naturalization Service. Occasional admissions continued to take place thereafter, but inspectors were concerned mostly with checking crew members of foreign ships. In late 1971 or early 1972 (officials do not recall exactly when), the inspectors' office was moved to the U.S. Customs building next door and, five years later, to an office building in downtown Long Beach. According to the chief inspector, at most only a dozen people were admitted to this country through San Pedro between 1977 and 1984. All attention had shifted to what had been renamed on 11 October 1949, Los Angeles International Airport.

The airport discussion is based on Virginia Black: "Fact Sheet. Los Angeles International Airport" (unpublished, Los Angeles Department of Airports, March 1985); Black, "Brief History. Los Angeles International Airport and the City's Regional Airport System" (unpublished, Department of Airports, June

1984); Black, "Early History of Los Angeles International Airport" (unpublished, Department of Airports, March 1978); "Los Angeles Department of Airports; 50th Anniversary" (memorial pamphlet, n.d. but about 1978); and a telephone interview, 4 April 1985, with Joan Sewald, Los Angeles Department of Airports.

A recent statement addressing the specific issue of the emerging Pacific Rim economy and the place of Los Angeles in it can be found in "L.A.'s New Chief Planner Sees City as Key Link to Pacific Rim," *Los Angeles Times*, 19 June 1986.

20. Computed from table 5 of the INS *Annual Reports, 1950–1960*.

21. Bureau of Census, *U.S. Census of Population: 1960* (PC(1)–6A), vol. 1, *Characteristics of Population*, part 6, *California*, tables 32, 89, 90, and 99.

22. When the Vietnamese refugees arrived in 1975, they were conditionally admitted, "paroled in." After two years, they could convert their status to resident aliens, and it is for that reason that they appear in such great numbers in fiscal years 1978 and 1979. In those two years, 28 percent were in California or intended to reside there. In addition to public-use tapes for 1972 to 1979 from the INS, Tables 6 and 6B in the 1978 and 1979 volumes of the *Statistical Yearbook* were used here.

23. Also during that time, one-fourth of those crossing the Mexican border (94 percent of whom were Mexican), were going to the Los Angeles area, which, as I configured it, included the city and some half-dozen surrounding communities. Twenty-eight percent of the 190,082 who came through (or who were adjusted in) Los Angeles planned to reside in the city (versus 4.7 percent from throughout the nation) compared to 38 percent going to (or in) that larger Los Angeles area.

24. Based on the tapes, Table 5 in the 1977 *Annual Report*, and Tables IMM 5.1 and IMM 5.3 in the 1982 to 1985 volumes of the *Statistical Yearbook*.

25. See Tables IMM 3.1, 5.1, and 5.3 in the *Statistical Yearbook*, 1982 to 1985 volumes, and the table referred to in note 28.

Many writers have referred to Los Angeles as the new Ellis Island, although New York was not Ellis Island per se. Calling the city by the name of the island confuses the role of Ellis Island as a processing center for all immigrants with New York City as a major destination for many of those immigrants. Similarly, this reference has been made to Los Angeles because of the growing number of people naturalized there, although people were not naturalized on Ellis Island, and that, again, confuses its historic role.

As the nation's second most important processing center of newcomers—its leading one on the Pacific Rim—Los Angeles can aptly be called a sort of new Ellis Island. "Sort of" because none of the complex procedures that existed on Ellis Island, such as elaborate physical exams and hospitalization of diseased individuals, have usually been done on arrival since the 1924 legislation shifted visa-issuing responsibilities to American consulates and embassies abroad. An example of the confusion is the news story by Laurie Becklund, "Ellis Island West. 38,000 Immigrants in Two Weeks Will Take Citizenship Oath in Los Angeles," *Los Angeles Times*, 14 November 1985. Becklund begins, "In yet another sign that Los Angeles is the Ellis Island of the 80s" and goes on to speak about the forthcoming naturalizations.

26. Guatemalans replaced Indians in the rank order for destination, for Asian Indians often arrived in the city and dispersed, whereas Guatemalans remained more concentrated.

27. Two studies that have presented data on Los Angeles are Douglas S.

Massey and Kathleen M. Schnabel, "Recent Trends in Hispanic Immigration to the United States," *IMR* 17, no. 2 (1983): 212–44, and Thomas Muller, *The Fourth Wave. California's Newest Immigrants* (Washington, D.C.: Urban Institute Press, 1984).

28. Data for 1982 to 1985 are summarized in the following table for comparison with the one in text on the 1970s. It is derived from the INS public-use tapes for these years.

Immigrants Admitted/Processed in Los Angeles District, 1982–85

Country of Birth	Total Number	Percentage of District Total
	311,176	
1. Vietnamese	45,301	14.56%
2. Koreans	41,611	13.37
3. Chinese[a]	39,493	12.69
4. Filipinos	29,767	9.57
5. Mexicans	15,624	5.02
6. Iranians	15,283	4.91
7. Kampucheans	11,525	3.70
8. Salvadorans	9,905	3.18
9. Soviets (U.S.S.R.)	9,136	2.94
10. Asian Indians	6,419	2.60
11. British	6,233	2.00
12. Laotians	5,749	1.85
13. Thai	4,952	1.59
14. Japanese	4,834	1.55
15. Guatemalans	3,956	1.27
16. Rumanians	3,823	1.23
17. Canadians	3,059	.98
18. Lebanese	2,860	.92
19. Cubans	2,720	.87
20. Peruvians	2,177	.70

[a] Includes persons from Taiwan, Hong Kong, and Mainland China.

29. California's soaring place in American immigration history and that of Los Angeles are very much entwined today. State destination data do not exist for 1980 to 1981, but a preliminary analysis of the 1982 to 1985 data, the latest available (*Statistical Yearbook*, vols. 1982–85, tables IMM 5.2 and 5.3), indicates that California's share of all immigrants giving their intended state of residence rose to 26 percent, of whom more than one-third stated that they were going to live in the Los Angeles area.

In this overall analysis, I have, obviously and of necessity, not tried to name every group that has entered through Los Angeles, but the 1980s data in note 28 does bring the information here quite up-to-date. I have identified every significant group entering or going to Los Angeles. Interestingly enough, the only two others heading toward Los Angeles whose numbers steadily increased in the 1970s were the Israelis and Egyptians, There were also signs of some increases in Africans, such as immigrants from Burundi.

I have not dealt here with the issue of undocumented aliens because this chapter is based on the INS data of legal immigrants. Substantial numbers of undocumented aliens are in California, and the Los Angeles area in particular, but they would be amplifying the groups I have identified and not altering the basic patterns. I have also excluded them because my focus here is not the economic nor social services impact of immigration, and only relatively small percentages of these immigrants (especially Mexicans, who comprise half or more of all such persons) appear to remain, legalize their status, and integrate via naturalization, a major concern of this study. The impact of the 1986 amnesty law is also obviously beyond the scope of this essay.

Jeffrey Passel and Karen Woodrow have recently estimated that in 1980, 28.25 percent of all legal resident aliens and 49.8 percent of all undocumented aliens resided in California (1.52 million and 1.024 million, respectively), over 45 percent of whom they estimate had arrived between 1975 and 1980. While half the legal Mexicans went to the state, two-thirds of the undocumented Mexicans did, too. In contrast, the researchers estimate that one-fifth of all other legal immigrants also went to California and 28 percent of undocumented non-Mexicans. They further calculated that 106,000 of the undocumented were from other places south of the border and 83,000 were from Asia. "Geographic Distribution of Undocumented Immigrants: Estimates of Undocumented Aliens Counted in the 1980 Census by State," *IMR* 18, no. 3 (1984): 642–71. Thomas Muller's recent study cites 320,000 legal immigrants going to Los Angeles between 1970 and 1980 (out of 782,000 to the state) and 566,000 undocumented (out of 1,086,000 statewide). Of them, 107,000 Mexican newcomers in Los Angeles were legally here, and 317,000 were not (statewide, 226,000 and 589,000, respectively; Muller, cited in note 27.).

See also Josh Reichert and Douglas S. Massey, "Patterns of U.S. Migration from a Mexican Sending Community: A Comparison of Legal and Illegal Migrants," *IMR* 13, no. 4 (1979): 599–623; Vernon Briggs, Jr., "Methods of Analysis of Illegal Immigration into the United States," *IMR* 18, no. 6 (1984): 623–41; and Frank Bean et al., "The Sociodemographic Characteristics of Mexican Immigrant Status Groups: Implications for Studying Undocumented Mexicans," *IMR* 18, no. 3 (1984):672–91; "The Half-open Back Door—Illegal Migration to the United States," chap. 9 in *Staff Report of the Select Commission on Immigration and Refugee Policy, United States Immigration Policy and the National Interest* (Washington, D.C., 30 April 1981), 457–558; Jorge A. Bustamante, "Immigrants from Mexico: The Silent Invasion," in Roy Simon Bryce-Laporte, ed., *Sourcebook on the New Immigration* 140–45; and Wayne Cornelius, "Mexian Migration: Causes and Consequences for Mexico," Ibid., 69–84.

We have also not made any effort to estimate emigration, either out of the state or the country, for such data have not been recorded since 1957. Robert Warren and Jennifer Peck estimated that 1.14 million foreign-born residents left this country during the 1960s, including 16 percent of those who had arrived during that same decade. However, they could not break down that data by either nationalities or ports of embarkation. "Foreign born Emigration from the United States, 1960 to 1970," *Demography* 17, no. 1 (1980): 71–84; and Robert Warren, "Volume and Composition of U.S. Immigration and Emigration," *Sourcebook*, 1–14. Note, too, Charles Keely and Ellen P. Kraly, "Recent Net Alien Emigration to the United States: Its Impact on Population Growth and Native Fertility," *Demography* 15, no. 3 (1978): 267–83.

Finally, with respect to Mayor Bradley's proposal for a Los Angeles Statue of Liberty, see "West Coast 'Statue of Liberty'," *Los Angeles Times*, 19 July 1986, part 2, 2.

30. See Witold Krassowski, "Naturalization and Assimilation Proneness of California's Immigrant Population: A Statistical Study" (M.A. thesis, University of California at Los Angeles, 1963), 8 and 79, and especially the discussion of background variables on 72–78, 116, 136–37.

31. In Los Angeles district, the percentage of people naturalized in the 1972 to 1977/1980 period, who had arrived or were adjusted to permanent residence—and who then began their required waiting time in the 1970s—was much higher at the outset because of the large number of Filipinos qualifying via their military service. During the years studied, the figures for new citizens in Los Angeles who had arrived beginning in 1970 were:

1972	5.3%	(644)
1973	5.6	(608)
1974	10.9	(1308)
1975	13.5	(1917)
1976	29.0	(3495)
1976TQ[a]	38.6	(1416)
1977	46.4	(5766)
1980	64.5	(14649)
	TOTAL:	29,803

[a] 1976TQ: Transitional quarter when the government switched from 1 July fiscal year to 1 October.

In view of the fact that between 1970 and 1975, 103,780 people said they intended to reside in Los Angeles and persons naturalized there did not live in only the city itself, it is difficult to determine the precise proportion in Los Angeles who sought such rapid citizenship. It would also be necessary to deduct the first half of fiscal-year-1970 arrivals, the unknown number who out-migrated and who emigrated, and those who died, and so forth, and add in those who had resettled in the Los Angeles area before applying for citizenship in order for us to arrive at a reasonable net eligible population.

32. In the New York District, 18.4 percent of all new citizens were sworn in. While the Los Angeles percentage of all naturalizations was twice the number of California's immigrants going to Los Angeles, New York's was only 86.4 percent of New York state's immigrants residing in the city. We cannot yet say if the greater proportion in Los Angeles was due to more eagerness there or the resettlement of larger numbers of immigrants who were subsequently naturalized.

33. Assuming, of course, that divorced persons were not disproportionately more likely to seek citizenship than married people, which we do not yet know.

34. While it is true that the district witnessed the naturalization of far more people than just those residing in the city, the rank orders of immigrants to the state and city are very close to these. There is a little more variation in terms of the Los Angeles area destination figures via Los Angeles, but the top five naturalized groups were among the top seven going there, and the other two are discussed later. On Mexican naturalization patterns, see Elliott Barkan and Nikolai Khokhlov, "Socio-Economic Data as Indices of Naturalization Patterns in the United States: A Theory Revisited," *Ethnicity* 7, no. 1 (1980): 159–80; Select Commission on Immigration, 265–70; Barry Siegel, "Immigrants' Story Not Always a Tale of Success," *Los Angeles Times*, 13 December 1982, 1+, but es-

pecially 17. On Asians, see Barkan and O'Brien "Naturalization Trends"; Barkan, "Whom Have We Integrated?"; and "1 of every 3 new Americans is Asian," *Asian Week*, 14 July 1983.

35. See, for example, Guy Poitras, "Return Migration from the United States to Costa Rica and El Salvador," in William F. Stinner, Klaus de Albuquerque, and Roy Simon Bryce-Laporte, eds., *Return Migration and Remittances; Developing a Caribbean Perspective, RIIES Occasional Paper No. 3* (Washington, D.C.: Research Institute on Immigration and Ethnic Studies, Smithsonian, 1982), 97–128.

36. Again, their overall figures are quite small. Indeed, in 1981 and 1982, their tiny percentages declined further, whereas the increase in Iranians reflects the influx during the late 1970s and mounting political unrest in Iran.

37. The Los Angeles–Long Beach urbanized area—as opposed to SCSA and SMSA—had 9,479,643 people in 1980. Bureau of Census, *1970 Census of the United States. General Social and Economic Characteristics*, vol. 6, *California*, table 81; *1980 Census of Population. Characteristics of Population. General Social and Economic Characteristics, U.S. Summary*, PC80-1-C1, tables 246–50.

Muller claims that 886,000 foreign born migrated to Los Angeles out of 1,868,000 in all of California during the 1970s and that, with natural increases of 556,000 and net out-migrations of native-born people of 1,008,000, the city's population rose by 435,000 (Fourth Wave, 18).

38. One-fifth of these immigrants in the city (171,402) were of "Other Spanish Origin" and certainly included the growing number of Central and South Americans. They made up only 16.2 percent of the Los Angeles Basin's Spanish-origin group; Cubans and Puerto Ricans represented 3.8 percent and 4 percent, respectively; Mexicans equaled over 75 percent in the city and nearly 80 percent in the greater area. The author has not yet used the census tapes for the city, but 63 percent of Salvadorans, Nicaraguans, and Guatemalans were in California in 1980 and, based on the immigration data, I believe they were heavily concentrated in the Los Angeles area. See the *1980 Census of Population. Supplementary Report PC80-S1-10. Ancestry of the Population by State: 1980*, table 3.

39. The seven major single-ancestry groups are English, French, German, Irish, Italian, Polish, and Russian. There were also thousands of Dutch, Hungarian, Portuguese, Swedish, and Scotch people listed but in much smaller numbers. The six principal mixed ancestry European groups included those listed as part English, French, German, Irish, Italian, or Polish.

40. See the map in the 1983 *Time* story, cited in note 1.

41. Bill Sievert, "California may be America's First 'Third World' State," *Los Angeles Times*, 11 December 1977; Barry Siegel, "Immigrants: Sizing up the New Wave," *Los Angeles Times*, 12 December 1982, 14; and Barry Siegel "Aliens' Role: It Depends on Who[sic] Is Asked," *Los Angeles Times*, 14 December 1982; "Asians in the U.S. in the year 2000," *Asian Week*, 9 December 1982; "L.A. County the Largest U.S. Asian Community," *Asian Week*, 16 July 1983, 1; "L.A.'s APA Population Jumps in 5 Years," *Asian Week*, 29 November 1985, 1; "Asian Pacifics May Total 800,000 in L.A. County," *Asian Week*, 21 February 1986; "Asians Approach 10 percent of State Population," *Asian Week*, 7 March 1986; "Asians' Political Impact in L.A.," *Asian Week*, 14 March 1986; Patt Morrison, "Western Avenue. East Meets West Where Thorofare Slices through Koreatown," *Los Angeles Times*, 14 February 1985, part 2, 1–3; "Orange County #3 in state for Chinese," *Los Angeles Times*, 28 September 1984; Penelope McMillan, "L.A.'s Chinatown Turns from Tourists to the Chinese," *Los Angeles Times*, 18 September 1977, part 2, 1,

and her "Vietnam Chinese Give Chinatown a New Look," *Los Angeles Times*, 24 November 1984, part 2, 1; Jacqueline Debarets and Linda Holland, "Indo-chinese Settlement Patterns in Orange County," *Amerasia Journal* 10, no. 1 (1983): 23–46; Eui Young Yu, cited in note 17; Robert Lindsey, "For New Asian Arrivals, California Is Simply Like Home," *New York Times Week in Review*, 23 June 1983; and Ethel Taft, "Absorption of Soviet Jewish Immigrants," *Journal of Jewish Communal Services* 54, no. 2 (1977): 166–67.

42. Kevin Phillips, "New Immigrants for the Next America," *Los Angeles Times*, Opinion Section, 11 May 1986, 1–2. Some of his remarks about political attitudes among Latinos and Asians are apparently derived from Bruce E. Cain and D. Roderick Kiewiet, "Minorities in California," public symposium at the California Institute of Technology (Pasadena, 5 March 1986).

"Immigration through the Port of Los Angeles": A Comment

Douglas S. Massey

During the early 1980s, an average of nearly 600,000 immigrants entered the United States each year, a figure exceeded only during the first decade of this century.[1] Although New York City remained the principal port of entry, Los Angeles became increasingly important, and New York state has already lost its dominance to California. In 1984, approximately one-quarter of all immigrants intended to settle in California, compared to only 20 percent in New York, and of those going to California, by far the largest share planned to reside in Los Angeles.[2] As the most important point of destination in the largest immigrant-receiving state, Los Angeles has become the urban symbol of the new immigration to the United States.

Nevertheless, focusing on Los Angeles as a port of entry or place of intended residence understates its importance in the immigration process. As Elliot Barkan's article makes very clear, the salience of Los Angeles cannot be appreciated from immigrant entries and intentions alone. Instead, its current dominance, in symbol and in fact, stems from its role as a mecca for immigrants rather than a gateway. Throughout its history, Los Angeles has drawn more immigrants than data on entries and intentions suggest, and at present, its foreign-born population is relatively larger and more rapidly growing than New York's.[3]

Given the rising importance of Los Angeles as an immigrant city, and New York's historical importance in that role, comparisons between the two cities are inevitable—hence the rhetorical question in Professor Barkan's article, "Los Angeles: the new Ellis Island?" Drawing on historical and contemporary evidence, Barkan's essay answers this question with a firm no. Los Angeles has never been, is not now, and probably will never be the most important port of entry to the United States. Even today, three times more immigrants enter the United States through New York than through Los Angeles.[4] But if we reformulate the title's rhetorical question to read "Los Angeles: the new melting pot?" the answer is more ambiguous. As an immigrant city, Los Angeles plays a role very similar to New York's in the past, and Los Angeles has clearly usurped New York's preeminence as a symbol of contemporary immigration. Current social and economic conditions in Los Angeles, however, are quite different from those prevailing in New York at the turn of the century, and the two cities—historical New York and modern Los Angeles—provide very different contexts for immigration. In this brief comment, I elaborate on the theme of comparative similarities and differences, touching on issues raised by Barkan's perceptive article but also broadening the view to consider Los Angeles as an immigrant city as well as a port of entry.

In spite of obvious differences between the two epochs, immigrations now and at the turn of the century have the same basic causes, and New York and Los Angeles have played parallel roles in the process. Immigration originates in profound structural transformations within sending societies.[5] Economic development invariably leads to wrenching economic, political, and social changes. The substitution of machines for hand labor creates a surplus of workers and disrupts traditional social structures.[6] The penetration of modern ideas through mass education and the media undermines traditional values and culture.[7] Disparities in wealth created by uneven development generate political and social tensions that lead to social unrest, violence, and displacements of population.[8] The end result of these interrelated changes is the creation of a mobile mass of people responsive to economic opportunity and the chance for a better life.

Some of these people are absorbed by expanding urban sectors of their own countries, but in every case, both historically in Europe and currently in the Third World, some share of the population has sought to migrate abroad.[9] Traditionally, the United States has been the primary destination of people so displaced through development, and one particular U.S. city has always stood as the main pole of attraction. At the turn of the century, that city was New York, and within the last two decades, it has become Los Angeles.

As magnets for immigration, both urban areas have attracted a diverse cross section of their respective immigrant flows. Virtually all groups represented in the great European migrations were present in New York before 1920;[10] and nearly all groups in the new immigration are present now in Los Angeles.[11] Although certain groups have tended to concentrate disproportionately in each city—Jews in New York and Mexicans in Los Angeles—and larger contingents of other groups have gone to different cities—Poles to Chicago and Cubans to Miami—these facts do not gainsay the importance of New York and Los Angeles as the preeminent immigrant cities of their times. In the early twentieth century, no city possessed a greater number of immigrants nor a wider variety of ethnic groups than New York, and within the past two decades, this distinction has gone to Los Angeles.

Both New York and Los Angeles bring together a bewildering variety of ethnic groups in a concentrated area, and in both places, immigrants have been received by natives with the same peculiarly American blend of hostility and respect. Thus, while Asians are widely held up as a model minority, the U.S. Civil Rights Commission notes a spreading pattern of anti-Asian violence;[12] and while Mexicans are welcomed to pick crops, they are resented for their widespread and very public use of Spanish. Americans have always been hopelessly ambivalent about immigration, and the love-hate relationship is as typical of Los Angeles in 1980 as it was of New York in 1920.

Thus, at a superficial level, immigrations to New York at the turn of the century and to Los Angeles today are remarkably similar. The fundamental causes have not changed much, and both cities attract a diverse cross section of immigrants who are received with classic American ambivalence. Yet in spite of these overt similarities, the historical roles of New York and Los Angeles are quite different, owing to contrasts in their historical and structural situations.

While forces stimulating immigration are essentially the same, the dynamics are now much more intense. Advancements in medical knowledge and public health have reduced mortality rates throughout the developing world, but because fertility has remained high, population growth has soared well above levels that prevailed in Europe during its period of development.[13] Therefore, processes unleashed by economic development—enclosure, mechanization, capital substitution, social breakdown—operate on much larger and more rapidly growing populations. Pressures for migration are also heightened by technological change, which has boosted both agricultural and industrial productivity, so that development now displaces more rural workers but absorbs fewer of them into the industrial sector.[14] At the same time, improvements in transportation and communication have reduced the costs and difficulties of movement and greatly facilitated the formation and operation of migrant networks.[15] Thus, developments since 1920 have simultaneously increased the number of potential migrants and made international migration easier.

The dramatically increased potential for migration to the United States contributes to another salient difference between the historical circumstances of New York and Los Angeles—the time horizon of immigration. Immigration through New York was concentrated in a forty-year span between 1880 and 1920 when some 23 million immigrants entered the country, primarily from southern and eastern Europe.[16]

This period of mass immigration was followed by a forty-year era of consolidation and adjustment. Between 1920 and 1960, the United States received only eight million immigrants, mostly from northern and western Europe, giving the country four decades of breathing space when it could accomplish the painful and often traumatic task of incorporating immigrants and their children into the fabric of national life.

We are currently in another era of large-scale immigration. At least ten million immigrants entered the United States between 1960 and 1980, and given the accelerating pace of entry over the past two decades, more than that number will probably come in the next two decades, surpassing the record 23 million immigrants enumerated between 1880 and 1920.[17] In this case, however, immigration probably will not end after forty years. As the process of development continues to spread throughout the world, many more people will be displaced by economic, social, and political upheavals, creating millions of potential migrants and generating tremendous pressures for immigration. Once a few migrants from a sending area gain entry to the United States, immigration streams will emerge and acquire momentum as networks develop and become institutionalized.[18] Innovations in transportation and communication will further encourage the process of international migration.

Mass immigration, therefore, will continue well into the twenty-first century. Although immigration to the United States was successfully blocked once before, it was by only an unusual series of events that is unlikely to be repeated: a world war, the galvanization of public opinion behind exclusionary immigration policies, global economic collapse, and a second world war. In the late twentieth century, none of these events is likely to occur singly, much less in combination; and in all probability, Los Angeles and other targets for the new immigration will not have forty years of breathing space within which to undertake the difficult task of incorporating millions of new immigrants into American society.

Perpetual immigration will also create unusually diverse ethnic populations crosscut by social class and generation. Because European groups entered the United States within a fairly narrow span of years, at any point in time, they were relatively homogeneous. Such groups as Poles, Jews, and Italians were dominated by at most one or two generations that occupied similar positions in the socioeconomic hierarchy. Perpetual immigration disrupts this homogeneity, as it has for Mexicans, the group with the longest history of immigration to the United States. As a result of eighty years of immigration, the Mexican population includes people from the first to the fifth immigrant generation, and from every socioeconomic background.[19] This diversity has created a fragmented sense of group identity, reflected in the multiplicity of terms denoting Mexican ethnicity on U.S. census surveys—Chicano, Mexicano, Mexican, Mexican-American—each favored by a different generational-socioeconomic group.[20] The Mexican experience will become increasingly typical and by the twenty-first century will characterize most, if not all, immigrant groups in such cities as Los Angeles. Ethnicity will be a far more complex, problematic, and multidimensional phenomenon than we have known to this point.

A third contrast between the historical situations of New York and Los Angeles is that immigration is now subject to numerical limitation. Throughout the period of peak European movement through New York, immigration was virtually unrestricted. If an aspiring immigrant met a few minimal criteria, he or she was allowed to enter immediately, without waiting in an endless queue or working through a complex preference system. Now, however, the number of immigrants is held to a statutory maximum of 20,000 per country, with a world ceiling of around 270,000.[21] Although some immigrants, such as wives and children of U.S. citizens, are not subject to these limitations, there is nonetheless a powerful barrier to entry that did not exist before 1920.

As a result, there is a sharp imbalance between the demand for legal visas and their supply, creating the historically novel phenomenon of undocumented migration. The potential for clandestine migration was created when immigration quotas were first introduced in the 1920s, but for a variety of reasons, widespread undocumented migration did not materialize until the 1950s, and it became chronic only during the 1970s. Thus, while about eight million documented immigrants entered the United States between 1960 and 1980, over the same period at least two million people entered without legal documents, comprising 20 percent of total immigration. The ratio of undocumented to total immigrants has been growing, climbing from 18 percent in 1960 to 1969 to 29 percent in 1970 to 1974, to 37 percent in 1975 to 1979. By far the largest number of these undocumented migrants go to California and within that state, to Los Angeles. Of the two million undocumented migrants counted in the 1980 census, half were in California, compared to only 11 percent in New York.[22] Now and in the future, a large share of the immigrants to the new melting pot of Los Angeles will, therefore, face a legal barrier to assimilation almost never encountered in the old melting pot of New York.

The process of immigration is rendered even more complex by the economic transformation of the United States that has occurred since the Second World War. Over the years the labor market has increasingly segmented into a capital-intensive core of high-paid skilled workers and a labor-intensive periphery of poorly paid unskilled workers.[23] At the turn of the century, the economy was undifferentiated and technology was such that most sectors were labor intensive, including immigrant-employing industries producing steel, automobiles, and textiles. As these industries adapted to unionization and economic flux, they became increasingly oligopolistic, highly paid, and capital intensive, and in doing so, they provided an avenue of upward mobility for European immigrants and their children. But new immigrants now face a labor market that is highly segmented between a primary sector of well-paid jobs in capital-intensive industries, skilled services, and high-tech light manufacturing and a secondary sector of poorly paid jobs in unskilled services, labor-intensive manufacturing, and agriculture.[24]

Reflecting the segmentation of the labor market, immigration itself has bifurcated.[25] At one extreme is a relatively small group of documented immigrants who enter the United States with significant human or financial capital and take positions in the core economy or achieve positions of advantage in the peripheral sector. At the other extreme is a much larger group of poorly educated, often undocumented migrants who move chiefly to the bottom rung of jobs in the peripheral economy. Thus, unlike European immigrants in New York, the vast majority of the new immigrants in Los Angeles are concentrated in jobs that are relatively unlikely to provide opportunities for advancement and economic improvement.

Structural conditions in the late twentieth century render the process of immigrant absorption problematic in Los Angeles, one quite different from that experienced historically in New York. Compared to the latter, Los Angeles will receive a larger number of immigrants from more diverse origins, who will arrive in a growing, perpetual stream. Many of these immigrants will not have the legal right to live and work in the United States, and most will be employed in the secondary sector of a segmented economy out of which mobility will be extremely difficult. The continuation of immigration in the long term will, in turn, produce ethnic populations fragmented by generational and socioeconomic status, so the identification of ethnic interests will be increasingly ambiguous. In sum, comments inspired by Barkan's article portend a future for the new melting pot of Los Angeles that is at once tumultuous and fractious but also dynamic, bold, and uniquely American.

Notes

1. Immigration and Naturalization Service, *1984 Statisical Yearbook of the Immigration and Naturalization Service* (Washington, D.C.: U.S. Department of Justice, 1984).

2. Ibid.

3. U.S. Bureau of the Census, *1980 Census of Population and Housing: Census*

Tracts, PHC80-2-226 (Washington, D.C.: U.S. Government Printing Office, 1983).

4. See Note 1.

5. Zvonimir Baletic, "International Migration in Modern Economic Development," *International Migration Review* 16 (1982): 736–56.

6. See Celso Furtado, *Economic Development of Latin America* (New York: Cambridge University Press, 1970); Cynthia Hewett de Alcantara, *Modernizing Mexican Agriculture: Socioeconomic Implications of Technical Change, 1940–1970* (Geneva: United Nations Research Institute for Social Development, 1976); Lourdes Arizpe, "The Rural Exodus in Mexico and Mexican Migration to the United States," *International Migration Review* 15 (1981): 629–49.

7. Alex Inkeles, "Making Men Modern: On the Causes and Consequences of Individual Change in Six Developing Countries," *American Journal of Sociology* 75 (1969): 208–25.

8. See Baletic, "International Migration"; and also Michael Teitelbaum, "Forced Migration: The Tragedy of Mass Expulsions," in Nathan Glazer, ed., *Clamor at the Gates: The New American Immigration* (San Francisco: Institute for Contemporary Studies Press, 1985), 261–84.

9. Lawrence Cardoso, *Mexican Emigration to the United States 1897–1931.* (Tucson: University of Arizona Press, 1980); Brinley Thomas, *Migration and Economic Growth* (London: Cambridge University Press, 1954).

10. Ira Rosenwaike, *Population History of New York City* (Syracuse, N.Y.: Syracuse University Press, 1972).

11. See Elliot Barkan's essay in this volume.

12. Peter I. Rose, "Asian Americans: From Pariahs to Paragons," in Nathan Glazer, ed., *Clamor at the Gates*, 181–212; "Asian Americans Victims of Violence around the Nation," *Population Today* 14, no. 7/8: 4–5.

13. Ansley J. Coale, "The History of the Human Population," *The Human Population* (San Francisco: W. H. Freeman for Scientific American, 1974), 15–28.

14. See Arizpe, *Rural Exodus*, and also Francisco Alba, "Mexico's International Migration as a Manifestation of Its Development Pattern," *International Migration Review* 12 (1978): 502–13.

15. Douglas S. Massey et al., *Return to Aztlan: The Social Process of International Migration from Western Mexico* (Berkeley and Los Angeles: University of California Press, 1987).

16. Douglas S. Massey, "The New Immigration to the United States and the Prospects for Assimilation," *Annual Review of Sociology* 7 (1981): 57–85.

17. See Immigration and Naturalization Service, *1984 Statistical Yearbook*, and Jeffrey S. Passel and Karen A. Woodrow, "Geographic Distribution of Undocumented Immigrants: Estimates of Undocumented Aliens Counted in the 1980 Census by State," *International Migration Review* 18 (1984): 642–71.

18. Massey et al., *Return to Aztlan.*

19. Frank D. Bean and Marta Tienda, *The Hispanic Population of the United States* (New York: Russell Sage, 1987).

20. John A. Garcia, "Self-Identity among the Mexica-Origin Population," *Social Science Quarterly* 62 (1981): 88–98.

21. Charles B. Keely, *U.S. Immigration: A Policy Analysis* (New York: The Population Council, 1979); Panel on Immigration Statistics of the Committee on National Statistics, "Immigration Policy: Past to Present," in Daniel Levine, Kenneth Hill, and Robert Warren, eds., *Immigration Statistics: A Story of Neglect* (Washington, D.C.: National Academy Press, 1985): 13–25.

22. Passel and Woodrow, "Geographic Distribution."

23. A good review of the segmented labor market literature may be found in Alejandro Portes and Robert L. Bach, *Latin Journey: Cuban and Mexican Immigrants in the United States* (Berkeley and Los Angeles: University of California Press, 1985).

24. Michael J. Piore, *Birds of Passage: Migrant Labor and Industrial Societies* (New York: Cambridge University Press, 1979).

25. Massey, "New Immigration."

Contributors

ELLIOTT R. BARKAN, professor of history and ethnic studies at California State University, San Bernardino, received his Ph.D. degree from Harvard University in 1968. He has published essays on French Canadians in the *Harvard Encyclopedia of American Ethnic Groups*, on the immigration and naturalization patterns of Asian newcomers to America in the *Journal of American Ethnic History* and *Ethnic Forum*, and on California public opinion regarding immigrants and refugees in *Migration Today*.

HILARY CONROY received his Ph.D. from the University of California at Berkeley in 1949. He is professor of far eastern history at the University of Pennsylvania. He has published numerous articles in scholarly journals and seven books, including *The Japanese Frontier in Hawaii* (1953) and with H. Wray, *Japan Examined: Perspectives on Modern Japanese History* (1983). Professor Conroy also serves on the Academic Advisory Council of the Balch Institute.

PHILIP C. DOLCE is dean of Social Sciences and Communication Arts and professor history at Bergen Community College. He holds a Ph.D. degree from Fordham University (1971), and from 1978 to 1986, he served as executive director of the Eastern Educational Consortium, consisting of forty-five colleges and universities in five states. He has written numerous articles and edited four books, including *Cities in Transition: From the Ancient World to Urban America* (1974) and *Suburbia: The American Dream and Dilemma* (1976).

DEAN R. ESSLINGER, professor of history and director of Faculty Development at Towson State University, received his doctorate from the University of Notre Dame in 1972. He is the author of *Immigrants and the City* (1975), *Friends for 200 Years* (1983), and coauthor of *Maryland: A History of Its People* (1986). Dr. Esslinger recently served on an Association of American Colleges delegation to the People's Republic of China.

LAWRENCE H. FUCHS received his Ph.D. from Harvard University in 1955. He is Meyer and Walter Jaffe Professor of American civilization

200

and politics and chairman of the American studies department at Brandeis University. The author of seven books and numerous articles on immigration and ethnicity, Dr. Fuchs served as executive director of the federal government's Select Commission on Immigration and Refugee Policy from 1979 to 1981. He is currently writing a book on *The Ethnic Kaleidoscope: Immigration, Ethnicity, and Public Policy.*

ALAN M. KRAUT, professor of history at American University in Washington, D.C., received his Ph.D. degree from Cornell in 1975. He has published three books and many articles on immigration and ethnicity and is presently writing a book on *Silent Travelers: Genes, Germs, and the Immigrant Menace, 1880–1940.* Professor Kraut has served on the Historical Committee of the Statue of Liberty-Ellis Island Commission, as an editor for the National Geographic Society, and he has also worked on television documentaries about immigration to the United States.

JOSEPH LOGSDON, professor of history at the University of New Orleans, has published, among other things, *Horace White: Nineteenth-Century Liberal* (1970) and *Audubon Park: An Urban Eden* (1985). He received his Ph.D. degree in history from the University of Wisconsin in 1966 and was a Danforth Postdoctoral Fellow from 1970 to 1971 and a Danforth Associate from 1973 to 1978. He is currently writing a history of public education in New Orleans.

DOUGLAS S. MASSEY is professor of sociology at the University of Chicago. He received his Ph.D. degree from Princeton University in 1978 and recently coauthored *Return to Aztlan: The Social Process of International Migration from Western Mexico* (1987). He has also written two books on American Hispanics for the National Commission for Employment Policy and several articles on related subjects.

TIMOTHY J. MEAGHER received his Ph.D. from Brown University in 1982. He is a program officer at the National Endowment for the Humanities. Editor of *From Paddy to Studs* (1986), he has written several articles on Irish-Americans in scholarly and popular journals, and he has also been visiting assistant professor of history at the Worcester Polytechnic Institute.

FREDRIC M. MILLER is curator of the Urban Archives Center and adjunct associate professor of history at Temple University in Philadelphia. He holds Ph.D. (1972) and MLS (1973) degrees from the University of Wisconsin and is a cofounder and codirector of the Public History Program at Temple. He recently coauthored *Still Philadelphia: A*

Photographic History, 1890–1920 and has written articles about British and Philadelphia social history and archival theory and management.

RANDALL M. MILLER received his Ph.D. from Ohio State University in 1971. He is professor of history and director of American Studies at Saint Joseph's University in Philadelphia. A specialist on the American South, Dr. Miller is the author or editor of nine books and over thirty articles. He is best known for *"Dear Master": Letters of a Slave Family* (1978) and *The Kaleidoscopic Lens: How Hollywood Views Ethnic Groups* (1980). Besides serving as chairman of the Academic Advisory Council of the Balch Institute, he is also writing a book on immigrants in the American South.

RAYMOND A. MOHL is professor of history and chairman of the department at Florida Atlantic University. He holds a Ph.D. degree from New York University (1967) and is the author of numerous books and articles, including *The New City: Urban America in the Industrial Age, 1860–1920* (1985) and *Steel City: Urban and Ethnic Patterns in Gary, Indiana, 1906–1950* (1986). An editor of the *Journal of Urban History,* he has received several research fellowships and has served as a Fulbright lecturer in Israel, Australia, and West Germany. He is currently writing a book on the ethnic and social history of Miami since 1940.

PHILIP SCRANTON earned his Ph.D. at the University of Pennsylvania in 1975. He is associate professor of economic history at Rutgers University-Camden. A specialist on the economic history of Philadelphia, particularly its textile industry, he has published several books and numerous articles in this field, including *Proprietary Capitalism* (1983), *Silk City* (1985), and with Walter Licht, *Work Sights: Industrial Philadelphia, 1890–1950* (1986). Dr. Scranton is a member of the Academic Advisory Council of the Balch Institute.

M. MARK STOLARIK received his Ph.D. from the University of Minnesota in 1974. He is president of the Balch Institute for Ethnic Studies in Philadelphia and Associate Director of the Temple University-Balch Institute Center for Immigration Research. Author of four books and over twenty articles on immigration and ethnicity, as well as producer of a film, he recently published *Growing up on the South Side: Three Generations of Slovaks in Bethlehem, Pennsylvania, 1880–1976* (1985) and coedited, with Murray Friedman, *Making It in America: The Role of Ethnicity in Business Enterprise, Education, and Work Choices* (1986).

CHARLES WOLLENBERG teaches history at Vista College in Berkeley, California. He received a Ph.D. degree from Berkeley in 1976 and among his publications are *All Deliberate Speed: Segregation and Exclusion in California Schools, 1855–1975* (1976) and *Golden Gate Metropolis: Perspectives in Bay Area History* (1985). He has also served as a researcher for a television series on Bay Area history.

Index

205